CULTURE AND EDUCATIONAL POLICY IN HAWAI'I

The Silencing of Native Voices

Sociocultural, Political, and Historical Studies in Education
Joel Spring, Editor

Spring • The Cultural Transformation of a Native American Family and Its Tribe

Reagan • Non-Western Educational Traditions: Alternative Approaches to Educational Thought and Practice

Peshkin • Places of Memory: Whiteman's Schools and Native American Communities

Spring • Political Agendas for Education: From the Christian Coalition to the Green Party

Nespor • Tangled Up in School: Politics, Space, Bodies, and Signs in the Educational Process

Weinberg • Asian-American Education: Historical Background and Current Realities

Books • Invisible Children in the Society and Its Schools

Benham/Heck • Culture and Educational Policy in Hawai'i: The Silencing of Native Voices

Lipka/Mohat/Ciulistet Group • Transforming the Culture of Schools: Yup'ik Eskimo Examples

Shapiro/Purpel (Eds.) • Critical Social Issues in American Education, Second Edition

Pugach • On the Border of Opportunity: Education, Community, and Language at the U.S.–Mexico Line

Spring • Education and the Rise of the Global Economy

CULTURE AND EDUCATIONAL POLICY IN HAWAI'I

The Silencing of Native Voices

Maenette Kape'ahiokalani
Padeken Ah Nee Benham
Michigan State University

Ronald H. Heck
University of Hawai'i at Mānoa

LEA LAWRENCE ERLBAUM ASSOCIATES, PUBLISHERS
1998 Mahwah, New Jersey London

Lawrence Erlbaum Associates, Inc., Publishers
10 Industrial Avenue
Mahwah, NJ 07430

Cover photo courtesy of the Hawai'i State Archives
and border design by Maenette K.P. Ah Nee Benham.

Library of Congress Cataloging-in-Publication Data

Benham, Maenette K. P. Ah Nee
Culture and educational policy in Hawai'i : the silencing of native voices / Maenette Kape'ahiokalani Padeken Ah Nee-Benham, Ronald H. Heck
p. cm.
Includes bibliographical references and index.
ISBN 0-8058-2703-X (cloth).—ISBN 0-8058-2704-8 (pbk.)
1. Hawaiians—Education—History. 2. Education and state—Hawaii—History. 3. Education—Social aspects—Hawaii—History. 4. Educational anthropology—Hawaii. I. Heck, Ronald H. II. Title.
LC3501.H38N44 1998
370'.899942—dc21 97-47700
CIP

Books published by Lawrence Erlbaum Associates are printed on acid-free paper, and their bindings are chosen for strength and durability.

Printed in the United States of America
10 9 8 7 6 5 4 3 2 1

This book is dedicated to
Kape'ahiokalani and Keonaonaonapua
(my great aunt and my mother)
and to all the *wāhine kūpuna*
(elder women) whose dreams I
will always reach for.

—Maenette Kape'ahiokalani

Contents

Foreword

David N. Plank
Michigan State University

Kwame Nkrumah told the story of colonialism this way:

> When the colonialists arrived in Africa they had the Bible, and we had the land. They said, "Hallelujah! Let us pray," and suggested that we pray with our eyes closed. When we opened our eyes we had the Bible and they had the land. (Folklore)

Maenette Benham and Ronald Heck tell a similar story about the colonization of Hawai'i. They characterize the exchange between American colonists and Hawaiian natives as one of land for so-called "civilization." The missionaries who came to Hawai'i believed they were bringing progress and enlightenment to benighted savages; their secular counterparts believed that they could make better use of the islands than could their original inhabitants. What the native of Hawai'i believed was of little moment to either. As in Africa (and Australia, Canada, Mexico, and the mainland United States among other places) the natives ended up with the Bible, or worse—in the words of a popular Hawaiian song, "Plenty of Nutting." The colonizers ended up with the land. To secure their control, they engineered the overthrow of the Hawaiian monarch and an illegal takeover of the islands by the United States in 1893, for which the United States president has belatedly apologized.

As Benham and Heck make clear, the civilization brought by the missionaries encompassed not only the Bible but Western schooling as well. The two were closely linked; both devalued Hawaiian ways of living and knowing, and sought to replace them with values more familiar and congenial to Whites. Partly as a result of these curricular choices, the educational system in Hawai'i perpetuated a racial hierarchy in which Whites predominated at the top and

Native Hawaiians at the bottom. Benham and Heck show how White political leaders established an explicitly dual educational system to ensure this outcome, in which a variety of high-status institutions (select schools, English-standard schools, etc.) served the mainly White elite while common schools served Native Hawaiians and non-White immigrants.

Benham and Heck provide a rich historical account of how schooling contributed to the disfranchisement and subordination of Native Hawaiians, but their book is of far more than local or historical interest. Instead, the story that they tell illuminates the painful political and cultural dilemmas that underlie the current debate over multiculturalism in U. S. schools. The essential dilemma resides in the fundamental ambivalence of subaltern peoples toward schooling. On the one hand, Benham and Heck show, enrollment in Western schools undermined the integrity of Hawaiian culture, devalued native ways of knowing and behaving, and legitimized the usurpation of Hawaiian sovereignty by Whites. On the other hand, as they acknowledge, exclusion from Western schools—or relegation to schools taught in Hawaiian or pidgin—condemned Native Hawaiians to economic and political marginality in their own country as the local economy came to be dominated by Western institutions and the islands were integrated into the global trading system.

In postcolonial Africa, Africans got most of their land back, and regained control of local political institutions. In Hawai'i, in contrast, the most important consequence of colonialism was the immigration of large numbers of non-Hawaiians, accompanied by rapid population decline among the native population. As a result, Native Hawaiians now represent a relatively small minority among their islands' population. The current movement in support of self-determination is handicapped by demography: Deprived of their sovereignty by illegal usurpation in the 19th century, Native Hawaiians can only reassert sovereignty by overriding the political preferences of a majority of their fellow citizens.

It is apparent that these postcolonial dilemmas are not unique to Hawaiians, but are shared to varying extents and in significantly differing ways by Native Americans, African Americans, Mexican Americans, and native peoples around the world. Enlisting schools to support an escape from these dilemmas would require the establishment of genuinely multicultural curricula that affirmed the value of plural traditions while simultaneously providing equitable access to material and political rewards. Benham and Heck describe some tentative steps in this direction that have been taken in Hawai'i, but there, as elsewhere, achieving the goal remains a distant aspiration. Their book shows how we arrived in our current fix and suggests how we might begin to think about extricating ourselves. It is a fascinating case study and an important contribution to current policy debates.

Preface

In this book, we provide a critical assessment of Native Hawaiian education, focusing on the historical, political, and cultural contexts and values that produced several institutionalized structures within the educational system. These institutions kept Hawaiians largely marginalized in the schools and the wider society. As an involuntary minority group, Native Hawaiians' culture stands in a very different position to the dominant culture in Hawai'i (and the rest of the United States) and the other various cultures of other voluntary immigrants to the islands (e.g., Chinese, Filipinos, Japanese, Koreans). Cultural differences between Hawaiians and other groups arose over time as Hawaiians became an involuntary minority group. In order to contend with prolonged discrimination and subordination by foreign values and political control, Native Hawaiians developed various coping methods. As Ogbu (1992) suggests, cultural boundaries are one mechanism developed to differentiate the dominated from their oppressors.

Unfortunately, however, some of these cultural boundaries have not equated well with achieving success within the institutional structures controlled by the state. In Ogbu's (1992) view, involuntary minorities have greater difficulty with school learning and performance, in part because they have greater difficulty crossing the cultural boundaries associated with formal schooling. School learning tends to be associated with learning the culture and language of the oppressors. The involuntary group may come to believe that in learning to act in the dominant manner, they will lose their sense of community lineage and self-worth. More powerful, however, are institutional structures that are developed to reinforce dominant views and ensure a comparative advantage over other groups in economic, political, and social spheres.

In the chapters that follow, we examine several of the institutions, or broad cultural scripts, that defined school policy and resulting educational experiences for Native Hawaiians, as well as many other minority children in the United States during the 1800s and 1900s. Although our work cannot be considered truly comparative because of space limitations, we show that the Hawaiian experience was part of a larger, dominant cultural ideology that shaped educational policy toward native cultures and immigrants, as the country expanded westward across open frontier lands and the Pacific. Moreover, we also look at the current attempts of Native Hawaiians to reclaim a part of their lands, their self-determination, and their education through political sovereignty and Hawaiian immersion education. We use the case of educational policy and politics in Hawai'i to explore how state context and history intersect with broader institutional perspectives that have defined U. S. policy towards those who were in some manner dominated.

It is our hope that, through a discussion of the processes that impact educational policymaking, we can contribute to an understanding of how social and political contexts over time operate to favor some and marginalize others. Such understandings may help us construct policies that will be responsive to the needs of a more culturally diverse population as well as redress some of the wrongs of the past toward specific groups.

Our method of examining these cultural ideologies and their impact takes us away from structural-functional approaches toward an interpretive (constructivist) lens in that we seek to understand the complexity of human interaction through examining the roots of these actions (Everhart, 1988). This is best accomplished through examining events as they have unfolded over time. Social relations are processes that may be dealt with as institutions which exhibit a multitude of consequences (Schatzman & Strauss, 1973). From this perspective, school policies can be seen not so much as organizationally derived but, rather, as reflecting larger sociocultural routines that affect students differently. Consequently, events, policies, and their meanings are multidimensional and must be examined as social fabric woven together to produce a greater whole (Everhart, 1988).

Researchers who investigate social phenomena are not just technicians trained to gather facts (Popkewitz, 1981). Rather, as Everhart (1988) reminds us, they are members of a culture and thus reflect "certain hopes, beliefs, and commitments to that which is, has been, and is seen as possible" (p. 712). In constructing this text, we consulted both Native Hawaiian and U.S. sources of history and also explored a variety of personal, " insider," or Native Hawaiian, experiences and understandings against the more detached, outsider view of the social scientist. We sought balance in presenting this material, as we attempted to hear the voices of those who have had little access to the educational policymaking process.

ACKNOWLEDGMENTS

Mahalo nui loa (thank you) to our *'ōhana* (family) at the Kamehameha Schools, Sarah Keahi, Kawika Makanani, LuAnn Fujimoto, and the staff at Midkiff Library Hawaiiana Collection, who guided the early days of this endeavor. *Aloha* to Donna Lindsey of the Department of Education and Vicki Rosser at the University of Hawai'i at Mānoa for their help and to those who generously and critically reviewed several versions of the manuscript: Joanne Cooper, David Plank, and Rob Rhoads.

Mahalo to Joel Spring, who believed in the *mana* (power) of this story and to Naomi Silverman, whose literary expertise and artful guidance helped give this dream shape. We are also grateful to the Hawai'i State Archives, Bishop Museum Collections, and the University of Hawai'i Mānoa Hawaiian Collection. Finally, *Mahalo* to Flora Ida Ortiz and Kathryn Au, who graciously encouraged us and enhanced the text with their suggestions.

A very special, heartfelt *Aloha pau'ole* to our *'ōhana*, Maenette's husband, Robert Kalani, and Ron's parents, Harvey and Dorothy, who love Hawai'i and its people. *Me ke aloha pau'ole!* (With all our love!)

Maenette K. P. Ah Nee Benham
Ronald H. Heck

A Note to the Reader On "Voice"

Maenette Kape'ahiokalani Padeken Ah Nee Benham

Because my mother passed away when I was 6, I never heard the stories of the women who came before me, who prepared my way. Much of my life has been a journey backward to understand the present and the future. About 2 years ago, I visited with my mother's sister, my Auntie Lily. The words, the pictures, and the voices she shared on that beautiful Hawaiian afternoon, in her home in Mānoa Valley, still resonate in my soul. As we ate salted black crab, *poki* (raw fish), and *poi*, and shared some bites of *manapua* and rice cake, my Auntie gave me my story.

My Hawaiian name is *Kape'ahiokalani*. Its literal English translation is the fan of the heavens. I have known this since I can recall coming to know anything about myself, but what I did not know was the Hawaiian meaning of my spirit. *Kape'ahiokalani* was the name of my great aunt, who was a cherished and skilled chanter for the court of King Kalākaua. As chanter, she was charged to tell the stories of the past, to teach the youth of their beginnings. It is said that Hawaiians from all parts of the islands came to hear her chant the stories of old Hawai'i and the ancestral lines of the great *ali'i* (chiefs). Her voice was clear and resonate, her retelling filled with passionate and vibrant technique. She was a master who was much adored and respected. The giving of a Hawaiian name is not done without thought (although today it is an exotic fad to give a Hawaiian name to a child), especially if one is to be named after a much-beloved ancestor. With permission, I carry the name of an extraordinary woman. I carry the responsibility of storymaking and teaching.

The native way of storymaking is an intellectual tradition that is articulated in a variety of texts—such as the Hawaiian *oli, kahiko, auwana,* in Hawaiian art and craft, and in Hawai'i's poetry and folklore. The work of the storymaker is to recollect and re-collect events, then reflect on the events' multiple meanings, both personal and public and within their time and across time. This reflection extends the mind not only to what is known, but to what is surprising. *Kaona* is the goal here, that is to tolerate ambiguity and shifting meanings in order to come to truth. As all things in Hawaiiana are practical, the process of storymaking presses the storyteller to make sense of these multiple thoughts within a current context; that is, to consider the political, the social, and the cultural. Once these thoughts are framed and articulated in a text, the storymaker must encourage—even propose—action.

Throughout this book, you will read a *Ha'awina No'ono'o* (sharing of thoughts). Most of these reflections are italicized to signal that it is my voice. This is my warrior voice, claiming my storymaker's responsibility. In telling these short stories and sharing my opinions, I attempt to frame how I think about the events comprising each of the case studies. Within the text, I grappled with how to tell the case of Hawai'i's educational history to best engage the reader in both a local as well as a global conversation. I do this to avoid the "quaint" and "exotic" stories often told about paradise. I have also worked hard to avoid the pitfall of essentializing the *haole* (foreigner) and the native experience.

This notion of voice is an interesting phenomenon throughout the cases presented in Part 2 of the text. Native Hawaiians, in the first case, are active in governance and thrive in schools, but in the following two cases (chapters 3 and 4) one may ask, "Where are the Hawaiians?" It is during this dark period that the dominant philosophy becomes a tool to corrupt the native mind, dismantling the spirit and nature of the Native community. This is the silence of the colonized mind. Although Native Hawaiians have suffered poverty, lost self-dignity and sovereignty over our governance and spirit, experienced hopelessness, and sustained the near devastation of our mother tongue and cultural traditions, the final case finds a resurgence of *Hawaiiana* (Hawaiian culture), of *Ha'awina 'ōlelo* (Hawaiian language), of *kūpuna* (ancestors), of *aloha* (love and care). The cases are of a journey, a hoop, that links Native Hawaiians to our roots and to the power needed for change.

This is also my journey as storymaker to recollect for you the events, to study these events through my lenses, and to make sense of these events within the contexts of history, memories, and current thoughts. Throughout the book, italicized text will signal you to my voice, my thoughts, my stories. It is my dream to be consciously political and an advocate warrior.

Kūlia i ka nu'u! (Strive for the summit!)

I

PUA I 'AKO 'IA (FLOWER THAT HAS BEEN PLUCKED)

1 'EKĀHI

The Case of Marginalized People: The Great Wave Cometh

> *He aupuni palapala ko'u, Aia i ka lani ke akua, O ke kanaka pono 'oia ko'u kanaka.* (My kingdom is a kingdom of knowledge, Its god is in heaven, The righteous man is my man.)
>
> —Hawaiian folklore

HA'AWINA NO'ONO'O (SHARING THOUGHTS)

We believe that the longest war in history has been the war against indigenous peoples. Modern, industrial countries have dominated, enslaved, and colonized, thereby defining the native role and place at the bottom of the socioeconomic hierarchy. In these primarily capitalistic economies, value is placed on property and economic gain, and the health of a society is measured by its gross national product, gross domestic product, and income level. With respect to the domination of native cultures in the United States, assimilation focused on replacing one set of cultural values with a new set of Euro-American values including, for example, individual rights and individual productivity to replace collectivism, ownership of private property instead of shared ownership, Christian doctrines to replace the previous spiritual practices and beliefs, and correct citizenship in a democracy (Adams, 1988).

For Native Hawaiians, who were involuntarily colonized beginning with increasing Western contact in the late 1700s and later conquered and annexed by the United States in 1893 (for which President Clinton recently apologized formally), the result of prolonged contact with foreign values and government has been perhaps most devastating. Western domination has largely stripped us of our language, customs, social position, self-governance, and cultural identity. In education, we have often been denied equal access to quality schools and, therefore, more promising economic and social status. Educational policies are often overtly, or covertly, racist and reflect wider cultural attitudes Euro-Americans hold about "other" ethnic groups.

To reveal some of the results of colonization in Hawai'i and its impact on Native Hawaiians, current data indicate that we face tremendous hardship fulfilling even the most rudimentary needs of living (Office of the Governor of Hawai'i, 1983). Employment statistics reveal that Native Hawaiians are underrepresented in white-collar jobs and overrepresented in service, low-status occupations (Alu Like & Office of Hawaiian Affairs, 1989). Health data compiled and evaluated by Alu Like and the Office of Hawaiian Affairs (June 1989) indicate that Native Hawaiians have lower life expectancies due to accidental death or significant illnesses such as diabetes, heart disease, hypertension, and cancer. Statistics regarding pregnancy for Native Hawaiians indicate high rates of teen pregnancy, illegitimate birth, congenital anomalies, insufficient prenatal care, and infant death. Many of these problems are attributed to a lack of local community dissemination of medical information and lack of personal income to pay for medical attention (E Ola Mau, as cited in Alu Like & Office of Hawaiian Affairs, 1989).

As one might therefore expect, data collected by a number of sources indicate a lack of educational achievement and aspirations among Native Hawaiians. Native Hawaiians rank well below other ethnic groups in the State of Hawai'i on standardized achievement tests (Kamehameha Schools/Bishop Estate, 1983). Conquered cultures often disdain dominant education because it is perceived as supporting the dominators. Where aspirations are present, institutional structures often prevent full participation and benefit for some groups. This lack of educational achievement has contributed to the Native Hawaiians' considerable overrepresentation in vocational and special education programs. This had led to overrepresentation of Native Hawaiians in blue-collar jobs (Alu Like & Office of Hawaiian Affairs, 1989) and higher poverty levels with subsequent welfare enrollment (Kamehameha Schools/Bishop Estate, 1983, 1993). It is estimated that 30% of Native Hawaiian adults are functionally illiterate (Kamehameha Schools/Bishop Estate, 1993).

Beyond the low academic achievement statistics and poverty numbers lies a more devastating truth; that is, cultural identity, or affinity to a cultural group, remains jeopardized by a lack of self- and cultural-esteem. We must caution that the accuracy of the data is contingent on the number of Native Hawaiians who declare themselves Native Hawaiians. While

Native Hawaiians make up about 24% of the population in the public schools and 23% of births, they only account for 12% of the State's population on the 1990 census (Kamehameha Schools/Bishop Estate, 1993). In fact, researchers have noted that, to their astonishment, not all Native Hawaiians consider themselves Native Hawaiians, but rather, white or of other ethnicities (Kamehameha Schools/Bishop Estate, 1993; Meehan & Meha, 1989). This attitude is a result of the colonizing effect on the Native Hawaiian mind. Alu Like's (1989) data indicate that a high proportion of Native Hawaiians suffer from social problems due to low self-esteem and ethnic stereotyping. Problems manifest themselves in the breakdown of the family and extended family unit, higher alcohol and narcotic use, increased social impairment and criminal acts, higher rates of suicide, and a large number of child abuse and neglect cases second only to Samoans.

This pattern of underachievement and social dysfunction represented by numerous statistics paints a gloomy picture. Sadly, the proud, beautiful Native Hawaiian that Mark Twain and Robert Louis Stevenson so artistically romanticized no longer exists. Today, Native Hawaiians as a cultural group have not been able to achieve positive self-esteem or self-actualization within the context of a Western inculcated island world. Similar to other groups of involuntary minorities (see Ogbu & Gibson, 1991), problems including financial instability, poor health, low self-image, and lack of adequate education and educational opportunity continue to be significant barriers to Native Hawaiian participation and social mobility. Historically, educational policy appears to have provided neither the cultural impetus nor the means for Native Hawaiians to fulfill their basic survival needs, maintain their culture and identity, and excel within the wider cultural boundaries of imposed (i.e., foreign) social norms. For Native Hawaiians, the public educational system has largely failed to help them reduce existing disparities.

AMERICAN EDUCATION AND THE CHALLENGE OF CULTURAL DIVERSITY

It is no coincidence that periodic calls for reform of the educational system in the United States over the past 100 years have been rooted in broad political, economic, and social (e.g., demographic) changes that have taken place. Because these trends affect political interests, participation in the system, and ultimately the distribution of political power among various groups, they affect the demands upon schools as well as expectations for education. Moreover, as Ward (1993) argued, schools are deeply affected by such demographic forces because trends in births, immigration, and migration patterns determine the nature and composition of the school population. Even with societal changes, the stability of our federalist system of governance itself, with inherent checks and balances and corresponding multiple points of access (e.g., courts, legislature, local versus state level), has typically ensured that the nation's institutions including schools remain intact and reflect the dominant social, economic, and political interests of the times (Benham & Heck, 1994; Iannaccone, 1977).

As Eulau (1972) argued, "If the political order is sound, stable, legitimate . . . , education and all that is implied by education, such as the creation of new knowledge or the transmission of traditional knowledge, flourishes. If the political order is in trouble, education is in trouble" (p. 3). The fundamental relationship between education and the political and social order, therefore, suggests using a longitudinal orientation for understanding how broader changes in cultural values and political ideologies may impact our schools. From the early days of the common school, communities recognized that education played a powerful role in the socialization of children. Therefore, school committees ensured that the curriculum content taught in schools functioned to shape the minds of students (Cody, Woodward, & Elliot, 1993; Finkelstein, 1978). The public and private schools, then, have always been potentially important instruments of political and social indoctrination in their replication of broader social class structures. Moreover, as Tyack and Cuban (1995) argued, over the past 100 years, U.S. citizens have commonly believed that progress was the rule in education and that better schooling would guarantee a better society.

Since the 1970s, however, we find that the public educational system has been increasingly challenged to upgrade its quality to meet the needs of a country changing from industrialism to information and high technology. This changing technology provides evidence that skills gained through education are becoming increasingly critical to the career success of students as they become adults (Reich, 1991). At the same time, policymakers and researchers have recognized that the United States is becoming more culturally diverse and, in many cases, poorer. While education is perceived as failing to meet the needs of the country as a whole, some (e.g., Adams, 1988; Banks, 1988; Cornbleth & Waugh, 1996; Ogbu & Gibson, 1991) have concluded that public education has failed also for particular groups of students (e.g., impoverished students, African American students).

The increasing cultural diversity of the United States and the perceived failure of the educational system are appropriate places to begin a discussion about past, present, and future schooling practices of our nation's children. An ideological focus is fundamental, because an erosion in consensus surrounding commonly accepted cultural doctrines may be the best indicator that a change in the structure of our institutions may be occurring (Iannaccone, 1977). Traditionally, public education in the United States has employed an assimilation model (Banks, 1988). While most would view this model as culturally neutral or reflective of the norms of the many in the country, it nevertheless embodies the Euro-American bias of the dominant U.S. culture (Banks, 1993; Brown, 1993). The model has been generally successful when applied to voluntary immigrants (e.g., Central Americans, Asians). As Ogbu and Gibson (1991) noted, however, the assimilation model has not been successful when applied to involuntary minorities in the United States (e.g., African Americans, Native Americans) or in other countries (e.g., Maories in New Zealand, Aborigines in Australia). One account of the success or failure of this public education model is related to how the specific group (with its cultural traditions and corresponding system of meanings) interacts with the dominant culture (Ogbu, 1992).

Voluntary immigration to a country provides immigrants with a very different orientation toward economic, social, political, and educational institutions in the new location (Brown, 1993; Ogbu, 1992). Because this group desires to achieve its goals (e.g., freedom, economic opportunity) in this new setting and the immigrants can compare their achievement to life "back home," cultural and language differences encountered in school are boundaries that are more easily crossed. Japanese immigrants to Hawai'i in the late 1800s, for example, used education to attain their goals of becoming acculturated into their new home and achieving upward social mobility (Tamura, 1994).

In contrast, involuntary immigrants are brought to their present condition through slavery or colonization. Most likely, they have been displaced from their homeland (e.g., African Americans) or their land has been taken over by foreigners (e.g., Native Americans, Native Hawaiians). Because of this, their comparative reference becomes the dominant group. Involuntary immigrants find themselves surrounded by the dominant culture and its measurement of success, to which they do not generally measure up satisfactorily. Over time, this leads to resentment as they perceive themselves as victims of institutionalized discrimination perpetuated against them by the dominant group and its institutions such as the schools (Brown, 1993). Moreover, they tend to realize that this condition is permanent.

Although cultural diversity has become a popular phrase in educational circles, exactly what the term means with respect to understanding our nation's past educational practices and establishing new goals for the education of the nation's various cultural groups has been openly debated (Banks, 1993; Marshall, 1993; Ogbu, 1992). In fact, different viewpoints regarding race, culture, and ethnicity have arisen since the decline of the liberal consensus favoring equity that largely shaped federal policy in the mid-1960s. Subsequent to this was the rise of a new conservative consensus emphasizing quality (Marcoulides & Heck, 1990; Marshall, 1993), beginning with the election of President Reagan in 1980 and corresponding with the re-segregation of U.S. schools. By the middle 1970s, many policymakers had lost faith in the equity experiment stemming from the Brown *v.* Board of Education Decision in 1954—that public education could be used to solve the nation's social and educational problems. As the 1980s closed, therefore, most of the districts that had been mandated to eliminate segregation through busing in the 1960s and 1970s had been released from their court orders (Marcoulides & Heck, 1990).

With the return to conservative values in policymaking during the 1980s, however, various groups that have long been marginalized by the educational system grew increasingly dissatisfied with the public education system's ability to meet their specific social and educational needs. This sentiment led to a number of recent policy initiatives, for example, single-sex schools for African American boys, voucher or choice systems for urban poor (e.g., Milwaukee), charter schools, and school-based management to give parents greater control at the local school level. While various groups currently contend politically for a piece of the educational pie, Ward (1993) suggests that the United States tends to see its own history as a series of individual events rather than as a product of long-term social trends which affect our economy, our politics, and our daily lives. Studies that examine political and social trends over longer temporal periods can therefore help illuminate the sources of current educational reform debates.

Less attention has been directed at the educational needs of Native Americans than whites. In fact, the experiences of minorities and Native Americans are conspicuously absent from the literature on educational reform. Mainstream literature on educational reform (e.g., effective schools movement) emphasizes a technical–rational (structural–functional) view of schools as organizations (Ogawa, 1992) and their related reform efforts (e.g., if standards are raised, outcomes will go up). Most often, this research focused on urban schools in low socioeconomic and ethnically segregated communities and assumed a minority-deficit model. This model proposes that if these schools change how they are organized, then their students will achieve similarly to Euro-American students. From this largely mythological view, the history of the United States has been one of continuous progress toward democratic ideals, with education playing a key role in assimilating ethnically diverse immigrants into U.S. values and institutions by giving them the tools to compete economically. Often these past historical narratives have been chronicled by those in power (Banks, 1993; Ogbu, 1992). Moreover, rational theories of organizational reform often ignore how larger trends and cultural contexts promote or inhibit change.

Newer critiques of the country's educational history argue for the need to re-examine the underlying assumptions embedded in our constructions of the past and, in some cases, to re-interpret conclusions previously drawn, as we strive to understand how cultural, social, and political contexts impact schooling and life experiences for some groups of people (e.g., Adams, 1988; Banks, 1988, 1993; Tamura, 1994). In contrast to a technical–rational explanation, the sociocultural approach examines how educational policies and practices are determined by these larger political, cultural, and ideological movements that have dominated the United States' past (Adams, 1988; Benham & Heck, 1994; Tamura, 1994). Such approaches allow us to see our educational history in more expansive and diverse ways.

HISTORICAL ROOTS OF THE AIM OF EDUCATION

In a stratified society such as the United States, educational institutions have a difficult time walking the fine line between the egalitarianism implied in many of our democratic ideals and their selecting or sorting function to provide labor for the economy (Iannaccone, 1977; Spring, 1989) and, thus, assure assimilation to the U.S. way of thinking and life. Historically, educational policy gradually took shape as fulfilling several interrelated dominant cultural values and functions. There is considerable agreement among scholars, especially since the 1970s and 1980s, about what some of these cultural values were (e.g., Adams, 1988; Banks, 1988, 1993; Tamura, 1994).

Adams (1988) argued that there were at least three broad cultural determinants of Native American educational policy during the 1800s and early 1900s. These factors formed a mutually reinforcing system with public education as the primary vehicle used to assimilate those who were perceived as different. These larger cultural ideologies are important to understand, for they also played a large role in defining educational policy toward Native Hawaiians. The first of these was Protestant ideology, which gave rise to the common school to instruct students in the Bible and elevate them spiritually through teaching about individual salvation and morality. The second cultural script was the widespread acceptance of a savage-to-civilization paradigm of social evolution. Policymakers believed that the native cultures (e.g., Native Americans) would either die out because of their cultural inferiority, or could be assimilated into white culture (Adams, 1988). They concluded that schools could be used to bridge the believed inherent inferiority of native cultures in one generation, as opposed to what might otherwise take many generations to do biologically. From their view, the only hope to save native cultures from extinction was to civilize them to the values of Anglo-American culture (Adams, 1988). The third ideological belief was Manifest Destiny, which provided a rationale for why lands must be taken and people assimilated as the United States expanded westward across the continent and Pacific Ocean. In fact, it was in the name of raising the natives spiritually and helping them to evolve upward from savages to civilized participants in democracy that justified taking and controlling their lands for economic reasons (Adams, 1988).

In chapters 2 through 6 we focus on several of these broad cultural institutions that have historically shaped educational policies and practices in Hawai'i. These include teaching religious doctrines of Christianity (e.g., Protestant beliefs about individual character, virtue, property, and work ethic) from contact with the missionaries and later "Americanization" to force Native Hawaiians and other immigrants to become assimilated into U.S. culture; the economic and cultural superiority of Euro-American culture as opposed to their own cultural heritage (i.e., to become civilized); and political socialization (i.e., to become a model citizen) within a republican democracy.

The formation of this interrelated cultural ideology and the corresponding role of education in developing a strong nation really began with the establishment of the new government after the United States Revolution. Thomas Jefferson questioned whether peace and stability in society were best preserved by placing energy in the government to control or by giving education to the people. The debate was not really about education but, rather, how people should participate politically in the new country. The new leaders were worried about possible rebellion creating political chaos (e.g., Shay's Rebellion between debtor farmers and city creditors, struggles between abolitionists and slave holders) before the country got a chance to get firmly established.

Jefferson believed in the potential to get such diverse groups to act in concert for the good of the country. As he argued, "Educate and inform the whole mass of people. Enable them to see that it is in their interest to preserve peace and order, and they will preserve them. . . . They are the only sure reliance for the preservation of our liberty" (as cited in Kemmis, 1990, p. 11). Jefferson concluded that an educated population was essential to developing the sense of community that was at the core of a republican democracy. He reasoned that an educated population would see and act upon the common good by placing the welfare of the society above their own interests. Jefferson's view of civic virtue and the need to encourage enlightened participation were partly behind his suggestion that tracts of land should be set aside for schools as the nation expanded westward. This would ensure community-based involvement and smaller governmental units.

Whereas the republican form of democracy placed high value on the engagement of all citizens in public life, in contrast, James Madison presented the Federalist view that argued for an elaborate system of governmental checks and balances (e.g., the procedural democracy) to minimize instability in society by balancing citizens' voices. As Sullivan (1982) suggested, the Federalist position urged abandoning the language of civic virtue. Instead, the language of the Constitution institutionalized the belief that politics in a democracy is about balancing diverse interests by protecting the working of a commercially competitive society (i.e., ensuring that the invisible hands of the economy can operate).

The Federalists believed the other key to ensuring tranquillity was the vast frontier itself. Where the republican position was that politics should be built around small units so all citizens could be involved, Federalists believed that the frontier was so expansive that geographical isolation would keep people relatively out of touch with each other. This isolation would keep them from developing too much common unity, thereby preventing rebellion (Kemmis, 1990). In the context of a geographically expanding country rapidly coming under the philosophical view of Manifest Destiny, Madison argued for a dispersed, disconnected citizenry that was kept in check by government. He reasoned that an expanding territory would tend to balance a variety of interests so that one view could not dominate. In contrast, Jefferson saw increasing territory as ensuring the republican goals of building civic participation in small communities.

With respect to the domination of native cultures, it is our belief that this political debate was played out consciously and consistently throughout the 1800s and 1900s. How to assimilate diverse groups into a dominant U.S. culture and how they would participate in society were issues at the core of social and educational policies (and institutionalized structures) aimed at those involuntarily conquered and those who immigrated, as the United States expanded westward and gradually shifted from an agricultural society to an industrial one. Schooling was an institution that could be used to rapidly indoctrinate and, hence, assimilate those who were different into a common set of Euro-American beliefs, goals, and behaviors.

Near the end of his life, Jefferson saw the westward expansion of the United States by conquering native cultures as inevitable, suggesting that if one began a journey from the Rocky Mountains to the eastern seacoast this would "in fact [be] equivalent to a survey, in time, of the progress of man from the infancy of creation to the present day" (cited in Pierce, 1965, p. 155). To take a more optimistic view of their motives, many felt that civilizing the Native Americans was the only hope to save them from extinction. Jefferson and others believed that because Native Americans were lower savages (with reference to the savage–civilization paradigm), they had too much land for their specific needs as civilized farmers (Adams, 1988). They reasoned that just roaming over the land (e.g., hunting) was not the same as owning the land, as when one farms a particular tract of land (Adams, 1988). Native Americans were, however, in need of the desired objects of civilization. As Jefferson argued, "When [Indians] shall cultivate small spots of earth, and see how useless their extensive forests are, they will sell from time to time, to help out their personal labor in stocking their farms, and procuring clothes and comforts from our trading houses" (as cited in Gibson, 1985, p. 14). On the other hand, whites had an abundance of civilization but were in need of land (Adams, 1988).

In Hawai'i, more specifically, this land issue became central soon after the arrival of the missionaries in 1820. Cultivating sugar cane had quickly become Hawai'i's dominant industry by 1835. With the growing economic importance of Hawai'i, the Great Land *Māhele* (division) of 1848 was engineered to end the communal land tenure that had been practiced in the islands under the Hawaiian system. It was replaced with the concept of private property ownership, a concept foreign to Hawaiian culture but consistent with the teachings of Protestant ideology. Of course, this opened the door for sugar plantations to control vast tracts of land that they had been unable to acquire previously and, shortly after, led to the Masters and Servants Act of 1850, which made it legal to import contract laborers to deal with increasing labor needs (and a population of Native Hawaiians rapidly declining due to disease).

Taking land, or exchanging land for civilization, it appears, became a U.S. institution as the country expanded to meet its economic needs during the 1700s and 1800s. As Turner accurately concluded in 1894 (as cited in Kemmis, 1990), "The peculiarity of American institutions is that they have been compelled to adapt themselves to the changes of an expanding people—to the changes involved in crossing a continent, in winning a wilderness" (p. 27). It is interesting to note that Turner's conceptualization of the West and democracy established a prevailing view for much of this century, which revisionist historians now argue was largely a myth, that the wilderness was the main source of U.S. democracy (Banks, 1993).

Sadly, however, the history of the educational experiences of Native Americans, Native Hawaiians, and other minority groups in this country document this long-standing policy toward the taking of lands and forced assimilation in the process of westward expansion. Added to the taking of land were various racist policies (e.g., citizenship, property ownership) toward those attempting to immigrate or who had immigrated to the United States from parts of Europe and Asia, especially during the 1800s and early 1900s (Tamura, 1994). Thus, political and economic needs soon gave rise to political debate over the function of education as part of the assimilation process—as freeing, in Jefferson's sense of building a truly democratic society, or enslaving (Spring, 1989), in the sense that it has served to reinforce the stratification of the country socially, politically, and economically. As Spring argued, segregated schools as education policy functioned to keep minority groups down in the lower social and economic strata, as well as politically disconnected. In contrast, integrating education such as through the Brown Decision was based on a belief that equal educational opportunity was essential to eliminating large differentials in political and economic power and social status and, thus, ensuring participation in society. In various forms, this argument has been made by Mann's notion of the common school, labor unions during the 19th and 20th centuries, progressive educators and social reconstructionists in the 1930s, and the Civil Rights Movement of the 1960s (Spring, 1993). Unfortunately, however, the goals of integrated education do not match with the perpetuation of elite power, privilege, and socioeconomic standing.

Segregated schooling was an essential part of Manifest Destiny in that it contributed to the ability of the dominant culture to maintain control, ensure a continued supply of labor, and maintain a stable socioeconomic class structure, thereby minimizing the chances of rebellion (Spring, 1993). In fact, Mann's common school appealed to the privileged business interests as serving to maintain their power while, ironically, the poor saw it as an opportunity to change existing socioeconomic disparities (Spring, 1993). In Hawai'i's colonial environment, segregated schooling soon was institutionalized as the first common and select schools were established. Kaestle (1983) argued that a primary reason for establishing the common-school system was to ensure that Protestant republican culture would prevail over Catholicism. In Hawai'i, this battle and efforts to quickly establish a common-school system corresponds with the Protestant missionaries' efforts to have the Catholics removed from the islands. Beginning with the first school leaders in Hawai'i, we document the efforts of the administrative elitists and progressives to implement school policy that reinforced this vision of educational progress and social stability. While formal segregation in Hawai'i's schools was replaced after World War II, its legacy has remained to this day in various forms. For example, Hawai'i has the highest percentage of children in the United States attending private schools (averaging nearly 20%)—some of which are 100 to 150 years old.

In fact, the history of the United States was not one of continuous progress toward integrating education with democratic ideals. It was instead a cyclic quest defined by conflict, struggle, violence, and exclusion

(Banks, 1993; Zinn, 1980). One must ask, in looking at our educational past, progress for whom (Tyack & Cuban, 1995)? As Spring (1989) argued, minority groups have always had to battle government-sponsored public schools to try to gain equal educational opportunity; this battle has never been fully won. These pockets of resistance are important in hindering attempts to dominate (Aronowitz & Giroux, 1985; Spring, 1993). As we have suggested, government always had an interest in education in the United States; at times, this interest has been expressed more directly (e.g., National Defense Education Act, categorical grants) and at times, more indirectly (e.g., block grants, student loan programs, goals for educational programs).

Addressing Diversity

Whether educational policy denigrates one culture in order to elevate another or enhances the proliferation of contrasting cultures is a dilemma both policymaker and society must address. Unfortunately, educational policy in the United States historically has failed miserably to attend to the needs and rights of native groups whose cultures were well adapted to this land for thousands of years before colonization. The basic human needs of Native American cultures to maintain their unique cultural ties as well as to live successfully within a foreign culture have been largely unmet by educational institutions instead charged with acculturating them with dominant cultural values and political beliefs.

Cultural background, religion, and gender all help develop particularized views of schooling (Banks, 1993; Dillard, 1995). Wealth and privilege in the United States led to understandings of race and ethnicity as a permanent part of the psyche of everyone in the nation (Bell, 1992). Historically, philosophy and action toward native cultural groups in the United States have been to isolate and contain their language and traditions, while promoting the salvation of their souls through a Western civilization and corresponding set of religious beliefs (Appleton, 1983; Ogbu, 1992). Because racism is a permanent structure in the United States, schools as institutions have often mirrored these larger intents through creating oppressive structures. Although attempts have been made to change this view, developing an attitude toward cultural plurality has been difficult.

Multiculturalists and biculturalists have made some impact on school curriculum over the past 20 years or so (Banks, 1993; Spring, 1993). For example, the 1960s and 1970s brought to the forefront educational equity policies which ensured native language instruction; however, in the 1980s, the bilingual education bills and subsequent programs were blunted by political pressure from both state and federal chambers (Crawford, 1989).

As Banks (1993) argued, multicultural education is for functioning effectively in a pluralist, democratic society. One of its major aims is helping students develop knowledge, skills, and attitudes needed to participate in reflective civic action. Certainly, this aim is consistent with Jefferson's version of republican democracy and the admittedly idealized role of education in ensuring full participation in society.

Emerging "Native" Voices

Cultural and institutional conditions stemming from prolonged colonialism have limited the involvement of Native Hawaiians and others in Hawai'i from participation in grassroots political and social change. Prior to statehood, the colonial social structure resulting from plantation agriculture favored elite domination socioeconomically and politically, with a White elite occupying the top of the class structure, an undersized middle class consisting of mainly White small business owners and crafts people second, and the majority of Pacific Islanders and Asians on the bottom supplying semiskilled labor (Tamura, 1994).

Despite this tradition of silence and marginalization resulting from colonialism, however, our book presents a struggle of determination. Hawai'i, like many other states, is currently attempting to implement significant changes in response to growing sentiments toward local governance, continued poor student outcomes, and diminishing fiscal resources. The centralized structure of its educational system, however, makes Hawai'i unique in the extent to which government has historically controlled, and continues to control, the educational system. While this entrenched centralized system remains difficult to reform, presently new voices are beginning to emerge, as Native Hawaiian groups become more vocal in seeking access to the sociopolitical system for political sovereignty and for the preservation of their culture through education.

Although a prevailing conservative mood toward social policy currently exists within the United States as evidenced by the trend toward removing affirmative action criteria in education and the workplace, we also see periodic demands for educational equity. This is not a new conversation; like the Hawaiian *honu* (turtle), it pokes its head out of its shell for momentary attention until the big fish coax or coerce it to withdraw into its shell. For some, the pursuit of educational equity for all cultural groups is a horned demon, for others it is a hero's quest. There seems to be a new twist on the demands, however. In some cases, we are seeing groups often demanding segregated services, as opposed to the liberal consensus of policymakers in the 1960s.

Recently, the subject of Native American rights has coaxed the *honu* once again. During the 1990 Congressional Session, Senator Daniel K.

Inouye (D-Hawai'i) introduced a last-minute amendment to S2167 that declares that United States policy concerning Native American languages is "to preserve, protect, and promote the rights and freedoms of Native Americans to use, practice, and develop Native American languages." The Native American Languages Act (1990) reversed an unofficial policy dating to the last years of the Indian Wars that sought to denigrate and eradicate the use of Native American languages as a means of assimilating Native Americans into the mainstream. This popularly known Mother Tongue Bill once again fostered increased attention on philosophical differences concerning bilingual education and cultural plurality. This debate is important to the vitality and empowerment of Native American education policies and the programs they impact because it forces current dialogue about schooling to be inclusive of native voices.

With the advent of renewed controversy stemming from the Mother Tongue Bill regarding the place of Native American languages, prevailing attitudes are again being challenged. Policymakers are being asked to focus their attention on cultural uniqueness and the matter of pursuing particular value choices. In Hawai'i, for example, Native Hawaiian groups during the late 1970s and 1980s succeeded in changing the school curriculum at the elementary, secondary, and postsecondary levels to include Hawaiian culture and language study. More recently, Hawaiian groups forced the establishment of public Hawaiian immersion schools at several sites throughout the state. However, managing educational change requires clear insight into both external institutional values as well as internal pressures. What then is the impact of social institutions and shifting cultural norms and symbols on the activity of schools? How do these cultural scripts affect the educational and subsequent life choices of native peoples?

THE EDUCATIONAL POLICY SYSTEM IN HAWAI'I

Understanding the relationship among culture, ethnicity, and politics and the impact of these on educational decisions is a relatively new area of research. As Wirt and Kirst summarized (1982), the study of educational policy formulation over time or across cultural groups has not been voluminous. In fact, current policy literature rarely explores the context of policymaking decisions, as most research articles are focused on traditional politics of education research (Sachen & Medina, 1990). Furthermore, the study of Native American education policy has been given little attention. Perhaps, not coincidentally, it has failed to receive attention because it has been somewhat lost in the history of the United States, which has focused on the politics of cultural domination through acculturation (Banks, 1988; Cody et al., 1993; Freire, 1985; Ward, 1993).

Important to Native Americans, this lack of contextual (political and cultural) understanding of policymaking is further compounded by academic and social outcomes that negatively impacted nations of Native Americans, Native Hawaiians, and Pacific Islanders and jeopardized the future continuation and success of their native cultures. Therefore, our presentation explores the broader context in which policy decisions are made, the actual content of a sample of policy decisions, and the impact of the policy decisions on Native Hawaiians over time.

The issue of Native Hawaiian status as Native Americans deserves further comment. There is not complete agreement within the Hawaiian community as to the political status of Native Hawaiians. While some see sovereignty as leading to regaining some self-determination and economic autonomy, others suggest that Native Hawaiians are not Native Americans because they are not native to the Americas. Instead, they argue that United States citizenship was forced on them through annexation in 1898 and then statehood in 1959 (Blaisdell, 1997). We return to this issue in chapter 5.

If appropriate policy decisions concerning Native Hawaiians are to be made, an understanding of the political and cultural influences on the policymaking process including its outcomes is necessary. This requires an eclectic approach which draws from the fields of sociology, political science, and anthropology. A longitudinal approach is preferred, as this allows the study of broad trends over time and permits an assessment of how these trends impact the structure of the educational system, identifies reforms that have persisted, as well as the outcomes of this process for particular groups.

Recently, we undertook a longitudinal study of the educational policy process in Hawai'i (Benham & Heck, 1994). We attempted to determine who the policy influentials were and whether the policy influentials and their policy agenda changed over time. Because fundamental value conflicts often recur (Cuban, 1990; Heck, 1991–1992; Iannaccone, 1977), the study of changes in governance and policymaking processes over time can be used to determine whether patterns exist. Identifying such patterns as a function of state political culture can aid in understanding why educational reforms succeed or fail. We used theory derived from political science and anthropology to help interpret past events, policies, and practices in Hawai'i.

As Garms, Guthrie, and Pierce noted (1978), "The outcomes of public policy can be predicted to some extent by careful examination of the cultural system in which they are made" (p. 12). Marshall, Mitchell, and Wirt (1989) proposed that cultural values shape institutions and traditions, and that these are reflected in both formal and informal codes. They define a policy as "a set of values expressed in words, issued with authority, and reinforced with power (often money or penalties) in order to induce a shift toward these values" (p. 6). These ideas, which become educational policy, guide the behavior and actions of educators. Thus, as Marshall et al. (1989) suggested, "The ongoing activity of the policy actors is to transform cultural values into policy—to allocate values" (p. 5). Therefore, in order to study the educational policymaking process over time completely, we are required to understand the political–cultural evolution of a specific society. To do so requires learning more about predominant values that were translated into policy. We present the political–cultural context surrounding each specific historical case in greater detail in chapters 2 through 6.

We defined a pattern of state political culture (i.e., Hawai'i) in terms of which core policy values appeared in key educational laws within each of four turbulent reform periods studied. Marshall et al. (1989) validated four values which compete in the education political arena. Three values—quality, equity, and efficiency—were identified in an earlier work by Garms et al. (1978). The fourth choice was suggested by Mitchell, Marshall, and Wirt (1986) through their research on educational policy.

We selected four periods of time in Hawaiian history for their relevance to the theoretical propositions of our research. These were periods of social and political turbulence that resulted in sets of laws that reshaped the political direction of the society. The first period began with the arrival of Christian missionaries in 1820. With them came the activity of formal schooling and the intent of "raising up the whole people to an elevated state of Christian civilization" (Kittelson, 1981). The second historical period focused on the overthrow of the monarchy in 1893 and the creation of the Department of Public Instruction which institutionalized the use of English in the classroom. The third period highlighted Hawai'i's move toward statehood, the theme of Americanization in the formally segregated schools, and a political power shift from the dominant Republican party to the youthful surge of the Democratic Party in the 1950s through 1960s. The final period centers on current Native Hawaiian movements toward self-determination and efforts to press the schools to be responsive to their needs.

To trace the possible changes in policy values temporally, we focused on seven basic educational policy domains where political values are pursued (Marshall et al., 1989). From these analyses, we determined regularities in the policy process that emerged from our study of turbulent political and social periods. Thus, the conceptual framework of our previous study suggested that educational policy is the result of multiple and conflicting forces including special interest groups, professional elites, and social classes working within a particular organizational structure that seek to influence and control the educational policy process.

We briefly summarize our major findings here in chapter 1, so readers can develop some understanding of the educational policy process in Hawai'i. We believe this is important preliminary information to begin our exploration of how the policymaking system has impacted Native Hawaiians. Hawai'i has a governance process that is unique among the fifty states, owing to its prolonged colonial background involving discovery by the British and domination by U.S. business and military interests.

First, our data reveal that the Hawai'i educational policy process has been controlled by elites (e.g., Hawaiian nobility with U.S. missionaries in the mid-1800s, U.S. business interests and descendants of missionaries in a one-party system from the late 1800s through World War II, governor and a one-party state legislature presently), with only limited participation of others such as teachers, administrators, parent advisory committees, and unions. A review of policy insiders reveals that the head of government (i.e., monarch, president of the republic, territorial or state governor) and his inner circle advisors (e.g., minister of education) control the school system. Furthermore, business interests in the near circle of influence, depending to some extent on the political and economic conditions of each period, have exerted continual influence on school governance, policy, and, to a lesser extent, curriculum. Indeed, even the labor unions have promoted a single, centralized system of school governance. Although, since 1978, the single elected school board has provided opportunity for public voice in school governance, the presence of an elected board (without having fiscal control of schools) is still a symbolic expression of continued elite control. Although it is constitutionally accountable to the public, the board is still an executive department and therefore reports to the governor. Prior to 1978, the board was appointed by the executive leader—the governor. Fiscal power to appropriate extra money to individual schools is held by the legislature and the executive branch (Department of Finance). Moreover, elite domination tended to keep the policy process privatized during most of the periods. An exception to this is that during the most recent period there has been some socialization of conflict, as special interests such as unions and Native Hawaiian groups have sought greater access to the policy system.

Second, a review of political values pursued in the laws, resulting from changes in government within each turbulent period, strongly demonstrates that the political value of efficiency has dominated, with lesser attention to quality. This can be seen by studying our content analysis of the political values embedded in the statutes summarized in Table 1.1.

We concluded that most of these regularities have been bred from a long-standing heritage of elite power, excessive partisanship, and an

TABLE 1.1
Distribution of Values and State Policy Mechanisms (SPMs)

SPM	*Quality*	*Efficiency*	*Equity*	*Choice*	*Total*
In Chapter VII, "A Statute for the Regulation of Schools," Constitutional Laws of Hawai'i, 1842 (Kingdom of Hawai'i)					
Finance		6			6
Personnel	3	3			6
Testing					0
Program	1				1
Governance		4			4
Curriculum					0
Bldg. & facilities		1			1
Total	4	14	0	0	18
In Act 57, 1896 (Republic of Hawai'i)					
Finance		7			7
Personnel	2	2			4
Testing					0
Program	1	1			2
Governance	2	24		1	27
Curriculum	1	1			2
Bldg. & facilities		1			1
Total	6	36	0	1	43
In Hawai'i School Laws, 1966 (State of Hawai'i)					
Finance		7	1		8
Personnel		1			1
Testing					0
Program	3				3
Governance		15		1	16
Curriculum					0
Bldg. & facilities					0
Total	3	23	1	1	28
In Article X, Education, 1978 (State of Hawai'i)					
Finance		1			1
Personnel					0
Testing					0
Program					0
Governance		1		1	2
Curriculum			1		1
Bldg. & facilities					0
Total	0	2	1	1	4

immobilized citizenry. Hawai'i's school policies, therefore, have resulted from partisan political activity pursuing efficiency that consequently focused on the policy domains of finance (efficient allocation) and governance (efficient control). The rhetoric and changes that emerged during each of the periods resulted in educational policies and activities that were expressions of these values and preferences. Both policy domains tend to result in resource allocations expressing who is to benefit (Easton, 1965a, 1965b) and maintaining the status quo, as opposed to promoting change. Policies that persisted, therefore, tended to be structural add-ons pursuing more efficient operations that were relatively noncontroversial in that they were consistent with widely endorsed values, had the support of special interests, and were required by law (Tyack & Cuban, 1995).

Drawing on our previous study of the policy process in Hawai'i, we found that several broad cultural scripts or institutions emerged from the data that were played out in the educational practices from the turbulent periods we studied. We discuss each of these institutions and their impact on Native Hawaiians in further detail in chapters 2 through 6. Interestingly, we found that these themes were also being institutionalized simultaneously in other parts of the United States, suggesting that national trends also impact the formulation and implementation of state educational policy. The dominance of efficiency as a political value served Hawai'i's increasing economic importance and institutionalized a clearly defined social hierarchy. Schooling became a primary method through which advantage was attained and maintained. In the first period, American missionaries saw a heathen society in need of Christian values and thus employed education as a means of devaluing native culture while creating their own heaven on earth. Much like on the plains of the Midwest, early education in Hawai'i was dominated by various Christian churches who contributed to colonialization of the islands and competed among themselves for political power as a means of institutionalizing their religious beliefs through educational practices (Friedberger, 1996).

A by-product was the creation of common schools in 1840 (reflecting the dominance of this primarily Protestant institution across the United States) for Hawaiian students and select schools for the children of Hawaiian royalty and missionary descendants. Thus, racism became institutionalized quickly in the schools of colonial Hawai'i. This first institution (or cultural script) left a legacy to this day: the direct descendants of the select schools are the private schools.

Dominating U.S. business elites overthrew the independent and sovereign Hawaiian monarchy in 1893, creating both a governance structure to ensure that their economic desires were met and a school system that gave whites privileges over Hawaiians and Asians, which characterized the second period. Coinciding with the municipal progressive reform that swept the United States from 1890 to 1920, the domination of business interests consolidated power in professional administrators, created a more centralized school system with fewer individual schools, and abolished the Hawaiian language for classroom instruction.

The third period, which was between the World Wars, also produced institutions within the school system. In 1924, elite business leaders instituted a formal segregated school system for standard English speakers and lesser schools for the majority of immigrants and Native Hawaiians. This change was tied to social policies directed at "Americanizing" Hawaiians and other recent Asian immigrants. Corresponding efforts resulted in extensive tracking practices with respect to access to curriculum, attempts to limit bilingual education, and charging high school tuition for those who were not United States citizens or could not prove their sole allegiance to the United States (Tamura, 1994). In 1920, for example, 98% of Japanese children attending public school in Hawai'i also attended Japanese-language school after hours (Tamura, 1994).

After World War II, however, *nisei* (second generation Japanese Americans) returning from fighting the war in Europe took advantage of GI benefits as well as changing attitudes about them. In contrast to Native Hawaiians, this group of voluntary immigrants who had grown up on plantations perceived education as a means to attain land ownership and economic prosperity. They moved into influential positions in governance (leading to the emergence of Democratic control) and the Department of Education. Various Asian immigrant groups also received citizenship rights between 1946 and 1952. Such political changes led to the abolition of formal school segregation in Hawai'i before the Brown Decision in 1954.

Finally, the fourth period, which has coincided with growing Native American political activism, has resulted in Hawaiian culture being infused into the curriculum at the elementary, secondary, and postsecondary levels. As Article X, section 4 of the State Constitution reads, "The State shall promote the study of Hawaiian culture, history, and language. The State shall provide for a Hawaiian education program consisting of language, culture and history in the public schools" (p. 16). Concurrently, both Hawaiian and English were recognized as the official languages of the state. In fact, Native Hawaiians voted in late 1996 on whether to proceed with political sovereignty. Results favored sovereignty by a 3 to 1 margin, but the vote was boycotted by several key groups who resent state control of the sovereignty process. To many, however, the implementation of Hawaiian educational policies has not been fully realized, nor have policies extended far enough to redress previous wrongs. Moreover, special programs must compete with all other programs in the Governor's budget. With an undiversified and slumping economy, education's share of the state budget declined from 28% in 1966 to 15.5% in 1991, and Hawai'i's rank in per capita educational spending among the 50 states has similarly fallen from 9th to 47th (Staff, Honolulu Advertiser, 1994).

On the other hand, in the 1980s and 1990s, increasing activism led to the creation of Hawaiian language immersion schools on all of the islands, where classroom instruction is conducted in Hawaiian. Similarly, the Hawaiian Studies department has grown over the past decade at the University of Hawai'i at Mānoa and University of Hawai'i at Hilo. Native Hawaiians are somewhat more proportionally represented in leadership positions within the Department of Education, for example as school principals. In 1986, Hawai'i elected its first Hawaiian governor, who served two terms. As the system became more open, however, other groups also became involved in legislating reform. One of these was the Business Roundtable, which was largely responsible for the institutionalization of school site-based management. As Borman, Castenell, and Gallager (1993) argued, it is organized across the 50 states and has tended to be dominated by White males. Such corporate efforts in changing schools were encouraged and actively supported under two conservative presidents, Reagan and Bush. Of course, in Hawai'i the Roundtable's reform efforts in 1988 were dominated by nearly all of Hawai'i's new and old major corporations, with very little representation from educational practitioners and scholars. As this suggests, considerable educational clout is still wielded by business due to its strong influence on the legislature and governor via campaign support and contributions.

THEORETICAL AND METHODOLOGICAL INTENT

It is one thing to collect the facts, but they do not explain or lead to the understanding of the actual event (Easton, 1953). What must be done, then, is to order the facts around a theory "which may explain, analyze, and predict the 'confusion of reality' " (Marshall et al., 1989, p. 4). Studying the policymaking process over a period of time requires an understanding of the political-cultural values of Hawai'i in each specific period of time sampled. In this last section of the chapter, we briefly discuss institutional theory and how we employed the theory as a means of making sense out of the data in our four turbulent historical periods. As Selznick (1957) argued, theories of educational reform should be rooted in a theory of social groups. After completing our previous study on the educational policy making process in Hawai'i (Benham & Heck, 1994), we wondered why waves of reform have been similar in Hawai'i to those across the United States, but political processes at the local and state levels were often quite different, ranging from elite-dominated and closed to pluralistic and relatively open emphasizing bargaining among diverse interests (Plank et al., 1996).

Educational changes are often an organizational response to the need to adapt to common changing environmental conditions (Ogawa, 1992).

These changing conditions lead organizations such as schools to develop along similar lines in spite of wide variability in political processes of educational reform found in specific settings. As Plank, Scotch, and Gamble (1996) forcefully argued, this variability is shown in various case studies of educational reform across the United States. Interestingly enough, in studying the implementation of progressive reforms that occurred between 1890 and 1920 across the United States, Plank et al. found that larger school districts in the East and Midwest decreased the size of school boards and expanded the size of their administrative staffs in response to the growth in enrollment size and complexity of their school systems. These innovations were soon adopted elsewhere in smaller cities and in other regions (e.g, the West). As Plank et al. maintain, districts often imitated each other to gain social legitimacy, even if they did not face the same growing school enrollment pressures. This echoes Turner's statement in 1894 that U.S. institutions were uniquely shaped by the need to adapt to changing environmental conditions as the country expanded westward.

The conceptual frameworks that researchers and policymakers employ are important for they tend to emphasize different features and provide somewhat different explanations of events (Ogawa, 1992; Wagner, 1993). Rational perspectives on organizations dominated most previous research and practice regarding educational reform. Such views suggest that organizations are formal structures organized around the pursuit of goals. Reform from this perspective is seen as altering formal structures to improve performance or goal attainment (Ogawa, 1992). In fact, the essence of reform would be to enhance the quality of the school system through making the delivery of schooling more efficient. As we found, the values of efficiency and quality are exactly what dominated in looking at the policymaking history of Hawai'i. As Tyack and Cuban (1995) argued, efficient management, professionalism, and the belief in continual progress gave the appearance that educational policy was the result of rational planning, as opposed to political bargaining.

An alternative view on educational reform is offered through the institutional perspective, which derives from institutional theory of social organizations in sociology. In fact, we believe this to be very close to a political-cultural view of society from anthropology. Because we were interested in how the school system as an organization responded to broad cultural values, however, we chose to emphasize institutional theory. While not new to sociology, it has recently re-emerged, in part in opposition to the bureaucratic rational and goal focused view of organizations (Ogawa, 1992). The theory stresses the influence of societal values, cultural theories, ideologies, and perceptions as defining organizational structures and practices. As Meyer, Boli, and Thomas (1987) argued, "Institutions define the meaning and identity of the individual and the patterns of appropriate economic, political, and cultural activity engaged in by those individuals" (p. 12). Political action by policymakers and organizational behavior, therefore, are the enactments of broad institutional or cultural scripts (Ogawa, 1992). Thus, theory is more useful in tracking possible changes in the educational system temporally.

An institutional perspective focuses on the impact of the environment on a particular type of organizational action: the adoption of structural features such as decreasing the size of school boards and increasing the size of administrative staff. Dimaggio and Powell (1983) argued that both competitive and institutional factors contribute to the structural similarities seen among organizations such as school systems. With respect to competition, organizations facing similar problems commonly respond in like fashion. Successful innovations can enhance survival and growth.

In contrast, the adoption of institutions may have less to do with efficient operation (despite the considerable rhetoric embedded in the laws) than on conforming to wider rules and myths that confer social legitimacy. Because these structures embody widely held beliefs, organizations can ensure social legitimacy with stakeholders such as politicians and policymakers. This legitimacy is required if stakeholders are going to continue to invest resources in the organization, which contributes to its survival and effectiveness. Moreover, organizations may also adapt structures to gain social legitimacy, in part, because legal and ideological norms of prudence and accountability require them to employ professionals who share similar backgrounds and common values (Plank et al., 1996). Both of these means help explain why districts and states tended to follow suit in mandating teacher tenure, mandating kindergarten, adopting the comprehensive high school, lengthening the school year, and ensuring stronger accountability policies for teachers and administrators, to name a few reforms. From this perspective, policymakers act as implementers of widely endorsed cultural norms. Their policies and actions reflect tinkering with the system, as opposed to pursuing widespread social and educational change (Tyack & Cuban, 1995).

This adaptive feature of organizations is a key point with respect to the history of schooling in Hawai'i because, for example, the common and later public schools have never been seen as completely legitimate, nor well supported. To illustrate, today many employees (e.g., teachers, administrators) of the Department of Education and politicians, who are charged with making or implementing educational policy for the state, send their children to private schools.

DiMaggio and Powell (1983) suggested three ways that organizations such as schools adopt institutional structures. First, coercive means result from pressures by other organizations on which the organization is dependent. This could explain, for example, some typical school responses to pressures exerted by local businesses that depend upon graduates. Second, organizations tend to mimic successful changes made by other organizations. Schools were particularly prone to mimicking each other, for example, in adopting the tenents of the municipal reform, including the belief in a unitary community, the professional neutrality of administrators, and the separation of politics and education (Iannaccone, 1977; Tyack, 1974; Plank et al., 1996). Finally, organizations may use normative means, that is, adopting norms because of the influence of professions (or others higher on the social scale) surrounding them (as members within the organization aspire to that social standing).

DiMaggio and Powell (1983) argued that, through these three means, organizations become more homogeneous in their particular field. Through several means of adopting wider cultural values, therefore, schools have become rather homogeneous in structure over time. Tyack and Cuban (1995) referred to these same phenomena as cycles of *policy talk* and institutional trends that interact to produce, at best, incremental changes to schools. We argue that institutional theory offers to explain why many of the educational reforms we identified over time in Hawai'i mirror those in other states across the United States, despite considerable political differences across settings. Not surprisingly, the effects of these institutions on Native Hawaiians has been similar in scope and power to those perpetuated on other Native Americans.

Methodological Approach

As critical theorists and postmodernists remind us, personal, cultural, and social factors influence the formation of knowledge. Researchers are often unaware of how their personal experience and position in society influence the knowledge they produce (Banks, 1993). With respect to understanding the relationship between Native Hawaiians and the dominant culture, we believe, like Merton (1972), that the perspectives of both insiders and outsiders are needed to gain a more complete view of social reality. On a personal level, we found this to be true, as we consulted both Hawaiian and U.S. sources of history and also explored a variety of personal (e.g., Native Hawaiian) experiences and understandings against the detached outsider view of the social scientist in attempting to find balance in presenting this material.

Because institutional scripts are socially constructed by the dominant cultural values in society, our methodological approach is necessarily constructivist. To examine these trends, we drew largely upon institutional theory, which focuses on how organizations such as school systems adopt widely held cultural or institutional values as a means of gaining and maintaining social legitimacy with stakeholders such as politicians, policymakers, business interests. Applying the theoretical lens, we examine how particular institutions were introduced (e.g., through laws, policies) and accepted into the school system in Hawai'i, and how they continue be shaped and maintained in the 1990s.

Our methodology, therefore, shifted away from the structural-functional explanations that have dominated the literature on school reform, and more toward an interpretive lens, focusing on the socially constructed meanings surrounding educational policy (e.g., as embedded in laws) and how particular cultural values became institutionalized in the schools. To conduct our analysis, we consulted a variety of data sources including journals of missionaries, newspaper accounts, and archival data consisting of school records, laws, and educational policies.

Bell (1992) noted that racism is a permanent structure in U.S. society, and schools as organizations have mirrored this, often through creating oppressive structures. Our intent is to examine how some of these structures have impacted educational processes in Hawai'i for Native Hawaiians, with the ultimate aim of creating better possibilities for a more open and democratic educational system in the present.

II

CASE HISTORIES

'ELUA

The Fortuitous Arrival of the American Missionaries, 1820s–1840s

If a big wave comes in, large fishes will come from the dark ocean which you never saw before, and when they see the small fishes they will eat them up.

—David Malo (Malo, 1898)

HA'AWINA NO'ONO'O (SHARING THOUGHTS)

The ways of knowing and living of the Native Hawaiian are rich, complex, and deeply embedded in nā akua (gods), the ali'i chiefs—who connect the people to nā akua , and the 'āina (land) that gives life. Princess Nahi'ena'ena's struggle between Native knowledge and tradition and the ways of the Western world is symbolic of the tragic clash of two cultures—one delicate, free, and sophisticated but to some primitive, the other equally proud and powerful, but with the might of modern institutions. Her life becomes the metaphor which aptly illustrates the story of colonialism.

Princess Nahi'ena'ena, Kamehameha I's only sacred daughter, whose name means fiery blaze, was symbolically linked to her two brothers on both a physical and psychic level. She and her brothers gave life and hope to the islands because they were descended from the akua and personified stability, eternity, and human skill. A union between Nahi'ena'ena and her brother Kauikeaouli (Kamehameha III) would assure the eternity of the islands. Nahi'ena'ena's life and destiny, however, would be changed by the arrival of the brig Thaddeus in 1820 which carried the first wave of American missionaries. Three years later, in 1823, a second ship, the Thames, brought the missionary William Richards. Upon the death of Nahi'ena'ena's mother, Keopuolani, William Richards was charged with the education of the young princess. Keopuolani, a convert to Christi-

anity, directed him to wean the native princess away from traditional Hawaiian rituals and toward the new ways of the Western world and Christian life.

The conflict between the world she was leaving and the one that was coming to dominate her thoughts tore at Nahi'ena'ena's soul. In a letter to a missionary wife, she wrote, "One day my thoughts are fixed on God; another day I am ensnared [by Christianity] and thus it is continually" (Sinclair, 1995, p. 132). Her love for her brother and duty to the Hawaiian people led to a secret marriage. Living the life of a Native Hawaiian, Nahi'ena'ena flourished in the hula and traditional rituals while enjoying rum that flowed freely from visiting ships. In an effort to save her Christian soul, Nahi'ena'ena was persuaded by Richards to relinquish her incestuous relationship and enter into a more solemn Christian life. She eventually married another ali'i, Leleiohoku, a marriage which was sanctioned by the Church. The princess died on December 30, 1836, at the age of approximately 21. On her death bed, missionary wives prodded her to repent her digressions, but there are no records that reveal that she sought mercy from a Western god.

Embedded in this story is a dilemma that I and current generations of Native Hawaiian youth have yet to solve. The destruction of traditional Hawaiian practices and principles over time by Western science, education, and economics has resulted in loss of life, loss of understanding of family and community, and loss of a cultural script that records process and experience. Indeed, the philosophic assumption that schools are bastions of democracy is a far cry from what is upheld and assessed in schools and society. And, for many Native groups including Native Hawaiians, this gap continues to grow as recent movements toward one homogeneous culture become more prevalent.

Education as a tool for transformation has sought to replace Native ways and Native thinking with foreign ontologies. In essence, foreign (non-Native) epistemological beliefs have guided educational policy and practice. In so doing, Western schooling has replaced Native ways of knowing (for more information see chap. 3). Table 2.1 provides some examples of this duality. The information has been drawn from Native Hawaiian scholars and kūpuna (Kame'eleihiwa, 1992; Meyer, 1996; Pukui, Haertig, & Lee, 1972).

So, what happens after 13 years of formal U.S. education during which one's role in community is defined? If the socialization of school is complete, the Native becomes silent, fulfilling the colonialistic rite. At first, I was silent, disregarding the tensions I felt between the ways of my kūpuna and the road of modern Hawai'i. Over time, through my own efforts of study and soul-searching, I recognized my need to both educate and challenge educational institution's values and processes which were in conflict with Native Hawaiian history, culture, language, and tradition.

So, how does a Hawai'i-raised and Western-educated woman go about making change? Like Nahi'ena'ena and many Native Hawaiians, when confronted with new ideas coupled with the might and technology of a colonial power, I struggle

TABLE 2.1
Native Hawaiian and Western Rationale

Concept	*Native Hawaiian Ways*	*Western Rationale View*
Intellect	Na'au: Thinking comes from the intestines; the "gut" links the heart and the mind. Thus, feelings and emotions are not separate from knowing, wisdom, and intelligence.	Separation of intellectual activity (cognitive domain) and emotion (affective domain). Thinking comes from the head/brain.
Spirituality	The source of knowledge comes from the 'aumakua and kumupa'a (spiritual guardians and guides). This spirituality is interwoven with knowledge and experience that frames cultural experience and context of knowledge (see Kame'eleihiwa, 1992; Handy & Pukui, 1972).	Knowledge is measurable in some fashion or can be rationalized by some set of objective assumptions that are not linked to mythical origins.
Boundaries	Boundaries are fluid. Because knowing is sensory bound, the boundaries between the physical and mystical are fluid. One is connected to the environment and to the supernatural. Thus, knowledge can be received in dreams.	Boundaries are clearly defined. Categorization of facts, disciplines, and bodies of knowledge provide for clearly defined intellectual thought that are supported by a variety of "textual" (written) affirmations.
Relationship	"Aloha mai no, aloha aku" (When love is given, love should be returned) (see Pukui, et al., 1983). Because one is spiritually and physically connected to others, good relationships and reciprocity are highly valued. The connections between people must remain unbroken, harmonious, and correct.	Individuals are disconnected from each other. Because knowledge is seen more as a concrete set of ideas and skills that can be quantified, individuals grasp of knowledge is highlighted. This creates a commodity quality to knowledge that leads to individual focused learning and being.
Knowledge	All learning must have aesthetic or practical use. Knowledge must link the spirit and the physical, and maintain relationships.	Knowledge for knowledge's sake has problematized Western education as the bridge between theory and practice has not been resolved.
Analysis	Kaona. This establishes a tolerance for ambiguity often viewed in the use of symbol and metaphor, "the illusion of mind/body split with regard to intelligence" (Meyer, 1996, p. 41).	Concrete analysis and objectivity clearly explain subject matter.

daily to negotiate messy, abstract, ever-changing borders that serve to restrict, to liberate, and to change. Through it all, I strive to maintain a sense of balance between what is Native and what is Western. How I have come closer to grasping the meaning of education and its implication on my life and the lives of many Native Hawaiians is to retell the history of education in Hawai'i. Understanding what has been lost and what has been gained, I believe, is a beginning to breaking the context and constructs of colonial oppression still imposed upon Native Hawaiians today.

"MY KINGDOM SHALL BE A KINGDOM OF LEARNING" (KAMEHAMEHA III)

The domination of Hawai'i's political, social, and economic institutions by the first wave of Western explorers and missionaries created a cultural and political schism among the Hawaiians. Some maintained their passion for the traditions of Hawai'i Nei while others, many more, aligned themselves with the Native elite who followed the teachings of a Christian god. This radical cultural change from what had been Hawai'i and what was Hawaiian allowed the seeds of Western culture to spread into almost every firmament of governance and economic growth. In this chapter, we examine the beginning of Hawai'i's colonial roots, focusing on how political and economic changes produced cultural values that became institutionalized in the early school system. These institutions were religious-dominated education and separate schools that mirrored a stratified social structure. We then present an analysis of the scope of the impact of these changes on the educational and life experiences of the Native Hawaiians.

Interaction with the missionaries, primarily Congregationalists and Presbyterians of the American Board of Commissioners for Foreign Missions (ABCFM), produced a number of quick changes in the internal affairs of Hawai'i. While the missionary effort among the Native Hawaiians was quite similar in tenor to the prosyletization of Native Americans, there is a notable difference. The missionaries in Hawai'i taught literary skills, Christianity, and civilization in the Hawaiian mother tongue, not in English. This, to the Native Hawaiians, gave the initial appearance that the Hawaiian language was an integral element of learning, that being Hawaiian was valued, and that Christianity was compatible with native thinking. This notion of compatibility might explain why Native Hawaiians, much like the Rio Grande Pueblos who embraced Catholicism, accepted the religious beliefs of the American missionary so readily and why other indigenous groups, like the Western Pueblo, forcefully and violently rejected missionary activity. It was only after the content of education became too complex for the missionary's Hawaiian language literacy that the English language was used. The introduction of English as a medium of instruction would create a social caste system between those who spoke English and those who did not.

By the end of the 1820s, the missionaries had encouraged the Hawaiian rulers to mandate schooling for all children. As might be expected, this produced the rapid adoption of New England values and structures explicitly revealed through schooling. The school structures created separate common and select schools for children of different social standing and ethnic backgrounds. Common schools (attended by the commoners) had a somewhat tenuous existence, as they were sporadically supported by local chiefs and the work of local laborers. Supplies at the common schools were scanty and the Native teachers, educated by the missionaries, were trained to teach only rudimentary skills which became tiresome to their students (Wist, 1940). Steuber (1981–1982a) noted that much of the curriculum focused on Western moral ethics. In fact, the curriculum "reflected a mixture of the Calvinistic theology and worldly asceticism expressed through work and delayed gratification, the teachings of Poor Richard and other lessons formed in the hardy New England environment and carried to Hawai'i" (p. 21).

In contrast, the select schools taught by the missionaries were well supplied and presented a well-prepared Western curriculum. The majority of children attending the select schools were the offspring of the chiefs, half-Hawaiians, and a few selected Christian-Hawaiian children of commoners (Steuber, 1981–1982a). Missionary children were educated at home and then sent to schools on the continent. The common and select schools had separate missions, thereby institutionalizing, almost immediately, racism and classism in Hawai'i's schools.

Because the school is an effective and often appropriate means for social transformation and cultural teaching, its religious and political philosophies taught new ways of thinking about self and status, land and individual property, and cultural value. Separate schooling ensured that social structure would remain stable, with missionaries and other foreigners at the top and others well below. The effects of these institutionalized structures were almost immediate, powerful, and have been long-lasting on the educational opportunities for particular groups of children in the state.

COOK'S ARRIVAL IN HAWAI'I, 1778

Prior to the rediscovery of Hawai'i by Western explorers, the Hawaiian perspective of reality was a relatively limited one (Makanani, interviews, 1991–1992).[1] This is not to say that Hawaiian culture was not well articulated. Before white contact, Hawaiians had formed a rather complete and complex social structure supporting a large population that was as highly efficient as any other stone age society. The Native population of approximately 300,000 (LaCroix & Roumassett, 1984, p. 154)[2] lived on eight islands—Ni'ihau, Kaua'i, O'ahu, Lana'i, Moloka'i, Maui, Kaho'olawe, and Hawai'i—which were further divided into feudal chiefdoms and stratified into three distinct social classes: the *ali'i* chiefs, the *kahuna* (special class of priests, specialists), and the *maka'āinana* (commoners).[3] Land, the source of power and control, was distributed among the *ali'i* and could only be redistributed if it were won through warfare by another *ali'i* (Kuykendall, 1938, p. 10).[4]

The political and economic stability of this early culture was bound to the *kapu* system, a system of religious law. The strength of this system in integrating Hawaiian society was the key to the success of the American missionary and the U.S. form of governance. This strict code of conduct was deeply ingrained in the political governing culture of Hawai'i. The importance of the *kapu* system cannot be underplayed, for the *kapu* system further provided a structured method of allocating valuable resources (e.g., land) to an *ali'i* class, whose position to make decisions was sanctioned by the gods (LaCroix & Roumassett, 1984, p. 155). Violations against the *kapu* system resulted in harsh punishments—death being common. Prior to Captain Cook's arrival, the Hawaiians established and maintained a rather exclusive political order in which a small group of individuals, the *ali'i*, were able to maintain control over a much larger population of *maka'āinana* through the religiously grounded *kapu*.

Upon his arrival, Cook found an indigenous society with a highly developed pattern of social, economic, political, religious, cultural, and ecologically balanced ethnology (Steuber, 1981–1982a, p. 19).[5] For the most part, learning was conducted through the process of "observing family members in their daily activities and eventually trying tasks for themselves" (Kelly, 1981–1982, p. 4). The goal of this informal schooling, a similar objective in today's school rostrum, was "to prepare children for full participation as functioning members of society" (Kelly, 1981–1982, p. 4).[6] There was no written language to be learned, only the values promulgated by the social-political order enforced by the *kapu* system which were learned through oral transference of knowledge. The *ali'i* class, under the tutorship of the *kahuna* class, however, had a more formal, orally instructed education that included such topics as "politics, economics, warfare, and the rights and lore of religion. They also learned medicine, astronomy, navigation, surveying, the chiefly genealogies, sport and game, and the dance or hula" (Steuber, 1981–1982a, p. 20). Marion Kelly (1981–1982) best summarized education in ancient Hawaiian society as:

> practical, skill-oriented, socially-useful, in tune with reality, environmentally-aware, conserver-cognizant. Regarding the process of learning there seems to have been a strong emphasis on learning-by-doing—one might say, on-the-job learning—together with memorization and rote. All the while education was in process the participants were practicing socially-acceptable roles that were commensurate with their abilities; they were contributing members of society and accepted as such from the time they entered the "age of responsibility," and through that relationship achieved a positive self-image. (p. 13)

Cook's landing on what he named the Sandwich Isles marked the end of Hawai'i's isolation and the beginning of a new societal order that would thrust Hawai'i into an era of turmoil. This is not to say that the chiefdoms had not experienced any social and political turmoil prior to Cook's arrival. In fact, historians (e.g., Kamakau, Kuykendall, Malo, Sahlins, & Kirch) wrote that during the earlier days of antiquity, there were numerous periods of political warfare for resources, which reshaped and defined the native social and political order. In contrast, however, the turmoil brought by the coming of the white was one in which the Hawaiians faced an entirely new set of cultural values—a new way of seeing life—one that threatened their very existence.

Once the Hawaiians overcame the initial impression of Cook and his men as being gods or messengers sent by the gods, they realized that these foreigners brought novel ideas and material objects, in particular modern weaponry. The Age of Iron had come suddenly to the sandy shores of Hawai'i. This iron god carried a double-edged sword. One edge was a forceful means through which the *ali'i* could gain greater power and more land resources. On the other side of the blade, bowing to this new deity meant deep cultural change; therefore, the warrior was forced to rethink and redefine who he was and what his world would be. The consequences of Cook's arrival and the introduction of a new and powerful Western technology created in the Hawaiian mind two ideas. The first notion was "that every belief they had, that they had developed over the years, that they had put their faith into were based on falsehoods" (Makanani interviews, 1991–1992). In short, Hawaiians began to realize that their perception of reality was limited. The second realization was that there existed other people with modern technical knowledge; unfortunately, this began the myth that the Hawaiian was inferior to the white.

Cook's arrival and subsequent foreign ships brought to the tiny island kingdom new technology and ideas. This began to change the Native Hawaiian perspective of reality and, therefore, the way in which the people were governed and educated. Kamehameha I was able to marshal the usage of Western weaponry to gain control over all the islands and place them under one rule. Essentially, the now united islands remained a feudal autocracy which maintained a hierarchy with the king as the supreme head. Although the king had the power to make decisions, he was often advised by a loosely gathered court of chiefs (Kuykendall, 1938). The only administrative addition was the appointment of governors, his special representatives to other islands, through which his widespread control could be maintained.

Collapse of the *Kapu* System

Much of Kamehameha I's governing activity dealt with keeping the kingdom together and upholding the still practiced *kapu* system. The *kapu* was a system of rules that defined every element of daily life from childrearing, to work and recreation, to sexual intercourse, to ritual and ceremonies. Kanahele (1986) pointed out that because the *ali'i* were thought to be gods, their support of the *kapu* and the Native class was a just system. As we have suggested, the *kapu* system was central to the stability of the Hawaiian culture. As Allen (1982) argued:

> The *kapu* had been the guiding mores of the Hawaiian people, forming the essence of their economic, social, and religious life. The *kapu* system established the class structure and held it firm, keeping the *ali'i* apart from the *haole* and the commoner. (p. 24).[7]

Some historians pointed out that the intelligence of Kamehameha I lay in his ability to balance the traditions of the past while still incorporating the new (Daws, 1969).[8] Toward the end of his life, Kamehameha realized that the collapse of the traditional order, the *kapu* system, could be the downfall of his hard-fought Hawaiian kingdom. So, he appointed his favorite wife, Ka'ahumanu, a strong-willed woman of high rank, *Kuhina-nui* (prime minister), to govern the land with his son, Liholiho, who would become Kamehameha II (Kamakau, 1992).[9] His intentions of appointing a person who would uphold the *kapu* system, although well meaning, in effect acted in reverse.

By 1820, numerous foreigners had already visited Hawai'i, introducing Western traditions and values that often conflicted with many of the restrictive *kapu*. Hawaiians began to witness many of their *kapu* proven false. This is not to suggest in any way that Hawai'i's religion was made up of mere superstitions, but that some aspects of the *kapu* system that governed the actions of the people were clearly not consistent with what was observed in the new, Western cultural system. For example, a *kapu* prohibited a Hawaiian woman from eating bananas for, if she did, she would be struck dead. If she observed a White woman eating a banana who did not subsequently die, then this controlling social more would begin to erode.

Ka'ahumanu and Keopuolani (mother of Liholiho, Kamehameha II), a month after the death of Kamehameha I, broke the *kapu* system (Kamakau, 1992).[10] The effect of this action was to place Ka'ahumanu, as some historians suggested by her own design, as an emancipated woman (Daws, 1969). The breaking of the *kapu* also suggested that power and governance could be amassed through secular means. Needless to say, Ka'ahumanu became the powerful force that moved Hawai'i. Kamakau (1992), citing *Ka Nūpepa Ku'oko'a*, wrote:

> All followed her from the highest to the lowest because of the laws she had made which brought protection to the poorest. She took the blind Bartimeus as her friend, made counselors, companions, and friends of the religious, visited the missionary families in their homes, and spent her time reading those parts of the Bible which had been translated. In her old age she learned to read and write and figure. At her death there was no one her equal to fill her place. (p. 323)

Teaching of Native Hawaiian Values

Education practices prior to the American missionary arrival in Hawai'i are not well documented; however, sources suggest that education was more informal and oral, focused on socializing the young to their life roles, teaching values, preparing them for their responsibilities to the *ali'i*, and educating them about changing *kapu*. The belief *Nānā ka maka. Ho'olohe. Pa'a ka waha. Ho'opili* (Observe. Listen. Keep the mouth shut. Imitate) was the Native Hawaiian way of teaching young children (Pukui, Haertig, & Lee, 1972).[11] Children did not take written notes and did not question their *kumu* (teacher), but observed and practiced a skill repeatedly until they displayed proficiency.

The teaching of Hawaiian values was an essential component of a young child's life. Values were tied to mysticism as well as the practicality of survival. For example, a child learned to never make a face at anyone because the insulted person could be a sorcerer who would do the child harm, or the offended party could employ a sorcerer to do the child harm (Pukui et al., 1972, Vol. II). The mystic rationale of rude behavior and its consequences made a child think twice before wincing at a stranger. Among the many values taught the young Hawaiian was that of *hana* or work. The saying *E ho'ohuli ka lima i lalo* (The palms of the hands should be turned down; Pukui et al., 1972, Vol. II) best describes the importance of work. In essence, the phrase suggests to the child that when one's palms are facing upward (*i luna*), the palms are idle, and laziness was disgraceful. However, because most tasks were done with the palms facing downward *(i lalo)*, if the palms faced downward then one was working, and work was highly respected. Another essential value was that one must always complete a project to perfection before going on to the next, even if it meant redoing the work several times. Once the child achieved perfect quality, the skill was learned and would assure future quality-made objects (Pukui et al., 1972, Vol. II). *Nīnau*, or when to ask questions, was a fundamental lesson learned by all children. This meant that a child never asked a *Kupuna* (elder) a question unless given permission, and the question must always be a well-thought out, not frivolous, query (Pukui et al., 1972, Vol. II).

Changes in Hawai'i

To better grasp the political, social, and cultural turbulence of this period which forms the context for the setting of initial educational policies and institutionalization of the dual school structure, it is important to understand that prior to the arrival of the American missionary, Hawai'i underwent rampant upheaval of its social-mythological, economic-agrarian, and political-kinship foundation that existed prior to the arrival of Captain Cook in 1778 (Linnekan, 1985). Hawai'i was what anthropologists have termed a pristine rank society (Fried, 1967).[12] An examination of the social and political composition of the Hawaiian chiefdom revealed a hierarchical structure where there were a few coveted positions of authority and many with adequate skills who could fill the posts (Fried, 1967). Furthermore, this hierarchical structure was maintained through a complex web of kinship and mysticism. Unique to this structure was that the *ali'i*, who was linked to high rank through religious standing and mythical lineage, did not have the power to command. The *ali'i* was a symbolic leader, as the power rested in the ritual or the *kapu* (taboo or prohibition). For example, eating rituals held that men could eat certain foods that were *kapu* to women, that the men and women ate separately, and that the *ali'i* could consume certain foods that were *kapu* to the *maka'āinana* (commoner). Such *kapu*, therefore, clearly defined the complex system of status for men and women, *ali'i* and *maka'āinana*, in the traditional chiefdom.

Conflict, which resulted in political evolution (Carneiro, 1970),[13] occurred due to the need for more agricultural resources (Fried, 1967) and symbolic matters which dealt with lineage or mythical providence. Prior to white contact, the Hawaiian chiefdom evolved in isolation due to internal or indigenous factors (Fried, 1967), thus maintaining Hawaiian ideals, traditions, and beliefs. After the arrival of Cook and a steady flow of foreigners, however, Hawai'i underwent a complete breakdown of its cultural (*kapu*) system which had maintained Hawaiian ritual, political governance, and social structures. The symbolic ties of kinship between the chief and commoner that had formed the foundation of the Hawaiian belief system were replaced with a Western structure layered in an economic and political bureaucracy foreign to Native Hawaiians.

Jocelyn Linnekin[14] (1985, 1990) observed that, as Hawai'i's economic structure evolved "from production for subsistence and tribute to production for external markets" (p. 155), a new proletariat class of Hawaiians emerged. Competing among each other for resources, the chiefs subjected the commoners to abject slavery, decimating what was left of the kinship relationships. Although three classes later emerged, the proletarian-chiefs, the middle-class professionals, and the commoners, it was the latter group, the *maka'āinana* (consisting of the majority of Native Hawaiians), which comprised the lowest class. Identity was defined by class and level of acculturation to the behaviors, dress, arts, and other customs of the *haole* (foreigners). As the new Hawaiian proletariat vigorously replaced the *kapu* with Western rituals, the Native Hawaiian lower class realized little power to define their own destiny.

Within this period of political, social, and cultural upheaval entered the American missionary who, over a short time, institutionalized the ideals of colonialism upon the wider social and political systems of the islands through the educational system. Hawai'i's newly formed hierarchical structure under one ruler and lack of formal governing structure, which the *kapu* had provided, became fertile ground for the pastor, the teacher, and the businessman who sought to gradually mold Hawai'i into a Western society. The arrival of foreign colonialism produced a political, social, cultural, and economic domination that brought to an end Native beliefs and values as well as undermined the Native Hawaiians' economic control over their lands and sovereign governance of the islands' domestic institutions.

Colonialism was effective in Hawai'i due to changing economic conditions, Native depopulation, and the activities of the missionaries in their churches and schools. Although education was conducted in the Hawaiian language, the content of what was taught emphasized the values of a dominating Western culture while devaluing what was Hawaiian. Indeed, Hawaiian sovereignty was first lost in the one-room schoolhouse.

THE ARRIVAL OF THE MISSIONARIES FROM NEW ENGLAND, 1820

The years between the arrival of Captain Cook and the first American Missionaries left the Hawaiians culturally devastated (Steuber, 1981–1982b) due to the debilitating effects of labor exploitation (caused by the whaling and sandalwood trade) and the introduction of disease and alcohol. Additionally, the open violation of the *kapu* system set about an accelerated decline of its control over Native Hawaiian lives. The *maka'āinana*, recognizing that no harm befell the *kapu* breakers, began to disregard the restrictive ancient system of controls, maintaining only some fundamental practices of their religion, polytheistic idolatry, and respect for the land-owning *ali'i* (Makanani interviews, 1991–1992). This was a period best labeled as the Dark Ages of Hawai'i, for it was a time of conflict between indigenous traditions and the values of an encroaching materialistic imperial power from the West.

It was not a coincidence that the zealous New England missionaries arrived at a time of great social, cultural, and political turmoil. They brought with them the spirit and intent of deculturation and enculturation which also drove the effort of missionaries working with Native American peoples (Coleman, 1993). Allen (1982) wrote that "the missionaries sailed into a religious vacuum in 1820. The old gods were officially gone, Ka'ahumanu saw a way to provide new laws and fill the obvious need of the people for a 'god' " (p. 25). A fortuitous arrival indeed! The first missionaries included two clergymen, a doctor, a farmer, a printer, two teachers, seven wives, five children, and three Native Hawaiians who had been educated in New England. They brought fundamental tools to promulgate change in Hawai'i's governing system, that is, formal Western education methods and a Calvinistic curriculum (Kuykendall, 1938). Similar to the work of missionaries on the North American continent, their methods used to gain cognitive control over the ways people make meaning (Spindler, 1968) included separating children from their families, conducting learning in an environment disconnected from daily living, introducing textual learning (often in another language, i.e., English), and deculturating to take away the Indian"ness," or in this case, the Hawaiian"ness" (Coleman, 1993).

Many authors have described the missionary, but none so eloquently as Mark Twain. In his *Letters from Hawai'i* (1966)[15] he described the American Missionary in this fashion:

> . . . the Sandwich Islands missionaries are pious, hardworking; hard-praying; self-sacrificing; hospitable; devoted to the well-being of this people and the interests of Protestantism; bigoted; puritanical; slow; ignorant of all white human nature and natural ways of men, except the remnant of these things that are left in their own class or profession; old fogy-fifty years behind the age; uncharitable toward the weaknesses of the flesh; considering all shortcomings, faults, and failings in the light of crimes, and having no mercy and no forgiveness for such. (p. 129)

Upon the missionaries' arrival, they were aware of two things: one, that the Hawaiians were heathens and in need of saving, as they were morally inferior; and two, that the Hawaiian rulers had strong ties to the U.S. nemesis, Great Britain. Examples of the missionaries' initial impression of the natives are gleaned from their personal journals. Mrs. Lucia Ruggles Holman (1986),[16] a member of the first missionary group, wrote:

> Sabbath, 7th (1820). I will now give you a brief description of their manners while with us.
>
> This first salutation was similar to our manner of introduction, that of giving the hand and Alohah, [*sic*] i.e., how do you do, or good morning. They took seats and began to admire the Ladies, asking if they had any children, calling us "piccaninny" (too little). The larger and fatter the women on Owhyhee [*sic*], the better. One of the old Queens weighs 350. . . . Not being accustomed to sitting upon seats, they began to be very uneasy, and ordering their servants to spread their mats, they flung themselves down, and rolled about the deck like so many hogs, requesting us to lie with them.
>
> They eat when hunger suggests, without any regard to time or place—indeed they make no account of time—they eat and sleep, and eat again, frequently 8 or 10 times in the course of 24 hours. . . . The sight of their wretched situation without firm confidence and faith in Jehovah, is enough to dishearten any one in their attempts to reform them. But the Lord has already done great things for this people. It appears that, he has already begun to put down the strong-holds of Satan—thus preparing a high way for his people. (pp. 18–20)

Mrs. Sarah Joiner Lyman[17] wrote in her journal of the Native Hawaiian and the mission responsibility:

> August 21, 1833. Letter to sister, Melissa Joiner, Royalton, Vermont. You have read that the men wear the Malo, but I presume you have not the least conception how it is put on, or what it is. It is a strip of cloth about three yards long and several inches wide. When folded together it is about the size of a skein of yarn. It is put perhaps twice around the body just above the hips, and then passed between the legs barely covering the private parts with the end fastened behind. This constitutes the whole clothing of multitudes. In my opinion, it would not be much worse to go naked. A great many of the females think no more of going with their breasts exposed, than we do our hands. All, or nearly all who do not wear a full dress, wear the kihe [kihei], which covers from the hips to the knees. Those who live near us have learnt that we think it not right to expose their nakedness, and are more modest about their dress. But neither class have the least sense of shame about them. Both men and women, if they have occasion for it will sit down in, or by the side of the road to do their duties, right

> before our eyes too. They seem to think no more about it than the dumb beasts. I am often put to the blush, but such things do not affect me as they did when I first arrived. Little boys and girls have as much intercourse as they please. Children are as wise as their parents. Things which are kept private from children at home are common talk among children here. Indeed there is nothing kept private from children. Whole families sleep in one apartment, and on the same mat; this is perhaps one of the greatest evils existing. The more I become acquainted with the people the more I feel the importance of labouring to elevate them. (pp. 56–57)

The mission's goal "was to supplement and implement the efforts of organized religious work to raise the Hawaiians from their alleged savagery and degradation and to help them pattern themselves as a people after their western teachers" (Steuber, 1981–1982b, p. 16). The significant ties between religion and education were fundamental to schooling. The educational mission, not unlike the educational purposes of New England colonists, was founded on the need to learn to read the Bible and to dedicate one's life to piousness. This limited view of education lay the foundation for the school's activities, which would work to destroy the Native Hawaiians' traditions, values, cultural heritage, and, in time, language. Among their first actions was to condemn *wā kahiko,* or the former times. This one show of domination firmly rooted U.S. intrusion into Native Hawaiian lives. Additionally, because the political powers of Hawai'i were partially influenced by the British government, the American missionaries, who had recently won their own independence, quickly looked for ways to supplant British influence.

Although many stories promote the event of Hawaiians eating Captain Cook, in reality, the Hawaiians were quite fond and deeply respectful of Cook and later Vancouver. In fact, this close affinity had been exemplified earlier by King Kamehameha I's interest in ceding the islands to King George and later by Kamehameha II's journey to Great Britain in 1823, which had been partially motivated by the desire of Hawaiian rulers to reinforce ties with Great Britain. It is essential to recognize that Native Hawaiian monarchs identified strongly with the British monarchs, seeing them as fellow monarchs. This endured up to the monarchical overthrow in the early 1890s. The American Missionary brought to the Hawaiian Islands an anti-British agenda and a form of government radically different from Great Britain's—a system that championed the ideals of voice in government and individual rights, individual rights to own land, rights to one's own body, and rights to one's own produce (Makanani interviews, 1991–1992).

In short, the missionaries brought not only a pious view of Christianity and civilization but also new political ideas of democratic liberalism. These two elements of their fundamental social beliefs functioned in unison to bring about both a new governing system and educational institutions which would socialize Hawaiian natives to Western social structures and Christian thought. Herein lies the irony of the duality of their action. The missionary had been directed to work only to Christianize and civilize the Hawaiians to Puritanical norms, but to refrain from involvement in the workings of government. Their instructions read:

> Your mission is a mission of mercy, and your work is to be wholly a labor of love. . . . Your views are not to be limited to a low or a narrow scale; but you are to open your hearts wide, and set your mark high. You are to aim at nothing short of covering those islands with fruitful fields and pleasant dwellings, and schools and churches; of raising up the whole people to an elevated state of Christian civilization; of bringing, or preparing the means of bringing, thousands and millions of the present and succeeding generations to the mansions of eternal blessedness (pp. 19–20). . . . But it is an arduous enterprise, a great and difficult work. To obtain an adequate knowledge of the language of the people; to make them acquainted with letters; to give them the Bible with skill to read it; to turn them from their barbarous courses and habits; to introduce, and get into extended operation and influence among them, the arts and institutions and usages of civilized life and society; above all, to convert them from their idolatries and superstitions and vices, to the living and redeeming God . . . to effect all this must be the work of an invincible and indefectivly spirit of benevolence. (American Board of Commissioners, 1838, pp. 27–28)

The directive avoids any mention of involvement with Hawai'i's governing powers. This was due in part to the political atmosphere in the United States. Since the colonies had recently gained independence from Great Britain, the missionaries were well aware of their people's repugnant attitude toward any government's overbearing governance of a colony. Therefore, the missionaries did not want to give the appearance that their intentions were in anyway similar to those of Great Britain. Ironically, however, if the missionaries were to change the Hawaiians, they could not change just one institution and hope not to influence other dependent institutions. Religion, political power, and economics of the land were, in the Hawaiian mind, heavily intertwined (as evidenced by the *kapu* system). One could not talk about politics without bringing up religion. It was therefore inevitable that the missionaries would impact the politics of Hawai'i. A direct connection between Hawai'i's governing forces (the *ali'i*) and the American Missionary was firmly established when Kamehameha I commanded that the missionary teach only the *ali'i*. Kuykendall (1938) wrote:

> From the beginning the chiefs were friendly to the missionaries; for the first few years, indeed, they practically monopolized the efforts of the new teach-

> ers. . . . Visitors to the islands in 1822 remarked that all seemed to hang on the word of the king; he said that by and by he would tell his people "that they must all learn the good word, and worship Jehovah; but that the Missionaries must teach him first, and themselves [the missionaries] get well acquainted with Hawaiian." (p. 104)

Allen (1982) wrote that the American Missionary had thoroughly infiltrated the decision-making processes of Hawai'i's rulers, "Kamehameha II was sadly remembered as a king who had listened too closely to the *haole*" (p. 26) and "Kamehameha III, whose only fault, many of the high chiefs thought, was listening to the foreigners" (pp. 25–26). Finally, American Missionary influence on Hawai'i's governance was formally confirmed with Reverend William Richards' appointment as an advisor to the king and his prescriptive instructions to the ruling *ali'i* in the drafting of the *Declaration of Rights* (June 7, 1839), the *Edict of Toleration* (June 1839), and Hawai'i's first written constitutional law, the *Constitution of 1840* (October 4, 1840; for review see Thurston, 1904).[18]

THE AMERICAN MISSIONARY'S CONTROL OF POLITICS AND EDUCATION: THEY CAME TO DO GOOD, AND DID VERY WELL!

The decades following the arrival of the American missionaries in 1820, was one of turbulence and transition for both the absolute monarchical government established by Kamehameha I and the religiously based educational system begun by the missionaries. Prior to 1832, the fearless and proud Ka'ahumanu and her high court of chiefs, being well counseled by the missionaries, governed Hawai'i with a heavy hand. During her reign, the zeal of Calvinism and Christian education spread rapidly. So powerful was her influence, however, that even after her death on June 5, 1832, many axioms of her rule, although tested in years to come, withstood every challenge.

Less than a year after Ka'ahumanu's death, the first challenge of her precepts was by Kamehameha III (Kauikeaouli). A rift between the two fountainheads of authority, Kamehameha III and the new *Kuhina-nui*, Kinau, began in 1833. Kauikeaouli, a young 18-year-old, became displeased with Kinau because she refused to approve his purchase of a brig. In a fit of rage, he declared the abrogation of all laws except those that dealt with theft and murder. Much to the displeasure of the missionaries, he declared the end of the moral law established by Ka'ahumanu and touted the life of drinking and incest. Daws (1969) wrote that Kauikeaouli was fast "becoming a monarch of misrule" (p. 92). This royal move brought out into the open many of the ancient pastimes considered by the missionaries and their followers to be the workings of the devil.

Under Ka'ahumanu's rule, power was shared between the King, the *Kuhina-nui*, and the court of high chiefs. Kauikeaouli, seeking to regain absolute monarchical power, worked to take away power from the chiefs and *Kuhina-nui*. In an address to the people, he declared:

> These are my thoughts to all ye chiefs, classes of subjects and foreigners respecting this country which by the victory of Mokuohai was conquered by my Father and his chiefs—it has descended to us as his and their posterity. This is more—all that is within it, the living and the dead, the good and the bad, the agreeable and the pleasant—all are mine. I shall rule with justice over all the land, make and promulgate all laws: neither the chiefs nor the foreigners have any voice in making laws for this country. I alone am the one. Those three laws which were given out formerly remain still in force, viz. not to murder, not to steal, not to commit adultery; therefore govern yourselves accordingly. (Kuykendall, 1938, p. 135)

He further sought to rid himself of his overbearing *Kuhina-nui* and her religious affiliations, creating a power struggle between himself and Kinau and her powerful older chiefs. For the next 2 years, Kauikeaouli vacillated between his control and the controlling power of the chiefs who were influenced by the teachings of the American Missionary. The battle for power ended in 1835, at which time Kauikeaouli left much of the power and decision making to Kinau and the high chiefs' court. Thus, the governing framework established by Ka'ahumanu and influenced by the American missionaries was maintained, increasing the influence of the missionaries on governmental figures. As an observer wrote in the latter part of 1836:

> Kauikeaouli (or Tamehameha) is now about twenty-three years of age and is possessed of more talent than almost any other native, but being of very indolent habits and excessively fond of pleasures he does not attend to the affairs of Government, but trusts Kinau his half sister with the reins, she is entirely governed by the American Missionaries who through her govern the Islands with unlimited sway. (Kuykendall, 1938, p. 136)

Despite the internal struggles for political control, Hawai'i faced an even greater foe, the threat of foreign rule. Once the central governing force was reestablished, attention turned to the important task of gaining recognition as a sovereign state. This concern was a benchmark in the changing governance of Hawai'i, as the little island nation began to take its place among the ranks of sovereign nations. David Malo, in a letter to Kinau, August 18, 1837, expressed his concern that attention be given to establishing treaties with foreign nations:

> I have been thinking that you ought to hold frequent meetings with all the chiefs . . . to seek for that which will be of the greatest benefit to this country: you must not think that this is anything like olden times, that you are the only chiefs and can leave things as they are. . . . This is the reason. If a big wave comes in, large fishes will come from the dark Ocean which you never saw before, and when they see the small fishes they will eat them up; such also is the case with large animals, they will prey on the smaller ones. The ships of the white man have come, and smart people have arrived from the great countries which you have never seen before, they know our people are few in number and living in a small country; they will eat us up, such has always been the case with large countries, the small ones have been gobbled up. . . . God has made known to us through the mouths of the men of the man-of-war things that will lead us to prepare ourselves. . . . Therefore get your servant ready who will help you when you need him. (Kuykendall, 1938, p. 153)

The Big Fish Within: Power Shifts

Whether or not the small Kingdom of Hawai'i was ready, it was to enter a new era. As David Malo (Kuykendall, 1938) so eloquently wrote, a big wave, colonialism, was fast approaching and with it a tide of economic pursuits, foreign intrigue, and new ideas. In order for Hawai'i to prepare itself for a new position in a global order, it was necessary that the monarchy be taught to formulate treaties and to deal with foreign governments. In 1836, Kinau and the high court of chiefs requested, through the American missionaries, that their friends in the United States send a teacher who could educate and advise the rulers of Hawai'i in economics and political science. A formal governing link between the American Missionaries and the rulers of Hawai'i was established on July 3, 1838, when Reverend William Richards, a member of the mission in Hawai'i, entered the employ of the king (Kuykendall, 1938).

Since the missionaries were enjoined not to participate in the actual workings of the government, to keep "from all interference and intermeddling [*sic*] with the political affairs and party concerns of the nation" (American Board of Commissioners, 1838, p. 28), Richards was relieved of his commission by the American Board of Commissioners for Foreign Missions so as not to give the direct appearance of any religious or U.S. meddling.

Reverend William Richards (1938)[19] wrote of this event in his journal:

August 1, 1838. After considering the subject for several weeks and discussing the subject thoroughly with the king and chiefs I at length accepted the appointment and now act as the "Chaplain, Teacher and Translator," for the king. They also expect from me free suggestions on every subject connected with government and on their duties as rulers of the nation, and in all important cases I am to be not only translator, but must act as interpreter for the king. (pp. 173–174)

Until this time, the governing forces of the Kingdom had not yet been formally wed to democratic ideals. During the reigns of Kamehameha II and the earlier years of Kamehameha III, Ka'ahumanu had only courted the ideals. With the appointment of Richards as the teacher and advisor to the King, the Hawaiian government adopted a distinctly Western form of governance.

Although Richards considered his appointment to be strictly as an advisor and teacher and his responsibilities to be either executive or administrative, his influence on subsequent laws and policies carried the unmistakable mark of U.S. ideologies. For example, in 1839, Richards worked diligently to formulate a declaration of rights and a constitution which accomplished two things: granted power to the *maka'āinana* (meaning a voice in the government to commoners) for the first time and distanced the monarchy from absolute rule. Although the *Declaration of Rights* (Kingdom of Hawai'i, 1839a) was penned by Boaz Mahune, a Native Hawaiian, missionary influence was obvious. Besides reflecting his education at the missionary-run Lahainaluna Seminary, Mahune's writing mimicked the ideals of U.S. independence. In part, the declaration reads:

God hath made of one blood all nations of men, to dwell on the face of the earth in unity and blessedness. God has also bestowed certain rights alike on all men, and all chiefs, and all people of all lands.

These are some of the rights which he has given alike to every man and every chief, life, limb, liberty, the labor of his hands, and productions of his mind.

God had also established governments and rule for the purposes of peace, but in making laws for a nation it is by no means proper to enact laws for the protection of rulers only, without also providing protection for their subjects; neither is it proper to enact laws to enrich the chiefs only, without regard to the enriching of their subjects also; and hereafter, there shall by no means be any law enacted which is inconsistent with what is above expressed, neither shall any tax be assessed, nor any service of labor required of any man in a manner or variance with the above sentiments.

These sentiments are hereby proclaimed for the purpose of protecting alike, both the people and the chiefs of all these islands, that no chief may

> be able to oppress any subject, but that chiefs and people may enjoy the same protection under one and the same law.
>
> Protection is hereby secured to the persons of all the people, together with their lands, their building lots and all their property, and nothing whatever shall be taken from any individual, except by express provision of the laws. Whatever chief shall perseveringly act in violation of this constitution, shall no longer remain a chief of the Sandwich Islands, and the same shall be true of the governors, officers, and all land agents. (Kuykendall, 1938, pp. 160–161)

Furthermore, it comes as no surprise that the *Constitution of 1840* both distanced Hawai'i from its past monarchical beginnings and decreed Hawai'i a Christian Kingdom. After all, U.S. feelings toward monarchies had always been antagonistic. The Constitution created an institutional structure which included, for the first time in Hawai'i's political history, a representative body of the people as part of a national legislature. Later, this question of power—power in the hands of the monarchy versus power in the hands of the legislature—would be challenged by King Kamehameha V and King Kalākaua. Nevertheless, because the early influence of the missionaries tightly grafted U.S. liberalism to Hawaiian thought, defiance against the system was often short-lived. Thus, the ideal of equity, a voice for all men, resounded. It should be noted, however, that "all" was defined as the male gender of middle to upper economic status and, for the most part, White and Christian. While the legislature consisted of both Native Hawaiian and White representatives, the majority of Hawaiians were educated by the missionary, thereby swaying governing decisions toward dominant colonial activity.

The values that informed Hawai'i's political leaders consisted of strong Christian undercurrents and U.S. democratic ideals which were foreign to traditional Native Hawaiian norms of governance and daily living. Inevitably, a variety of social programs began to replace the activities once cared for by *kahuna* (priests), *kūpuna* (elderly), extended families, and *kumu* (teachers). Foreign laws and rules even restricted the practices of Native Hawaiian dance, art forms, and religious practices. Formal schooling, which was essential for the Western improvement of the community, was now supported by a Hawaiian government advised by American missionaries. In effect, government's role was to be the purveyor of resources for the Christian good of all Native Hawaiians. The idea of government existing for the Christian good of the people became well ingrained in the political spirit of the day. The *Constitution of 1840* (Kingdom of Hawai'i, 1840) decreed:

> That no law shall be enacted which is at variance with the word of the Lord Jehovah, or at variance with the general spirit of His word. All laws

of the Islands shall be inconsistency [*sic*] with the general spirit of God's law.

As the Hawaiian Kingdom turned its sights outward to protect itself from foreign warships and threats by foreign governments to overthrow the kingdom (e.g., Russian threat), little was done to curb the growth of internal U.S. influence. One beautiful tropical morning in 1893, the Hawaiians would awake and see, to their astonishment, a beast living among them. By the end of Kamehameha III's reign, it was clear that the Americans were indeed a power with whom to reckon. David Malo and Samuel M. Kamakau, Hawaiian scholars educated at Lahainaluna Seminary who were held in high esteem by the rulers and chiefs, recognized the increasing numbers of foreigners in positions of authority. They further observed that Hawaiians were not being trained to step into these positions of authority, which were, for the most part, taken by the White foreigner (Makanani interviews, 1991–1992). Some foreigners appointed to positions of authority included Reverend William Richards (later appointed minister of public education), Dr. Gerrit P. Judd (appointed minister of foreign affairs), and John Ricord (appointed attorney general), to name a few. These advisors wielded a hefty amount of clout when dealing with both the internal affairs of Hawai'i and foreign affairs of diplomacy and economy. Fatigued by the stress of the dilemmas caused by the social, economic, and political change of his kingdom, Kamehameha III, after being approached by U.S. businessmen, considered selling his kingdom to the United States. Of course, the sale was not made, and history would soon tell the tale of the United States procuring Hawai'i without a bill of sale.

"They Will Eat Us Up": The Colonial Tide

The process of colonial rule never had as a goal the recognition of the validity of heathen cultures. Colonialism subjugated indigenous people, leaving them dispossessed of their own history and heritage. The key events of this period mark the beginnings of this oppression. With the introduction of modern Western goods and skills, the belief that the foreign way was superior to Hawaiian traditions began, and with the coming of the American missionaries, this belief was further supported. In order to participate in the activity of the island kingdom, Hawaiians had to measure up to the standards of Christian beliefs. There was no equity. For the American missionaries, there was only piousness or backsliding, heathen or Christian (Daws, 1969). There existed the rulers and the ruled, the educated and the uneducated. This lack of equity encouraged and institutionalized separatism in the school system. For example, two distinct school systems created an elitism in which, generally, those of European descent and those born of high rank attended the more serious and well-run select schools, while the commoners attended the more deficient common schools.

Knowing the values and the game of Hawai'i's political, economic, and educational institutions becomes instrumental to our understanding the patterns of power and influence between authority systems in both an explicit and implicit way. Because the American missionaries had an earlier beginning in Hawai'i than did other religious groups, they were able to position themselves with influential people, the ruling chiefs. Although not closely connected to either Kamehameha II or Kamehameha III (during the earlier part of his reign), the missionaries established strong ties with both *nā Kuhina-nui*, Ka'ahumanu and Kinau. They further enhanced their influence through diligent work with lesser chiefs.

By securing a broad base of support among a number of authoritative figures and U.S. businessmen, the American missionaries were able to establish criteria for appropriate political behavior based on both their religious codes and political philosophies. So strong was this political network that the missionaries were able to create policy that alienated the Catholic movement in Hawai'i. Eventually, opposing religions (e.g., Catholicism, Mormonism) and beliefs also found a home in Hawai'i, but the governing rules had already been clearly established. Only those who were connected to authority and upheld the value priorities of the elite group, composed primarily of the American missionaries and U.S. businessmen, were able to enact social policy allowing for the regulation of social and educational activities.

The importance of understanding the unique features of Hawai'i's political culture helps in shaping an accurate picture of how policy decisions were made and provides information that assists in linking broader institutional values to actual educational policy. Arguably, there were a number of special conditions that existed in Hawai'i at this time; however, two distinct aspects most influenced both the political structure as well as the core beliefs of Hawai'i's governing organization. First, there existed a chasm of confusion about how Hawai'i would be governed that was ready to be bridged. This was due in part to Kamehameha I's uniting of the islands under one king, which had literally moved Hawai'i politically from a chiefdom to an early state. The political evolution coupled with the shaky rule of Kamehameha I's successors, Liholiho and Kauikeaouli, and the overthrow of the *kapu* system challenged what Native Hawaiians traditionally thought to be truisms and expected rites and rituals of governance. These events, which included contact with foreigners all occurring over a short period of 50 years, left Hawai'i in a state of turmoil.

Hawai'i's vulnerable political state, created by the turbulence of the fall of the *kapu* system, was tailored to the ambitions of the American missionaries and the colonial ideals of Manifest Destiny. In fact, the second unique element which encouraged the acceptance of Western values, activities, and form of governance was that, in the Hawaiian mind, governance and religion were inseparable. Further, although this belief is now considered a myth, it was also in the Hawaiian mind that Western artifacts and ideas were better than Hawaiian products and beliefs. It was into this most fortuitous set of circumstances that the American missionary entered. They brought the tools, the ideas, and the dogged Calvinistic perseverance to fill the needs of the burgeoning kingdom.

Essentially, Hawai'i's policymakers were a tightly organized network of interests upholding a web of institutional structures that embraced both religious precepts and U.S. democracy, while also prescribing elite rule that controlled the Kingdom of Hawai'i. This domain of elite rule remained throughout Hawai'i's early history, although it soon left the hands of native rulers and fell into the outstretched arms of their U.S. advisors. In summary, Hawai'i's political events during the 1820s and 1830s created a powerful political culture driven by the early American missionaries employing the useful tool of formal education.

THE EDUCATION OF THE NATIVE HAWAIIAN

It is interesting to note that the American missionaries were not assured immediate admittance to Hawai'i in 1820. In fact, it was only after several days of deliberation that Kamehameha II (Liholiho) agreed to allow the missionaries to stay in Hawai'i, but only for a probationary 1-year period. Liholiho, after all, had only recently rid his kingdom of an oppressive religious order *(kapu)* and was not ready to replace it with yet another restrictive religion. Further, as Daws (1969) observed, the ruler did not live a model Christian life but continued to practice polygamy and incest as well as to find comfort in a good jug of rum.

Education of the Elite Hawaiians and the Adult Population

The purpose of education in Hawai'i, as the missionaries perceived it, was to define school-related activities that educated both Hawaiian royalty and the commoner in a rather narrowly determined manner. Schooling had been the answer to the "Indian problem" on the continent. Coleman (1993) wrote, "By the late 1820s the ABCFM's [American Board of Commissioners for Foreign Missions] eight schools among the Cherokees of the Southeast had become, according to William G. McLoughlin, 'an international showpiece,' visited by such dignitaries as

President James Monroe" (p. 40). He continued, "At the schools of the ABCFM and of other Protestant missionary societies, the goal remained the extirpation of tribal cultures and the transformation of Indian children into near-copies of white children" (p. 40).[20] David Wallace Adams (1995) affirmed this action quoting an observer, George Wilson, "The kind of education they are in need of is one that will habituate them to the customs and advantages of a civilized life . . . and at the same time cause them to look with feelings of repugnance on their native state" (p. 21). Similar to the missionary work on the continent, the duties of Hawai'i's newly arrived missionaries were to teach literacy (preferably in the English language) and academic subjects, to instill the value of accumulating personal wealth, to Christianize, and to teach U.S. citizenry (Adams, 1995).

The law of the land, at the time, was a curious mixture of remnants of the *kapu* system and a common law system (Sahlins & Barrere, 1973).[21] Much of the law lay in the word of the King. Kuykendall (1938) characterized Kamehameha II's rule writing, "He did not have to rule by ritual and he did not know how to rule by law, and so he ruled by whim, alternately despotic and delinquent" (p. 69). Nevertheless, the King, knowing that the American Missionary brought this "magic of reading and writing" (Makanani interviews, 1991–1992), recognized a real opportunity for the *ali'i* to attain this power. So naturally, the *ali'i*, seeing reading *(heluhelu)* and writing *(kākau lima)* as means of power, were the privileged first to possess this Western magic. This led the way for Hawaiian scholars such as John 'I'i and David Malo to be educated by the missionaries. Both men would become influential forces in the development of Hawai'i's future political structure.

Liholiho, who mistrusted the missionaries, kept them close to him and mandated they teach only the *ali'i*. A small group remained in Kailua, Hawai'i with the King. A second small group was allowed to settle in Honolulu with Ka'ahumanu, and a third group was sent to Kaua'i, where Kaumuali'i (chief of Kaua'i) welcomed his son who had traveled to the United States to be educated in New England and had returned with the first group of missionaries. The first months were very difficult for the first group of American missionaries, as they were limited only to the education of an *ali'i* class—many of whom looked upon the missionaries with mere curiosity while still practicing traditional values taught by the *kahuna* (Daws, 1968).

The English language was the medium used in the education of the *ali'i* for two reasons: first, the missionaries felt that the Hawaiian King and his chiefs should learn English in order to better communicate in the business affairs of the State, which by this time was monopolized by U.S. businessmen; and second, the missionaries had not yet translated the oral Hawaiian language into a written language. The only texts suitable for teaching were in English and, of course, the Bible was in English. The missionary intent was to teach and elevate all Hawaiians; however, within their first few years of labor, they had educated only some of the *ali'i* class, who had become well versed in several languages such as Latin, English, and French, thereby dispelling the commonly held myth among the *haole* that Hawaiians were intellectually inferior (Makanani interviews, 1991–1992).

Although formal education had begun in the English language, the missionaries sought to educate the *maka'āinana* in their own native tongue. The decision for this was motivated by simple logistics: that is, the Hawaiians were many and the missionaries few. To teach the entire population to first read and speak English, then to teach them Bible lessons would take an immense amount of manpower and time that the missionaries did not have. The only realistic decision was for the few missionaries to learn the Hawaiian language and then teach Hawaiians the Bible in their own language. Their work to reduce the oral Hawaiian language to a printed language was speeded along by previous missionary efforts that developed a written or Roman alphabet for the Tahitian language. The Hawaiian language was built on an orthographic base of 12 letters. By 1822, only 2 years after their arrival, they had printed the first 16-page primer in Hawaiian (the Pī-ā-pā). After the printing of the Hawaiian language, the chiefs became active learners, as reading became comparatively easier and more interesting in their own mother tongue.

Important to the success of education was the role of the *Kuhina-nui* (Regent). Ka'ahumanu, appointed regent by Kamehameha I before his death, had powerful influence over the political, religious, and educational future of Hawai'i. At first, Ka'ahumanu was not interested in the missionaries' religious zeal; in fact, many of the chiefs shied away from the religious teachings of the newcomers. The missionaries knew that without the support of the ruling *ali'i*, their goal of Christianizing all the native people would not be realized. Although they had labored diligently during their first year to persuade the king to allow public education and widespread Christianity, their intentions were not realized. Again, providence, some may say, stepped in. In 1821, Ka'ahumanu fell gravely ill, and by chance or, as the missionaries may have seen it, by divine intervention, Mrs. Sybil Bingham nursed Ka'ahumanu back to health. So grateful was Ka'ahumanu that she gained a new-found respect for the missionaries. Ka'ahumanu toured the islands burning the Hawaiian idols and became a diligent student of Christianity.

Ka'ahumanu's Christian devotion and open approval of the American missionaries were an important turning point. Soon after her conversion, Liholiho (Kamehameha II) and his queen (Kamamalu) embarked on an ocean journey to Great Britain. His absence only strengthened Christianity and created a gateway for U.S. political ideologies. With the sudden death, due to illness, of both the King and Queen in 1824 while in Great Britain, and the heir still a young boy, Ka'ahumanu literally became the sole ruler of the islands. In fact, the tenor of Kamehameha III's (Kauikeaouli) reign was established by Ka'ahumanu. Kamakau (1992) included in his account an example of Ka'ahumanu's influence on the 11-year-old ruler. In a speech given by Kauikeaouli, strong Christian values were communicated:

> Chiefs and people, give ear to my remarks. My kingdom shall be a kingdom of learning.
>
> I rejoiced when they said to me,
> Let us go to the House of Jehovah,
> Let us come and sing to Jehovah,
> Let us sing joyfully to Jehovah with psalms,
> For Jehovah is a great God,
> He is King over all the gods.
> We are the sheep of his pasture,
> And as sheep we are led by his hand.
>
> On this day when we hear His voice let us not harden our hearts, but let us give our hearts and bodies to Him, and our lives to Him, that we may live in peace in this world. . . . Let our hearts be holy before Jehovah our God, that we may go forth in His ways and keep all His commandments, in order that our souls may live in the world to come. Let us keep our earthly laws, in order that we may live here in peace, because our nation is His. . . . It is a right that we strive hard to learn letters and to understand His words, that we may know the nature of His message. Let us be diligent, men, children, women; let us be strong. Those of you who are teachers, be faithful in teaching your pupils. It is my great desire that the poor, the rich, the chiefs, the men, the commoners, and all the children of our nation acquire knowledge and know how to read the Word of God. . . . Therefore, let you, the chiefs, be educated by the judges of this earth. (Kamakau, 1992, p. 319, reprinted from *Ka Nūpepa Ku'oku'a*, Oct. 3, 1868)

With Ka'ahumanu at the government's helm, the power of the absolute monarch would soon end. Although not wanting to give the appearance of political meddling, the missionaries did much work behind the scenes in aiding Ka'ahumanu and her chiefs to establish a moral and punitive law. Ka'ahumanu even suggested that law be based on the Ten Commandments. Such a morally based law, however, was not approved by her high court of chiefs. In a sense, this event first exhibited the beginning of a democratic form of governance in which there existed a balance of power. Nevertheless, Ka'ahumanu's influence on governance was often unchallenged.

The devotion of Ka'ahumanu to the American missionaries enabled them to increase their impact on more of the Hawaiian people through a common school system. In fact, there was rivalry between religious groups to control political and educational institutions, similar to how religious denominations vied with each other on the frontier in the Midwest to establish common schools (Friedberger, 1996). The concept of public education was not widely held, but, due to the work of the American missionaries, Hawai'i might be seen as a forerunner in the public education movement. This interest in educating all the people was declared in April of 1824 at a meeting of the high chiefs, Ka'ahumanu, and her ministers at which they declared ". . . their determination to adhere to the instruction of the missionaries to attend learning, observe the Sabbath, worship god, and obey his law, and have all their people instructed" (Chamberlain, 1824, pp. 210–211).[22]

This decision, obviously influenced by the missionaries, enacted by the court of high chiefs with the enthusiasm of Ka'ahumanu, resulted in an increase of adult pupils. Schools were conducted by the best Native Hawaiian scholars who were educated by the missionaries and sent to a variety of locales by royal decree. Figure 2.1 reveals demographics that show that adult students numbered more than 1,600 by the end of 1824. Four years later, the number jumped to 34,000, and by Fall of 1831 there were 1,103 common schools taught in the Hawaiian language, serving 52,000 pupils (Kuykendall, 1938). A manuscript found among Asa Thurston's letters (March 6 through April 22, 1832), presented in Schmitt's, *The Missionary Census of Hawai'i* (1973),[23] provides additional accounts of adult scholarship.

The activity of schooling was so popular that, as Wist (1940)[24] suggested, it became a substitute "for lost indigenous social activities" (p. 26). In fact, the quarterly examination included much pomp and ceremony in which Natives eagerly and proudly participated. Reverend Rubin Tinker wrote in his journal on July 19 and 20, 1831:

> The shell horn blowing early for examination of the schools, in the meeting house. About 2000 scholars present, some wrapped in large quantity of native cloth, with wreaths of evergreen about their heads and ganging toward their feet—others dressed in calico and silk with large necklaces of braided hair and wreaths of red and yellow and green feathers very beautiful and expensive.
>
> It was a pleasant occasion, in which they seemed interested and happy. . . . The King and chiefs were present, and examined among the rest. They read in various books, and 450 in 4 rows wrote the same sentence at the same time on slates. They perform with some ceremony. In this exercise, one of the teachers cried out with as much importance as an orderly serjeant [*sic*] . . . and immediately the whole company began to sit up straight. At the next order, they stood on their feet. At the resting on the left arm as a musician would place his fiddle. At the next order, they brought their

Notes

Sandwich Islands—1832

About 900 schools
50,000 learners 50 pupils at the High School
About 500 members of churches

In O'ahu

About 29,000 inhabitants
10,000 connected with the Schools
(1 hour a day, perhaps) or about 1%–3% of the population
6,526 able to read
200 members of the church
85 admitted during the year
3,000 men connected with prayer meetings
3,000 women do
2,000 persons connected with the temperance society—but probably 19%–20% of the whole population do not drink spirits at all
700 Bible class—meet Thursday 5 P.M.

Kona, Hawai'i	
Kane	4,607
Wahine	4,670
Keikekane	1,559
Kaikamahine	1,569
Total	12,432

Ka'u, Hawai'i	
Kane	1,563
Wahine	1,604
Kamali'i	1,393
Total	4,560

Translations: Kane = male; Wahine = female; Keikekane = boy; Kaikamahine = girls; Kamali'i = children.

FIG. 2.1. School statistics, 1832. From a manuscript filed in HMCS vault dated Feb. 1941, B. Judd (Ed.).

pencils to bear upon the broadsides of their slates ready for action. Mr. Bingham then put into the crier's ear the sentence to be written, which he proclaimed with all his might and a movement of the 450 pencils commenced which from their creaking was like the music of machinery lacking oil. Their sentences were then examined and found generally correct. . . . Eight of the Islanders delivered orations which they had written and committed to memory. Gov. Adams (Kuakini) was among the speakers. (Kuykendall, 1938, pp. 108–109)

It appears that, at least in the beginning, Native Hawaiians held education and Christian religious activity in high regard, as they relished in the ritual. Accounts such as Reverend Tinker's, which recorded the Native Hawaiians' dedication to learning, their joy in and expertise in writing and oratory, and the self-pride exhibited through such public exams illustrate the success of the American missionaries' endeavors as well as the ability of the native.

The curriculum was quite rudimentary, including, as Kamakau (1992) related, the teaching of the Hawaiian alphabet, spelling, and simple reading. He recorded the rigidity of classroom lessons, subject matter, and religious currents in the early school rooms:

> The subjects taught were spelling in unison, reciting syllables of two letters; reciting a refusal to keep wooden gods; names of lands, names of months; a recitation relating the emotion of the people over the death of a king in a foreign land; portions of the books of Matthew, Psalms, Acts of the Apostles, and Luke; questions relating to God; the Ten Commandments; questions prepared for the exhibition; the desire of the rulers proclaimed at Honuakaha; the first hymn about 'Opu-kaha-'ia; and the arithmetical processes of adding, multiplication tables, division, and fractions. . . . Some schools taught how to get ready, to stand, to speak out, to take up a slate, how to place the pencil on the slate, thus. . . . King Kau-i-ke-aouli laid great stress on the progress of education among the whole people and he continued attending school. . . . The spread of knowledge was very rapid in Hawai'i. (pp. 270–271)

Writing, however, was taught to a limited number of students as writing utensils and supplies were scarce. The major text used was the *Pī-ā-pā*, an eight-page pamphlet consisting of the "alphabet, Arabic and Roman numberal [*sic*], punctuation marks, lists of words, verses of scripture and other reading matter, including a poem" (Kuykendall, 1938, p. 107). The school clientele consisted mostly of adults (schools for children did not begin until the 1830s), as their instruction was not only deemed important by the chiefs and the missionaries, but also because the adults were more forceful in asking for, often demanding, the new instruction. Furthermore, adult education as a means of control was prompted by the unruly behavior of the adults who missionaries perceived as uncontrollable children (Kuykendall, 1938).

Yet, even with all the troubles of their earlier years, the American missionaries had accomplished much. In a relatively short period of time, the missionaries were able to secure the trust of the Hawaiian rulers and establish their Christian and democratic ideologies. In addition, a small band of missionaries were able to teach the "three R's, instruction in geography, history, music and, of course, religion" (p. 45) to a large population of approximately 85,000 Native Hawaiians (Everly, 1965).[25]

Schooling for Children: Institutionalizing the Common and Select Schools

Toward the end of the 1820s, the missionaries began to encourage the *ali'i* to mandate schooling for children. When the mandate was delivered, the missionaries were prepared with *O ke Kumu Mua Nā Kamali'i* (The

Primer for Children). As we suggested in the beginning of the chapter, two types of schools were established that mirrored the social caste system; they were the common schools and the select schools. This division between the commoners attending common schools and the elite attending select schools produced two immediate and far-reaching effects: first, it refueled the myth that common Hawaiians were intelligently inferior to the White foreigner, and, second, it further divided the Hawaiians into two distinct classes of the elite and the underclass. Remnants of this attitude toward education and a class system still exist today in Hawai'i's unique phenomenon of private versus public schools.

In an article describing the common school's curriculum written in 1888, the authors commented that "the methods of teachers were of the rudest kind, and little was taught beyond reading, writing, elementary arithmetic and geography" (Alexander & Atkinson, 1888, p. 4).[26] Kamakau (1992) and Malo (1898) observed that, at the start, common schools were not the effective vehicle for teaching a new morality, much to the chagrin of the missionaries. This was not because of their weaknesses in curriculum and qualified teaching, but because of two other factors. First, because *ali'i* such as Kamehameha III often defied Christian ethics; the people often followed his example and left the boredom of the classroom to return to traditional pastimes. There are many Native accounts retelling how people were able to practice traditional activities when the missionaries were not around and, upon request, were able to bring out the Bibles and clothing with the fervor required by the missionary mentors. Second, attendance at common schools was mandated, but was only sporadically enforced by the local chiefs. For example, Governor Hoapili of Maui issued an edict in 1825 that all children 4 years and above should attend school; however, he had no means (e.g., manpower, technology) that could rigidly enforce his policy (Kuykendall, 1938). A culture of resistance was inevitable, but it would take 100 years of oppression for it to gain a voice.

As much as the common schools were found to be deficient, the select schools were found to be a haven of scholarship. Clearly, the separation of people was beginning to take root. The select schools, operated by the missionaries, became a resourceful method of enlarging the supervision of education under missionary influence. With attention on teacher education and printing, Lahainaluna Seminary was established on September 5, 1831, graduating many of Hawai'i's future policymakers. Some of the graduates included David Malo, who became the first superintendent of public instruction; D. H. Nahinu, District Superintendent for South Kona and member of the legislature in 1864, 1873–1874, and 1882–1886; Luther Aholo, Speaker of the House from 1876 to 1886 and Minister of the Interior from 1886 to 1888; J. Kakina, member of the legislature in 1874 and 1880; and L. S. Ua, member of the legislature, 1851–1853.

The opening of the O'ahu Charity School followed in 1832. This school is noteworthy for a number of reasons, but most importantly it was a free school; common-school students frequently paid a fee to support common schools. Supported by foreign residents and shipmasters, the O'ahu Charity School is considered to be the first legitimate public school in Hawai'i. Another notable school was the Female Seminary in Wailuku, Maui, which became the forerunner of girls' schools in Hawai'i. It is significant to note that Hawai'i's educational history was not gender biased, as the continental U.S. education was. Education for women was deemed essential by the strong women figures of Hawai'i's leadership. Thus, the girls studied right along with the boys (Makanani, 1991).

Although the select schools, and to a degree the common schools, offered the opportunity for intellectual advancement, schooling for children in the 1830s was not an easy task. Partially due to lack of monarchical and local chiefs' support as well as the rigid religious, moral curriculum of the missionaries, both native teacher and scholar began to lose interest in education. Two journal entries by Mrs. Sarah Lyman (1860) point to this disinterest and the problem of attendance:

> December 15, 1833. Some extra efforts have been recently made to awaken the church and Sabbath school teachers to more vigorous action. The result is many of the old schollars [*sic*] have returned and some new ones gathered into the school. . . . I would not distrust the Almighty, but I am sometimes led to fear that it is the novelty of the thing which has aroused the attendance of the people. They are pleased with new things, and a protracted meeting is something entirely new among them. (p. 61)
>
> September 4, 1834. I do not recollect to have ever felt a greater reluctance to engage in any undertaking than I did to commence the children's school. It seemed a hopeless task. The children are permitted to come and go at their pleasure. They are pleased to have school commence, but as soon as the novelty ceases, they cease to attend regularly. And this is one reason for my having a select school. I have selected 20 schollars [*sic*] from families who live near with whom we are well acquainted and over whom we have some considerable influence. The majority of them are children of, or reside with the members of the church. Another reason for my limiting the number is, that I may do most of the teaching myself. Native teachers are a source of vexation. They are exceedingly indolent and do not seem to possess a faculty of interesting their pupils. I have been engaged in no school since I came here to the island that has seemed so much like a school at home as this one. The children at first were very wild, would run about the school house during school hours like so many goats. If I gave directions to one schollar [*sic*] I would have to give to all, but they are beginning to be quite orderly and quiet. I find it far pleasanter to teach children than adults. Six of them have been in school before and are now learning arithmetic. Seven of the little girls are learning to sew on pieces sent out in the box last fall. (pp. 71–72)

The work of the missionaries both in educating the commoners and advising the rulers went undaunted. Further evidenced in 1834, the King and high chiefs agreed to set aside land for the construction of permanent schoolhouses. Additionally, land around the mission homes and schools was to support missionary work; hence, the first government allocation of land resources to education. It is essential to understand that this land grant meant different things to the parties involved. In the minds of the Hawaiian Chiefs, land was granted only for temporary use, not to be privately owned by someone else other than themselves. To the missionary, land ownership was a U.S. aspiration; the land grant did not mean they had to give it back. On the contrary, the land had become their own private property. Schooling and the American Missionary (and their descendants) had come to stay, for they were now tied to the land. Soon, with the appointment of Richards as the King's advisor, a written statute would mandate schooling.

Shifting Control of Schools to Hawai'i's Political Elite

The need to include education under government auspices came about at the same time as the first Hawaiian Kingdom's Constitution was being drafted. Prior to the written constitution, education, although sporadically supported by the chiefs, was mainly an activity conducted, monitored, and financed primarily by the American Board of Foreign Ministries (ABFM). The shift from missionary control to government regulation was due primarily to three reasons. First, a retrenchment circular distributed by the ABFM severely cut financing of foreign missions, which was a direct result of the United States' depression in 1837. The mission schools, therefore, needed public support in order to continue. Second, concerned by the phenomenal growth of Catholicism and their normal schools in Hawai'i, the missionaries thought that, if governmental law regulated schools, they could keep the Catholics' influence from becoming too strong. Finally, Hawai'i's movement toward a constitutional government and private land ownership required that the people become knowledgeable citizens. This task was, of course, left to the schools, which by this time had become the missionaries' most powerful tool in acculturating the Native people to Western ideologies. Realistically, the missionaries could not succeed in this endeavor without the support and enforcement of the government (Wist, 1940).

To understand how political values were transferred to educational policy and school-related activity we look first at what value themes dominate a political culture. Although democratic ideals such as the concept of commoners having equal voice in governance and the right to land ownership were not enthusiastically supported by the monarchy, these were strong, basic beliefs held by the American missionaries throughout this early period. There had always been rule by *ali'i* with mythical ties to the gods, and the concept of land ownership was foreign to the native. However, the cornerstone of democracy was instrumental in influencing the move of the kingdom from an absolute monarchy to a constitutional monarchy in 1840.

Another shift of values occurring at this time dealt with the ruling chiefs' definition of economic efficiency. At the time, efficiency was determined by how the chiefs could get the most out of their labor force so that they could purchase more Western goods. Because Western economics was still a foreign subject to the Native rulers, many *ali'i* became indebted to U.S. businessmen who controlled and regulated Hawai'i's commerce. To the American missionary, however, the value of efficiency had social, rather than economic, implications. The missionary shunned the exorbitant material luxuries of the Hawaiian elite and frowned on the slave labor conditions of *maka'āinana,* who labored in the sandalwood trade. For the American missionaries, efficiency defined their expeditious mission to civilize the Native Hawaiian and make Hawai'i a heaven on earth.

First School Laws

Over time, the missionaries, now cabinet members and the forefathers of schooling in Hawai'i, managed to reshape social and governing norms and create a school system that legitimated the process of deculturation and the teaching of new Christian and Western values. As DiMaggio and Powell (1983) suggested, wider cultural values are institutionalized by organizations in several ways including coercive means, mimicking other successful implementations, and the normative structure of those within the setting and organization. Strong support for this institutional perspective on the adoption of norms across wide contexts is provided by examining the values embedded in the school laws set up in Hawai'i after the arrival of the missionaries. These provided a legitimating function, ensuring that the schools operated in a manner that was culturally similar to the values and goals of those with power and influence in the community.

It is no surprise that, under the tutelage of William Richards, the first school laws of 1840 were similar in tenor to Massachusetts School Laws of 1642 and 1647 (Wist, 1940). For example, Hawai'i's law requiring that every village with 15 or more children establish and support a school was similar to the creation of school districts on the continent. Additionally, each community had to elect a local committee of three members to work with the missionaries and the tax collector in the operation of the school(s):

> 1. Wherever there is any number of parents having fifteen or more children of suitable age to attend school, if they live near each other, in the same

> village, or in the same township, it shall be the duty to procure themselves a teacher, which they shall do in the following manner. The tax officer shall give notice by a crier of the time and place at which all the male parents of the township, district or village shall meet, and they shall choose three of their number as a school committee for that place. (Kingdom of Hawai'i, 1842)

The specific structures adopted tended to mirror other successful innovations (DiMaggio & Powell, 1983). For example, the manner in which the school board was organized parallels the School Advisory Committees/Boards in Massachusetts. Further similarities are noted in the tasks of the board, which were numerous but essentially included regulation of hiring and paying of teachers and allocating resources (efficiency value) needed by the teacher(s):

> 2. Said school committee shall then apply to the general school agent, spoken of below, and they together shall lookout a teacher for that place. If there are but few children then there shall be but one teacher, if more, then two teachers, and if the children are very numerous, then there shall be three or more teachers as they shall think best.
>
> 3. When the teacher is obtained, then the general agent, the teacher and the school committee shall agree as to the wages. If the teacher have no land and they shall agree in the opinion, that it is important that he should have some, then the general school agent shall endeavor to secure some which is not occupied, and that land shall be given to the teacher, but not in perpetuity. When he shall cease to act as teacher then the land shall revert to government. But if the land do not afford the teacher a full support, then they shall furnish him with as much more as they shall agree to be necessary. It shall be furnished from the avails of the King's labor days and from the yearly tax, but not the poll tax. (Kingdom of Hawai'i, 1842)

Attendance laws, specifically compulsory schooling for children between the ages of 4 and 14, were another similar regulation:

> 9. The proper ages for children to go to school shall be considered to be from four years and upwards to fourteen years of age. If any man have a child of suitable age to go to school, but below eight years of age, and do not constantly send him to school, then that parent shall not be freed from the public labor of the King and the land agent, but if a child be more than eight years of age and do not go to school, then the fault shall not be considered as the parent's only, but the child's also. That child shall go to the public labor of the King and land agents on all labor days. No child (over eight years of age) who does not go to school, shall be freed from public labor; they shall all go to work. (Kingdom of Hawai'i, 1842)

Hawai'i's first school laws reflected the values of its continental counterparts seeking two objectives: first, to establish an organizational structure which would enable schools to efficiently and adequately acculturate the Native Hawaiian citizenry to Christianity as well as democratic social and political norms; and second, to hold local school boards, teachers, parents, and students accountable to the laws. As noted in the four school regulations previously quoted, although local communities chose their own school boards and had some say in school governance, suggesting a decentralized system of local control, the monarchical hierarchy maintained a centralized policy apparatus so that school-related activities could be monitored by the high *ali'i* and their missionary advisors.

The majority of Hawai'i's first school laws, comprising 20 regulations, were written to assure efficient acculturation of Native Hawaiians, disregarding native customs, oral traditions, and lifestyle. For example, policies were formed to establish, enforce, and monitor appropriate behaviors and attitudes toward learning new Western mores. Two examples that describe particular student behavior include:

> 4. Furthermore, it shall be the duty of the children to be generous to their teacher, and aid him by working on his land, according as they shall agree, or according to their good will.
>
> 10. Children when at school are required to be quiet, and listen to the instruction of the teacher. But if any one is mischievous, the teacher shall be allowed to administer to him proper correction, but not improper. (Kingdom of Hawai'i, 1842)

Supplementing Chapter VII, Additional School Law, Chapter LII, further directed the children's behavior in schools:

> Another evil is that the scholars in the schools are noisy. It is the duty of teachers to instruct the scholars in this particular, and to consult with the school committee on the measures to be pursued. The Government will always support the teachers and school committee, while they do well. For a school is of little value if the scholars are disorderly. There is but one right way, and that is for the scholars to kindly and faithfully regard the instructions of the teacher. If the scholars conduct improperly they must be punished as the law requires. (Kingdom of Hawai'i, 1842)

Student behavior policy coupled with parental responsibility for a child's education provided some assurance that a school's atmosphere would be more conducive to learning new social norms:

> 12. It shall be the duty of the school committee to encourage the parents in whatever will promote the education of their children, and shall themselves encourage the children to go to school and acquire knowledge, and shall aid the teacher in whatever is necessary for the prosperity of the

> school. (Kingdom of Hawai'i, 1842)
>
> It is important that parents should have so much sincere regard to the welfare of their children as to influence them to attend to instruction. For if they are unable to read, they can neither marry husbands nor wives, they can never act as land agents nor be employed in any office over others. The parents too must suffer inconvenience, for their lands cannot be increased, they cannot fish gratuitously nor take timber from the mountains without paying for it. It is therefore important that parents should consider this subject well, and stimulate their children to learn. It is also the duty of parents to aid in supporting the teacher in such manner as shall be mutually agreeable, and should do it generously lest the Government be burdened. (Kingdom of Hawai'i, 1842)

Student and parent responsibility made for important educational policy, but more essential policy dealt with teacher efficacy and accountability. After all, teachers were the pivotal instruments through which new values could be transferred. For example, in regulation 6, the law reads that only "exceedingly laborious" teachers "should be paid a high price," suggesting that quality education would be measured by the efforts teachers made in acculturating the Natives to new values. Teachers were held accountable to this lofty charge in regulation 11. We mention three examples that regulate teacher work.

> 6. It is not proper that all teachers should be paid alike. A very wise teacher who is exceedingly laborious in his business, and has many pupils, should be paid a high price, while he who is less wise and less laborious in his business should be paid a lower price, but no person is by this law considered a teacher unless he have a teacher's certificate from the general school agent.
>
> 11. If a teacher fail of doing his duty, and become negligent or guilty of a crime, then he shall be brought to trial before the school committee and general school agent of the place, and they shall decide respecting him.
>
> 18. Furthermore, it shall not be proper for the general school agent to give the teacher's certificate to ignorant persons, not to persons known to be vicious or immoral. If a man can read, write and understands geography and arithmetic, and is a quiet and moral man, and desires a teacher's certificate, it shall be the duty of the school agent to give him one, and not refuse. (Kingdom of Hawai'i, 1842)

These regulations may, at first glance, seem harmless; in fact, to some they made perfect sense. However, a heavy dose of moral values seen in regulations 6 and 18 is suggestive of Protestant disdain for the growing Catholic schools. Attempts by the Protestant missionaries to prevent Catholicism from taking root in Hawai'i was a battle of political wit. For instance, prior to the writing of the 1842 laws, Protestant missionaries were advisors to the Kingdom's school board. Political positioning was vital; consequently, only native teachers graduating from Lahainaluna Seminary, a Protestant School, or natives of the Protestant persuasion were given government approved teaching certificates, thereby alienating Catholic teachers. As expected, the Catholic contingency objected vehemently. The missionary advisor role was eventually replaced with the secular position of school agent. However, the expectation of upholding Protestant Christian values was already fixed in the fiber of school governance.

By 1842, a school agent was appointed on each major island along with a *luna* (superintendent). The duties of the school agents, which included management of the teachers, encouraging students, interpreting school laws, and responding to the *luna*, assured efficient operations of the schools:

> 13. There shall also be annually appointed certain men of intelligence as general school agents, as follows, one for Hawai'i, one for Maui, one of Moloka'i, one for O'ahu, one for Kaua'i, and one superintendent of the whole. They shall be appointed by the legislature at their annual meeting. These persons shall be the school agents for the year.
>
> 14. The business of the general school agents shall be to consult with the school committees and teachers in accordance with what is before stated. The general school agents shall superintend, manage and provide for the teachers, and shall encourage them and their scholars. They also shall be the judges of the law in relation to schools. The Supreme Judges are the only persons above them. They shall report to their superintendents their various acts, and the result of their observation, and the superintendent shall report to the legislature at the annual meeting. (Kingdom of Hawai'i, 1842)

Economic efficiency in the running of schools was also built into Hawai'i's first school laws. This is addressed in several regulations but most prominent in the areas of school construction and teacher pay are regulations 8 and 9:

> 8. At all places where the children are in want of a school house, the tax officer shall notify the people, and they shall build it under the direction of the school committee. And inasmuch as the labor is not such as concerns the chiefs only, but is alike for the benefit of the people and the rulers, it shall be considered as national work, then even transient persons and servants shall labor.
>
> 19. Furthermore, all the tax officers are required to listen to the commands of the general school agents, when they give orders for the payment of the

> teacher or teacher's [*sic*], in accordance with the requirements of this law. (Kingdom of Hawai'i, 1842)

As readers may recall, Table 1.1 presented a summary matrix of how the specific political values of efficiency, quality, choice, and equity were embedded in school laws across the four periods we studied. A detailed content analysis to determine what attitudes and behaviors were preferred over others within Hawai'i's educational laws were examined, and all items were coded first by what value it reflected and then by what policy domain was addressed. Utilizing Marshall et al.'s (1989) framework, Table 2.2 shows the translation of these particular values across policy choices in seven broad policy areas considered pertinent domains of educational policy. These domains include finance, personnel, student testing, program definition, governance, curriculum materials, and building and facilities. Through this analysis, one can determine how cultural or political values (e.g., efficiency) were institutionalized in specific policy domains within the school system.

As we see in Table 2.1, the value of efficiency was embedded in all of the preceding school regulations. Quite simply, the laws reflected the American Missionary ideal of how schools should be managed, who should teach, the responsibility of students, parents, and community to the school, and who would be held accountable. Efficiency was the primary value key to the success of the missionaries' task to acculturate the Native Hawaiian to Christian and U.S. democratic ideals. In contrast, the other values of quality, choice, and equity were referred to sporadically throughout the first school laws.

Although additional school laws included in Chapter LII alluded to the ideal that every Hawaiian citizen had the opportunity to get an education in a socially stratified system, such as the Hawaiian monarchy,

TABLE 2.2
Distribution of Values and State Policy Mechanisms in
Chapter VII, A Statute for the Regulation of Schools

Policy Areas	*Quality*	*Efficiency*	*Equity*	*Choice*	*Total*
Finance	0	6	0	0	6
Personnel	3	3	0	0	6
Testing	0	0	0	0	0
Program	1	0	0	0	1
Governance	0	4	0	0	4
Curriculum materials	0	0	0	0	0
Bldg. & facilities	0	1	0	0	1
Total	4	14	0	0	18

Source: Kingdom of Hawai'i, 1842, *Constitutional Laws of Hawai'i, 1842.*

equity was not a political, and certainly not a social, priority. Frankly, the law allowed for the establishment of a public school system for all, regardless of class or race; however, in Hawai'i's social system, two hierarchical school systems existed. At the bottom were the public or common schools, which were supported by the local communities with very little, if any, financial support from the King's coffers. It comes as no surprise that the public schools provided only what the community could afford, which was in most cases very minimal. On the other hand, at the top were the privately funded select schools, which were attended by the children of the missionaries, other White children, and the children of Hawai'i's *ali'i* class. These private schools provided extraordinary academic opportunities for those with the money and credentials (i.e., race or class) to attend. This is not unlike the common school ideas of Horace Mann in the 1830s (see 1876, 1957, and 1965 writings), who sold this identical idea to the rich as a means of maintaining their power. To the poor, the idea of schooling was sold as a means of enhancing their socioeconomic condition (Spring, 1989).

It is essential to note that "reading, writing, geography and arithmetic" (Kingdom of Hawai'i, 1842) were required of all Native Hawaiians in order to be married or to hold any high office. This regulation epitomized the political power that the American missionaries wielded and clearly linked the transference of their value system to that of the school. Further, this policy legitimized the stripping away of the Native Hawaiian's cultural identity, in that it essentially stated that a Westernized form of schooling founded on the canons of U.S. democracy and the new knowledge it afforded were more valuable than the Native Hawaiian's orally based schooling grounded in cultural traditions.

The first school laws issued under a constitutional monarchy established Hawai'i's first public school system only three years after Horace Mann secured similar school laws in Massachusetts. The idea and the structure of Hawai'i's public school system was a U.S. invention. And, identical to U.S. purposes, education was the tool used by governing powers to influence the social growth of their citizenry. However, Hawai'i's public school system did not fully mature until the late 1840s and well into the 1850s under the administration of Richard Armstrong.

THE IMPACT OF WESTERN EDUCATION ON NATIVE HAWAIIANS

There exists an overwhelming array of narrative data located in Hawai'i's state and private archives written by foreigners that provide diverse perspectives on the life of the Native Hawaiian prior to 1840. Because many volumes of information essential to the study of any topic regarding Hawai'i that were written in the Hawaiian language by Native Hawaiians have yet to be translated and organized, one can see that any picture of Hawai'i at this time is likely biased from a foreign perspective. In an attempt to provide a trustworthy account of the impact of educational policy on Native Hawaiians, it was necessary to access data from a number of sources, both of foreign and native origin.[27] The following analysis is arranged in two sections: first, academic achievement of Native Hawaiians, and second, economic and social standing of Native Hawaiians.

Academic Achievement of Native Hawaiians

Academic achievement during the 1820s and 1830s cannot be measured by today's statistical standards, for a student's scholarly ability was not determined by test scores but by that student's ability to be a good Christian. Further, Hawai'i's social hierarchical system required only minimal literacy and counting skills among the common people, while supporting advanced schooling for Hawaiians in high *ali'i* classes. Thus, measurement of knowledge by today's standards is not only inappropriate but would serve only to describe Hawai'i's caste system.

The American Missionary's rigid criteria (prior to 1837), which measured whether or not a heathen native had been unquestionably transformed to a model Christian worthy of admittance into the Protestant Church, prevented large church membership. Although literacy skills were a major requirement for membership, true change in character was a factor that many Native Hawaiians, in the eyes of the missionary, were incapable of attaining. There were however, 1,300 Native Hawaiians, all literate scholars, who were given church memberships (Schmitt, 1973). As the criteria for change in character relaxed between 1837 and 1840, nearly 20,000 literate Native Hawaiians were admitted to the church (Schmitt, 1973). It is essential to note that the use of the terms "literacy" or "literate" indicates that Native Hawaiians could read, write, and count in their Native Hawaiian language. Literacy rates by 1853 reveal that nearly three fourths of the Native Hawaiian population over the age of 16 years could read the Hawaiian language (Schmitt, 1977).[28] While it is difficult to judge these figures by today's literacy standards, they suggest that this was a remarkable achievement, given the overall low literacy rates of the U.S. populace at this time.

There are several limitations to available data related to scholarship (Table 2.2). Specifically, for some years, the figures are only available for O'ahu with the result that some of these numbers are underreported to a significant degree. Further, the numbers presented do not distinguish the common school pupil from the select school student, nor do they account for other religiously affiliated schools. Also, the figures in Table 2.3 consider English literacy and not literacy in other languages (e.g., Chinese, Japanese, Portuguese, Filipino, or other Pacific Island languages).

Nevertheless, the data (Table 2.3) indicate an increase in number of scholars between 1822 and 1824 from 65 scholars to 1,600, and again by 1826, to 20,000 scholars. This growth in the number of Native Hawaiians attending school continued through 1831, reaching its highest peak at 52,882 pupils. This large population of scholars is attributed to the feeling of curiosity and desire of the Native Hawaiian to gain the power of reading and writing. The numbers tended to drop in the 1830s and 1840s due to several factors including: educational policy that began to focus on children, the depopulation of Native Hawaiians due to disease, and a

TABLE 2.3
Protestant Mission Schools, Teachers, and Enrollment, 1820–1849

Year	*Schools*	*Teachers*	*Scholars*	*Readers*
1820, Sept. 14[a]	1	NA	40	NA
1821, May 23[a]	1	NA	30	NA
1822, Feb. 1	NA	NA	65	NA
1824, Sept. 17	NA	50	1,600	NA
1825	NA	50	2,000–3,000	NA
1826	NA	NA	20,000	12,000+
1827, Jan.	NA	NA	25,000+	NA
1828, July–Aug.	NA	500+	34,395	17,000
1830, Feb. 20	674+	NA	39,208+	20,000
Date unspec.	NA	NA	41,183	NA
1831	908	900+	44,895	20,989
December	1,103	NA	52,882	NA
1832, June	NA	NA	NA	23,127
1833, June	NA	NA	NA	20,184
1834, June[b]	NA	NA	NA	10,608+
1838, June	NA	NA	8,100–9,100	NA
1839, June	200	NA	14,000	NA
1840, May	NA	NA	15,000	11,000
1841, May	357	505	18,034	5,514
1842, May	305	438	15,228	5,526
1843, May[b]	202	246	8,827	3,926
1844, May[b]	346	294	12,678	6,569
1846, July	NA	NA	15,393	NA
1847, April	496	495	16,528	NA
1848, May	341+	262+	16,387+	NA
1849, April	393+	NA	12,009	NA

[a]Figures are limited to O'ahu. [b]These figures are underrepresented.

Source: From *Historical Statistics of Hawai'i* (p. 211) by Robert C. Schmitt, 1977, Honolulu, Hawai'i: University of Hawai'i Press. Copyright 1977 by the University of Hawai'i Press. Reprinted by permission.

general feeling of boredom among Native Hawaiians toward the ill-supported common schools.

Clearly, the link between policy and educational outcomes is significant when assessing literacy rates. The 1820s witnessed growing numbers of Native Hawaiians, encouraged by their chiefs (following Ka'ahumanu's lead), learning the new power of reading and writing. As Table 2.3 indicates, the number of schools in 1831 reached 1,103 with as many as 52,882 pupils. Although the records show plummeting school enrollment figures in the 1830s, the value of the new literacy was not lost as evidenced by the substantial education laws of the *Constitution of 1840* (Kingdom of Hawai'i, 1840) that placed legal restrictions on an illiterate citizen. In fact, Hawai'i's literacy rate was one of the highest in the world; only Scotland and some of the New England states surpassed the tiny Kingdom (Kamehameha Schools/Bishop Estate, 1991).

This surge in literacy is reflected in the February 14, 1834 printing of Hawai'i's first newspaper, *Ka Lama Hawai'i* (The Hawaiian Luminary), which was also the first newspaper printed west of the Missouri River. This weekly paper, published until December 26, 1834, was printed for Lahainaluna Seminary scholars as a means ". . . to communicate to them the ideas on many subjects directly and indirectly, such as we should not put into sermons, nor into books written formally for the Nation" (Andrews, 1835, p. 146).[29]

The popularity of this newspaper spawned a flurry of printed newspapers, many written by missionaries. For example, *Ke Kumu Hawai'i* (The Hawaiian Teacher), provided a means through which missionaries could present enlightening world information as well as encourage native scholars to write articles which would convince their countrymen and women to improve themselves (Andrews, 1835). Other popular missionary-inspired newspapers included Reverend Richard Armstrong's *Ka Nonanona* (The Ant, 1841–1845) and *La 'Elele Hawai'i* (The Hawaiian Messenger, 1845–1855), both of which targeted children and their parents. The content of many of the papers provided readers with civilized ways of living (i.e., proper personal hygiene, housekeeping, home building, and agricultural methods). These early newspapers, filled with American Missionary values and ethics, established the moral and political instruction of the day.

More importantly, the growing literacy rates among Native Hawaiians saw a proliferation of newspapers written by Native Hawaiians—up to 100 at one given time. Many voiced the concerns of Native Hawaiians toward growing foreign influence in the islands, expressed alternative ideas on controversial topics, served as a means of perpetuating Hawaiian traditions, and cataloged many of Hawai'i's presently extinct biological phenomena.

Economic and Social Standing of Native Hawaiians

Assessing the impact of educational policy on both the social and economic status of Native Hawaiians presents similar problems to studying its impact on educational success. To understand these impacts, we drew on a variety of sources that account for Native Hawaiian demographics, such as population, health, occupations, skills, financial debt, and land ownership. Of course, the impact of educational policy on these demographics is at best indirect through the actual school experiences that were provided.

The social status of the common Native Hawaiian can only be understood if it is described within the context of the native chiefs' economic exploits. During the early 1800s, *nā ali'i* (chiefs) displayed a growing appetite for foreign luxuries that translated into a substantial need for sandalwood to pay for the new Western expense. Much has been documented about the effects of the sandalwood trade on Hawai'i's environment and its people. Simply, the *maka'āinana* who worked the land for the *ali'i* become a docile work force. Thus, power for the *ali'i* meant control of this labor force. Since many chiefs had run themselves into debt purchasing the wares of the Western world, they literally forced the commoners into slave labor. David Malo wrote in *Hawaiian Antiquities* (1898), "The condition of the common people was that of subjection to the chiefs, compelled to do their heavy tasks, burdened and oppressed, some even to death" (pp. 60–61). The draconian methods of the *ali'i* forced the commoners to work with little in exchange for their labor. This provided very little time for the people to tend to their dwindling food supplies. Inevitably, great famine resulted in a severe population decline.

The process of colonization pays little attention to the demise of native people due to economic abuse or disease. Teaching personal hygiene, how to build a house, or how to store food could not stop the rapid depopulation of Native Hawaiians. In two statistical tables (Tables 2.4 and 2.5) provided by Schmitt (1968) in *Demographic Statistics of Hawai'i 1778–1965*, he reported that the 1850 census showed a relatively low number of children, who accounted for only 29% of the population, and a median age of 32.2 years. From this standpoint, all the previous years of education had not helped the Hawaiians to fend off the aftereffects of foreign intrusion.

Table 2.4 provides two estimates of population demographics. Comparing population data available between 1778 and the census taken in 1850,[30] we can reasonably conclude that increased contact with whites was wiping out the Native population due to the introduction of foreign diseases. Additionally, foreign capitalism had devastating effects on Native Hawaiians as evidenced by their poor Western education, disenfranchisement, and little economic opportunity. Within a short period of 72 years

TABLE 2.4
Total Population: 1778 to 1850

	Population[a]			
Date	Series A	Series B	Date	Population
1778	300,000	300,000	1823	134,925
1796	280,000	270,000	1831–32	124,449
1803	266,000	0	1835–36	107,954
1804	280,000	154,000	Jan. 1849	87,063
1805	152,000	0	Jan. 1850	84,165
1819	145,000	144,000		

[a]Schmitt notes that the "Series A" and "Series B" labels used for two estimates completed by different research groups.

Source: From *Demographic Statistics of Hawai'i, 1778–1965* (p. 41) by Robert C. Schmitt, 1968, Honolulu, Hawai'i: University of Hawai'i Press. Copyright 1968 by the University of Hawai'i Press. Reprinted by permission.

more than 75% of the Native Hawaiian population had died. Not surprisingly, the number of children, those who were destined to carry on the bloodlines, was extremely low. In fact, some writers of the middle 1800s feared that there would soon be no person of Hawaiian ancestry left. This expressed fear corresponded with policymakers' views in the United States that native cultures would inevitably become extinct because they would be left behind technologically. Therefore, their thinking went, Natives should be efficiently acculturated because it would be good for them. Table 2.5 records the meager number of youth in 1850 who comprised only 29% of the total population.

The decaying health of Native Hawaiians resulted in an imbalance of Native Hawaiian births to deaths (Table 2.6). Why this is so can be attributed to a variety of reasons; however, we could conclude that Ha-

TABLE 2.5
Population[a] by Age and Sex, January 1850

Sex	All ages	Under 18	18 to 30	31 to 30	53 and over	Median (years)
Both sexes	80,539	23,366	15,747	22,065	19,361	32.2
Males	42,203	12,983	7,995	11,018	10,207	31.2
Females	38,336	10,383	7,752	11,047	9,154	33.1

[a]Excludes 754 blind and deaf persons and 2,872 foreigners or dependents of foreigners.
[b]Schmitt quotes this data from the *Polynesian*, May 4, 1850.

Source: From *Demographic Statistics of Hawai'i* (p. 43) by Robert C. Schmitt,[b] 1968, Honolulu, Hawai'i: University of Hawai'i Press. Copyright 1968 by the University of Hawai'i Press. Reprinted by permission.

TABLE 2.6
Estimated Birth and Death Rates[a] of Hawaiians and Part Hawaiians by Series[b]: 1778–1850

Series & Period	*Length in years*	*Decrease in population*	*Annual rates per 1,000*		
			Natural decrease	*Births*	*Deaths*
		Series A			
1778–1796	18	20,000	4	35	39
1796–1804	8		0	33	33
1804–1805	1	128,000	457	25	482
1805–1819	14	7,000	3	29	32
1819–1823	4½	10,050	17	25	42
		Series B			
1778–1796	18	30,000	6	34	40
1796–1803	7	4,000	2	33	35
1803–1804	1	112,000	421	20	441
1804–1819	13	10,000	5	28	33
1819–1823	4	9,000	17	25	42
		Both Series			
1823–1825	2	3,950	15	25	40
1825–1832	7	6,551	7	29	36
1832–1836	4	16,495	35	25	60
1836–1848	13	12,498	9	30	39
1848–1850	2	8,863	48	22	70

[a]Includes persons absent at sea. [b]Series A and B account for two different censuses taken at the same time. The rationale is not provided by Schmitt and could not be located in archival data.

Source: From *Demographic Statistics of Hawai'i* (p. 45) by Robert C. Schmitt, 1968, Honolulu, Hawai'i: University of Hawai'i Press. Copyright 1968 by the University of Hawai'i Press. Reprinted by permission.

waiian women could not or would not give birth due to several factors: their dwindling health, the health of the men, and a social environment which threatened their native traditions of day-to-day living.

Schools, therefore, played a prominent role in upholding traditional hierarchical structures which supported the subjugation of Native Hawaiians through the institutionalization of various educational practices that foreshadowed curriculum tracking. To illustrate this, schooling provided the majority of Hawaiians, the *maka'āinana*, with only rudimentary literacy and counting skills; while only a minority, usually of the upper ranks, were provided advanced scholarly opportunities or vocational education. The common schools, then, did not provide the Native Hawaiian commoner with the skills to compete in a new Western, capitalistic system.

French Captain Vaillants' report of 1836 on the status of the common Native Hawaiian is particularly telling, ". . . for the father of the family has no hope of doing anything that will increase the well-being of his wife and children, since the more he acquires, the more the chiefs demand of him" (as cited in Sahlins & Kirch, 1992, p. 27). Whereas the educated *ali'i* class was able to establish itself in commerce with the United States and European countries, the *maka'āinana* maintained their traditional roles, faithfully following the lead of their chiefs, and did not (or were not allowed to), as a group, aspire to a higher occupation.

CONCLUSION

The settling of foreigners on Hawai'i's shores produced profound changes in the lives of Native Hawaiians. The cultural vacuum resulting from the demise of the *kapu* system provided an open arena in which the American Missionary successfully engineered political and social reform. In a little fewer than 60 years, Hawai'i's governing structure changed from an agrarian chiefdom to a constitutional monarchy and clearly linked education to political status and property rights.

The slow, yet effective, foreign takeover of Hawai'i mirrors the goals of Manifest Destiny in subjugating the Native Americans as the country expanded westward. The removal policy pressed Native Americans to restructure their governing systems to align with those employed by the states and federal government. A promise was made that such an alignment would assure smooth relationships between Native Nations and the United States. In effect, many tribes modified their governing structure. Although the Cherokee Nation was the most successful example of democratic governance which assured Native Americans political status and property rights by treaty, the State of Georgia took their lands and moved them onto reservations. In the end, the Supreme Court ruled in favor of the State of Georgia saying that the Cherokees did not have practical education to be self-governing, so must be considered wards of the state.

The practical education that both the Native Americans and Native Hawaiians received was always at their own expense and to the profit gained by their trustees. This education included the indoctrination of Western thought and beliefs through Christianity. The rationale for doing so was the perception that these cultures were less civilized and desired Western values and materials. Underneath the moral uplifting, however, was the intent to secure Native lands for economic gain.

The only remnant of Hawai'i's Native governance, suiting the needs of the colonial leaders, was the institutionalized governing caste system which maintained a fundamentally centralized form of governance and allowed the White elite to govern. The stability of this system, coupled with educational policy emphasizing assimilation of the Native culture, ensured against the possibility of rebellion while maintaining a supply of labor for the plantations.

Institutional theory has provided a lens for us to observe that the political culture during this period of political and social turbulence favored efficiency and quality in an effort to quickly acculturate Native Hawaiians to Christian beliefs. At the same time, however, these religious intentions reinforced the stratified governing structure, replacing the *ali'i* with American missionaries and businessmen. With predominantly Protestant values and beliefs at the helm, laws which governed Hawai'i's social institutions (e.g., education) were steered towards satisfying the needs of U.S. citizens, especially the business element. Assimilation thus resulted in the gradual acceptance among Hawaiians of individual rights and property, Christian spiritual beliefs, and political socialization toward democracy. As we argued, these policies resulted from the interplay of Protestant ideology, the belief that native cultures were inferior and likely to become extinct, and the economic need to control conquered lands (Adams, 1988).

The new values resulted in the institutionalization of several important structures within the early schools. First, the missionaries succeeded in teaching the Native how to read and write in their Native Hawaiian language, and the curriculum, even in its rudimentary stages, provided necessary information and instruction which prepared them for roles within a new Christian Hawai'i.

The impact of the educational laws of 1840 served to establish schools as an efficient tool through which appropriate beliefs and Western skills could be taught. Although records show that many Hawaiians still practiced the traditions of their ancestors, the seeds of social and political change were effectively planted by the schools. The idea that "West was best" was entrenched in the beliefs of the Native Hawaiian, and, as it goes with many beliefs, no matter how false, many Native Hawaiians soon accepted it as truth. The structure of this system—with separate schools and curriculum for commoners, Hawaiian royalty, and missionary children—ensured that Hawaiians would soon be (and remain) at the bottom of the social, political, and economic hierarchy. Echoing Madison's argument about government, a disconnected citizenry could easily be kept in check, and Euro-Americans certainly had the ears of Hawai'i's rulers to ensure its governance remained closely aligned with U.S. values and economic goals (Kemmis, 1990).

The message of Princess Nahi'ena'ena's life story, that of a sacred daughter of Hawai'i born to sustain a rich past within an era of tumult which witnessed the onslaught of Western ways and attitudes, shared at the beginning of this chapter is not lost. The dilemma is clear: How do we rebuild the crumbling walls of our Native Hawaiian heiau (temple) yet employ new ideas brought by foreigners? No doubt, the legacy of U.S. education has produced great technological and scientific achievements that have resulted in enormous profits as well as global prestige and power. While the American Missionary brought new ways of seeing the world and skills which proved useful for negotiations as well as land claims and use, it did not offer structures to maintain the insight and epistemology of Hawaiiana. As the pueo (owl) warns of the morning and the twilight, so too, Nahi'ena'ena's short life was a harbinger of what would soon be lost.

ENDNOTES

1. Interview with Russell Kawika Makanani, teacher and scholar of Hawaiian History and Culture at Kamehameha Schools. He described the political culture of the time, the influence of the American Missionary, and conflicting cultural values between the Hawaiian and the foreigner. He spoke also on education policy and school-related action that was deemed valuable by both the *ali'i* and the missionaries. At the core of his discussion, Makanani pointed out that the American missionaries played a significant role in the political as well as educational atmosphere of Hawai'i.
2. Sumner J. La Croix & James Roumassett, "An Economic Theory of Political Change in Premissionary Hawai'i," *Exploration in Economic History 21*, 151–168 (1984). This article provided secondary data accessed to add insight into the economic impact on social and political change.
3. For the translation of Hawaiian language, we utilized Mary Pukui, Samuel Elbert, & Esther Mo'okini, *The Pocket Hawaiian Dictionary* (Honolulu: University of Hawai'i Press, 1975).
4. Ralph S. Kuykendall, *The Hawaiian Kingdom 1778–1854, Vol. I* (Honolulu: University of Hawai'i Press, 1938). A noteworthy Hawaiian historian, Kuykendall craftily chronicled the history of Hawai'i from a brief sketch of ancient Hawai'i through the downfall of the monarchy and establishment of a provisional government in 1893.
5. Ralph Steuber, "Hawai'i: A Case Study in Development Education 1778–1960," doctoral dissertation, University of Wisconsin (1964), provided invaluable insight into the understanding of Hawai'i's educational governance over a 182-year period. Employing the works of current scholars as secondary sources offered additional perspectives. Also, reference is made to Steuber, R., "Twentieth-Century Educational Reform in Hawai'i," *Educational Perspective 20*:4 (1981, 1982b, Winter) 4–19. Steuber, R., "An Informal History of Schooling in Hawai'i," *To Teach the Children: Historical Aspects of Education in Hawai'i* (Honolulu: Bishop Museum, 1981–1982a) 16–34.
6. Kelly's writing presented ideas which reveal a conflict between Hawaiian traditions and Western values.
7. Allen favored the Native Hawaiian perspective and utilized a variety of sources, especially interviews and personal journals, to develop her narrative.
8. Gavan Daws (1969) *Shoal of Time: A History of the Hawaiian Island*. Honolulu: University of Hawai'i Press.
9. Samuel Manaiakalani Kamakau's writing is essential reading and an important resource for all Hawaiian scholars, as it brought to print the rediscovery of the islands and the impact of the American Missionary through the early 1800s (through the reign of

Kamehameha III). Kamakau, of Native Hawaiian descent, is considered to be Hawai'i's greatest historian. His voluminous work, spanning almost 34 years, was printed in Hawaiian language newspapers and later translated into the English language. Kamakau's work stands strong as a Native Hawaiian perspective among the many volumes of work by Non-native historians. Kamakau, S. M. (1992). *Ruling Chiefs of Hawai'i* (Revised Edition). Honolulu, HI: Kamehameha Schools/Bishop Estate.

10. Ibid. Chapter XVIII, "Abolition of the Taboos Under Liholiho," pp. 219–228.
11. The writings of Mary Kawena Pukui, E. W. Haertig, & Catherine A. Lee provide substantial Hawaiian cultural information.
12. See specifically Chapter 4, "Rank Society," pp. 109–184, in Fried, M. (1967). *The Evolution of Political Society.* New York: Random House for further information.
13. See Robert Carneiro's theory of circumscription discussed in Robert B. Graber & Paul B. Roscoe, "Circumscription and the Evolution of Society," *American Behavioral Scientist 31*:4 (1988, March/April) 405–415. Also, refer to Robert Carneiro, "The Chiefdom: Precursor of the State," in G. D. Jones & R. R. Kautz (eds.), *The Transition to Statehood in the New World* (Cambridge: Cambridge University Press, 1980), pp. 37–79.
14. Jocelyn Linnekin is a profile scholar whose work has enlightened the field of Hawaiian Anthropology. Two of her texts are referenced in this study, they include *Children of the Land: Exchange and Status in a Hawaiian Community* (New Brunswick, NJ: Rutgers University Press, 1985), and *Sacred Queens and Women of Consequence* (Ann Arbor, MI: University of Michigan Press, 1990).
15. Twain's book added a unique perspective to Hawai'i's history and culture.
16. Mrs. Lucia Ruggles' journal recounts her 1-year encounter with the Native Hawaiian. Although short, it is important for two reasons: first, she was one of the members of the first missionary group, and second, she brought to the study a very different perspective of Hawai'i and Hawaiians. Constructing an authentic picture of Hawai'i's social-political culture during the 1820s and 1830s required the inclusion of the American Missionary perspective. Primary historical texts also cited numerous American Missionary journals. The Hawaiian Mission Children's Society Research Library in Honolulu is the primary depository of these journals. This archival library holds the largest collection of journals written by early American missionaries working in Hawai'i. Several journals have been published and are available in paperback; however, the majority of journals, letters, and other documents are for use at the facility only.
17. The information in Part I of this two-part edition is compiled from Sarah Joiner Lyman's journal, which begins with the chronicles of her journey to Hawai'i in the latter part of 1831 until her death in 1887.
18. The 1840 Constitutional Law was invaluable to this study, as it is the first written law documenting schooling. The law was retrieved from the Hawai'i State Archives in Honolulu. An excellent source for the study of Hawai'i's early laws is Lorrin Thurston (Ed.), *The Fundamental Law of Hawaii, 1840–1842* (Honolulu: The Hawaiian Gazette, 1904).
19. A transcript of Reverend William Richards' journals and letters are located in the Hawaiian Mission Children's Society Library, Honolulu. His journals are essential to the understanding of the politicalization of schools during the 1840s.
20. Coleman quotes William G. McLaughlin, *Cherokees and Missionaries, 1789–1839* (New Haven, CT: Yale University Press, 1984).
21. This journal article presents memos, letters, and artifacts belonging to Richards which help define the social and political conditions of Hawai'i.
22. A transcript of Levi Chamberlain's journals is located at the Hawaiian Missions Children's Society Library in Honolulu. This primary source added another perspective of missionary activity in Hawai'i.
23. Demographic information was essential to this study. Schmitt's texts provided, in one comprehensive compilation, a variety of data from several sources. Robert C. Schmitt,

The Missionary Censuses of Hawai'i (Honolulu: Pacific Anthropological Records, no. 20, Dept. of Anthropology, Bishop Museum, 1973). Further statistical documentation was found in Robert C. Schmitt, *Historical Statistics of Hawai'i* (Honolulu: University of Hawai'i Press, 1977) and Robert C. Schmitt, *Statistics of Hawai'i, 1778–1965* (Honolulu: University of Hawai'i Press, 1968).

24. Benjamin Wist was the Dean of the Teachers College at the University of Hawai'i. This source is the only comprehensive historical account of public education in Hawai'i prior to 1940. Factual data included in the text are sufficiently verified and the historical narrative provides detailed descriptions of education/schooling in Hawai'i.
25. This source includes a series of lecture transcripts presented during Kamehameha School's 75th Anniversary. The lectures, delivered by Dr. Everly, Dr. Sinclair, and Dr. Tuttle, provide rich information about Hawai'i's education history and its objectives for the future. *Kamehameha School's 75th Anniversary Lectures* (Honolulu: Kamehameha Schools/Bishop Estate, 1965).
26. This source presents information clarifying the purpose of schools, the progress of schools, and documenting school activity.
27. A number of historical resources employed by this study as primary sources have already been noted. The following is a listing of other primary sources. Lawrence Fuchs, *Hawai'i Pono: A Social History* (New York: Harcourt Brace, 1961). This text is devoted to the study of democracy in Hawai'i in the 1900s. Extracts from personal journals of primary American Missionaries include: Reverend Cochran Forbes, Reverend Hiram Bingham, and Sarah Bingham. These journals were used to provide description of Hawai'i's political, economical, and schooling activities. An essential source of information was the Hawaiian Historical Society. Located at the Mission Homes in Honolulu, this prestigious organization is devoted to recording the history of Hawai'i since 1881 and has contributed countless publications of scholarly historical accounts regarding all facets of Hawai'i's life in *The Hawaiian Journal*. Another important primary source, Dorothy Kahananui (Ed. & Trans.), *Ka Mo'o ōlelo Hawai'i* (Honolulu: University of Hawai'i, 1984), was originally published in 1838 with the first English translation published in 1984, provided a much needed Native Hawaiian perspective of Hawai'i's early years. This is an exceedingly significant work, as it was the first oral history project which documented Hawai'i's antiquity through the eyes of Native Hawaiian *kupuna* (grandparents, elders). Conducted by Lahianaluna Seminary students, the material is heavily slanted toward a Christian perspective; however, if one can see through the religious zeal of the young students, a picture of Hawai'i from a Native Hawaiian point of view can be assessed. Joseph Feher, *Hawai'i: A Pictorial History* (Honolulu: Bishop Museum Press, 1969) and Edward B. Scott, *The Saga of the Sandwich Islands* (Lake Tahoe, NV: Sierra–Tahoe Publishing, Co., 1968) provide ample photographic data. Additionally, replicas of teaching tools used by the missionaries added a sense of reality and life to the study. Artifacts can be found at both the Bishop Museum and Hawaiian Mission Homes Museum.
28. Schmitt utilized the following sources for his data: *The Missionary Herald* for August 1821, February 1822, January 1823, May 1825, January 1826, January 1827, January 1828, January 1830, October 1930, January 1831, January 1832, January 1833, January 1840, January 1841, and April 1841; the *Extracts From the Minutes of the General Meeting of the Sandwich Islands Mission* (for 1832, 1833, 1834, 1841, 1844, 1848, and 1849; *The Polynesian* for September 4, 1841, and December 28, 1844; and the *Report of the Minister of Public Instruction* for August 1, 1846, and April 28, 1848.
29. Lorrin Andrews, *Mission to the Sandwich Islands: Report of the American Board of Commissioners for Foreign Missions 20* (1835). Unpublished report. Honolulu: Hawai'i State Archives.
30. Accounting prior to 1850 can only be considered estimates because of a lack of scientific method of obtaining estimates.

'EKOLU

Hawai'i, No Longer for the Native Hawaiian

Hawai'i owes her present position in the world, her civilization, and her prosperity to the lovers of the early missionaries. . . . The danger . . . is now that they make too much of their success, and endeavor to drive where they should lead. That is the complaint of the lay element in Honolulu against the present missionaries, who still have predominating influence in the affairs of the Republic.

—*Literary Digest*, 1897, Vol. XIV, p. 499

HA'AWINA NO'ONO'O

By the 1880s, Native American tribes on the North American continent were either being confined to reservations or, like the buffalo, were near extinction. A prevailing attitude toward the Native Peoples was they were "fully capable of being transformed and assimilated once exposed to the 'superior' influences of White society" (Adams, 1988, p. 2). A similar fate awaited a tiny island kingdom, 2,500 miles across the Pacific. The Hawaiian Monarchy was being dismantled, replaced by an insurgent group of mostly U.S., with some British, German, and other European, businessmen and politicians. Following the arrival of the American missionaries in 1820 and the growing economic prosperity of haole businessmen, the indigenous people of the Hawaiian Islands were sufficiently assimilated through formal schooling to a Western, White Christian way of life that successfully robbed them of their land, the richness of their own history, and, indeed, their very soul.[1]

To view these events through the rose-colored lens of a Michener novel would ignore the exploitation of paradise and its people, dismiss the devastation of of Native traditions by Protestant ideology, and affirm the erroneous stereotype of the lazy, pagan, ignoble savages. What has been missed by scholars and policymakers is the deep harm suffered by indigenous peoples, in this case Native Hawaiians, who have been subjected to both administrative and legislative policies imposed by a foreign system. Past policy decisions have had such a negative impact on the integrity of the Native culture that widespread concern has demanded that current legislative actions not only improve the economic status of the Native Hawaiian, but also protect cultural beliefs and activity. Although education has been viewed as one tool through which both economic mobility and cultural integrity can be developed, it has not historically served the needs of this indigenous island group. Some suggest that because dominant political and institutional ideologies inevitably define the educational goals and curriculum of the schools, they reflect the beliefs and values of the controlling majority (Easton, 1965a, 1965b; Iannaccone, 1977; Kirst, 1984). In fact, the contrasting beliefs and values of those who governed schools and those who were being served, which inevitably defines school-related activities, accurately describe the nature of Hawai'i's educational policy process historically.

THE POLITICAL CONTEXT: STRUGGLE FOR THE *'ĀINA* (LAND)

The Economic Battlefield

It is important to mention the public context surrounding the formal shift of control in Hawai'i from the Native Hawaiians to the foreigner. The power of economics in determining social and political policy in Hawai'i became a reality during the last half of Kamehameha III's 30-year reign (1824–1854). During this period of time, economic alliances with U.S. business interests eventually led to enlarged political power for the U.S. citizens who controlled these businesses, due to the Hawaiian government's dependence on capitalistic endeavors to supply the treasury and pay for an increasing Hawaiian debt. It was inevitable that those who controlled the businesses and the wealth, either directly or indirectly, soon governed Hawai'i. By 1882, the *ali'i* oligarchy that ruled the Hawaiian Kingdom under the guidance of the American missionaries and U.S. cabinet ministers was largely replaced by a foreign element, mostly the U.S. business oligarchy.

The coalition of men who comprised this elite inner circle of power were White with professional or church interests. Many were born in Hawai'i to missionary parents, educated on the continent, and returned to Hawai'i to gain favor and economic opportunity from the Hawaiian chiefs. A short listing of names and occupations (Table 3.1) illustrates clearly the interests of those who influenced policy decisions by virtue of their governmental positions and economic activity. Hawai'i's governing interests did not reflect the voice or needs of Native Hawaiians but, rather, the desires and attitudes of a White, elitist society.

The transference of governing power from the Native Hawaiian monarchs to U.S. business interests can be attributed to two events. First, over time, the Hawaiian monarchs and lesser chiefs grew more reliant on their foreign friends' advice, which resulted in an ever-widening window of opportunity for the advance of U.S. influence on Hawai'i's governance. Second, this gradual shift in power was further enhanced because Hawai'i's mercantile business was entirely controlled by U.S. businessmen.

Throughout the early years of Hawai'i's growing kingdom, it was these U.S. businessmen who had opened avenues of trade between Hawai'i and foreign markets, provisioned passing ships with local agricultural products, and supplied Native Hawaiians with Western goods that filled the homes of the wealthy *ali'i*. However, by the 1850s, Hawai'i's whaling services and sandalwood trade were severely declining, and many U.S. businessmen began to look to other forms of commerce for their capital. A profitable commodity was found in the growing sugar industry. In fact, by the late 1840s, this burgeoning industry already began to lay claim to its future wealth.

One explanation of the sugar barons' eventual social and political supremacy in Hawai'i was founded on the acquisition of large, endless tracts of land and the formation of controlling conglomerations.[2] In order for the sugar industry to be economically feasible as well as profitable, growers needed large tracts of continuous land; however, U.S. businessmen did not feel secure under Hawai'i's land ownership laws, which allowed a person to occupy the land for only a prescribed period of time.

Traditionally, the ruling *ali'i* organized their *'āina* (land) along a hierarchical standard. Simply, higher chiefs ruled over the larger territory called the *moku*. The next chief in line oversaw the *ahupua'a*, which was a triangular piece of land that ran from its point in the *uka* (mountains)

TABLE 3.1
The Elite Oligarchy of 1882 (Allen, 1982)

Name	*Occupation*	*Name*	*Occupation*
William D. Alexander	President of Punahou Academy	W. L. Jones	Teacher at Punahou
William N. Armstrong	Attorney & Educator	Lawrence McCully	Judge
William R. Castle	Attorney	Amasa Pratt	Principal at Punahou
Sanford B. Dole	Attorney & Judge	Dr. C. T. Rodgers	Physician
Anderson O. Forbes	Clergy	Thomas Rain Walker	British Vice-Counsul
Charles M. Hyde	Clergy	Dr. John M. Whitney	Dentist & Educator

to its base at the *kai* (ocean). The next lowest land division was the *kīhāpai* (farmland; Sahlins & Kirch, 1992).[3] A chief's tenure over the land was always dependent on whoever the ruling *ali'i* was. Land tenure, then, was an ever-changing process dependent on the proclivity of the ruling *ali'i*, who almost always gave the land to relatives. Therefore, land that may have been given to a sugar planter under one chief could, at any given time, be taken away, thereby leaving the businessman's future at risk. Knowing that the success of the sugar industry would be dependent on private land ownership, an effort to change Hawai'i's land laws was pursued through the businessmen's established contacts and relationships of trust with Hawai'i's *ali'i*. Consequently, the land reform acts occurring from 1846 to 1855 by the Board of Commissioners to Quiet Land Titles (the Land Commission) executed the now infamous *Māhele*.[4]

Analyses by many historians (Kame'eleihiwa, 1992; MacKenzie, 1991; Makanani interviews, 1991–1992; Sahlins & Kirch, 1992) conclude that the *Māhele* replaced traditional rights of the *maka'āinana* (the children of the land, the commoners) to live and work on the land with the need to acquire a paper title to land ownership. The propaganda of the day fronting the pages of *The Polynesian*[5] claimed that the *Māhele* would teach the natives how to be profitable industrialists, would remove the commoners from the slavery of their ruling chief, and would allow larger land enterprises to become models of the Puritan ethics of industrialism and civilization. In reality, this alien concept concerning private ownership of land guaranteed future profits only to those who understood the law (such as government officials, sugar planters, and other Whites). For the commoners, land divisions and foreign ownership of lands were fatal to their social and economic well-being; in the final assessment, Native Hawaiians received less than 1% of Hawai'i's land (Thrum, 1900, p. 36).[6]

In short, those who controlled the lands also controlled the people. Within the larger scheme of colonizing the Hawaiian Islands, then, the taking of Native lands formed the base of a set of cultural values that ensured the demise of Native culture. The institutionalization of those values was accomplished through the widespread acceptance of Christianity and the inevitability of these inferior cultures' demise because of their contact with superior Western culture (Adams, 1995). David Wallace Adams wrote of the same ideology that drove the westward movement across the North American continent. He argued that "the very survival of the republic demanded that the Indians be dispossessed of the land. According to primarily Lockean theory, only a society built upon the broad foundation of private property could guarantee public morality, political independence, and social stability" (1995, p. 5).

Realizing the force of this idea, the sugar planters formed powerful conglomerates that centralized their power and control of Hawai'i's economic system. Many of their supporters took government positions and began to institutionalize their values in laws and policies. Some of the companies owned by the growing Missionary Party included H. Hackfield and Company; Castle and Cooke (started by two former missionaries); C. Brewer; and Walker, Allen, and Company—*all* U.S.-owned businesses. Throughout the middle 1800s, the sugar plantations prospered, providing the U.S. business interests the key they needed to translate their wealth into political power. The dream of Manifest Destiny, that it was the Whites' God-given right to take over Western territories from the lesser, subhuman Natives, enveloped the North American plains and the Pacific Ocean, devastating Native American tribes and Native Hawaiians. The taking of Hawaiian lands, coupled with the success of Hawai'i's sugar industry, prepared the way for future disenfranchisement of Native Hawaiians from their homeland.

The Ideology of Manifest Destiny

With the growth of agricultural opportunity in Hawai'i came thoughts of annexation to the United States. This was influenced by the policy of Manifest Destiny. The U.S. businessmen's loyalties lay not with the Hawaiian Kingdom but with their own homeland, the United States. Moreover, overall United States policy toward Hawai'i pledged interest and support in the tiny island kingdom. In fact, Daniel Webster confirmed the United States' interest in the islands:

> The United States [is] . . . more interested in the fate of the islands, and of their government, than any other nation can be; and this consideration induces the President to be quite willing to declare, as the sense of the government of the United States, that the government of the Sandwich Islands ought to be respected; that no power ought either to take possession of the islands as a conquest, or for the purpose of colonization, and that no power ought to seek for any undue control over the existing Government, or any exclusive privileges or preference in matter of commerce. (as cited in Stevens, 1945, p. 3)[7]

Further, recognizing the dominance of U.S. economic interests in Hawai'i, President Tyler followed Webster's comments in December of 1842, adding:

> Its forbearance in this respect, under the circumstances of the very large intercourse of their citizens with the islands, would justify the government, should events hereafter arise, to require it, in making a decided circumstance against the adoption of an opposite policy by any other power. (as cited in Stevens, 1945, p. 4)

The United States' interest in the Hawaiian Kingdom was established through economic lines, as the majority of Hawai'i's businesses were under the control of U.S. citizens. In addition, Hawai'i's governing structure, dominated by American missionaries and other U.S. businessmen because of missionary influence and control of the royal cabinet, was founded on U.S. beliefs. It was not surprising that the United States government made formal promises regarding the use of diplomatic power and pressure to protect the interests of its U.S. citizens.

Although an essential cornerstone for future action by U.S. businessmen, local economic events cannot be construed as the primary reason for the Hawaiian Kingdom's demise in the 1890s. More important was the larger imperialistic belief in Manifest Destiny embraced by many U.S. politicians, businessmen, and professionals both in Hawai'i and the United States. Pursuit of this goal was the prominent value from which all action and interest flowed. The first formal use of Manifest Destiny occurred in December of 1842, when President Tyler applied the ideology in pledging protection to Hawai'i against policies made by other countries contrary to the United States' interests. Moreover, in 1843, the United States refused to sign a pact with Great Britain and France that recognized the independence of the Hawaiian Kingdom (Daws, 1969). In fact, there were even rumblings of Kamehameha III selling the Kingdom to the United States.

The ideology of Manifest Destiny expedited a shift of power in the Hawaiian legislature from majority Native representation to increased representation of Euro-Americans. The desire for Euro-American control encouraged the formation of the Committee of Thirteen in the latter part of 1853, their objective being Hawai'i's annexation to the United States. Daws (1969) wrote that "a good many Americans in the kingdom were Manifest Destiny men, rabid nationalists, their minds inflamed by the election to the American presidency of the expansionist Democrat Franklin Pierce, who took office in 1853" (p. 147).

This transfer of power from monarchical to U.S. control was essentially a peaceful exchange with the missionaries playing an integral part. The acceptance of new governing methods and beliefs was easily established because many of the American missionaries, who had left the American Board of Foreign Ministries due to the missions' lack of funds, held prestigious and influential positions in the Hawaiian government. These former missionaries had always stood for Hawai'i's independence. Reverend Richard Armstrong first wrote in support of independence on December 29, 1848: "These Islands are becoming of great influence to Americans, and their independence should be sustained by the United States," and, "annexation we do not want, much less a protectorate, both or either would be submitted to as the lesser one of two or more evils.

What we do want is protection—and to be left alone" (as cited in Stevens, 1945, p. 26).

The missionaries' attitude affirming Native rule gradually changed over the next 10 years. Because the Native rulers and Native people still retained many of their objectionable traditional customs and had succumbed to Western vices of materialism and drink, the Missionaries became convinced that the rulers were incompetent. To this effect, Armstrong wrote in 1856, "Now you and the friends of the Hawaiian race in New England may as well take it for granted first as last, that the native chiefs can never govern this restless enterprising, and sometimes factious foreign population" (as cited in Stevens, 1945, p. 29).

Changing population demographics, new attitudes toward private fortune and land ownership, and growing sentiment toward U.S. annexation inspired by the "Westward Ho!" call of the Monroe Doctrine all contributed to shifting governing power in the Hawaiian Islands. Attempts by later monarchs to restructure the Hawaiian government and to rid the islands of the belief that the U.S. way was better were largely unrealized. Concerned about U.S. influence, for example, Kamehameha IV (Alexander Liholiho) introduced the Anglican Church in an effort to increase British presence. Related endeavors to place Episcopalians in governmental positions (e.g., the head of education) were unsuccessful, and, after the death of Kamehameha IV, the church was relegated to being just another minor denomination.

Refusing to endorse a proposed Constitution in 1864, Kamehameha V (Lot) was successful in writing a new Constitution that returned all monarchical power to the king (Kuykendall, 1953). The fundamental structures that had been written into law by previous supporters of colonialism, however, still littered the new constitutional pages. Governance by the elite did not change. The new constitution still excluded Native Hawaiians, as it continued to include a property test for voters and candidates, thereby filling the legislature with two factions—the very wealthy U.S. businessmen and the very wealthy Hawaiian *ali'i*. The political climate encouraged racism in the divided legislature, as the Hawaiians only spoke Hawaiian and the U.S. citizens only spoke English! While the political arena was locked in heated debates, which often led to dead ends, the U.S. agriculturists supplying United States' need for sugar profited from the Civil War (Makanani interviews, 1991–1992). With an economic base they perceived as stable, at least temporarily, the Manifest Destiny idealists were reasonably comfortable with Lot's temporary autonomous control, which ended with his death in 1872.

The Kamehameha Dynasty came to an abrupt end with Kamehameha V's death. With no heir named, a vote of the Legislative Assembly was required. This touched off heated political debates between at least four high *ali'i* and framed the beginnings of rudimentary political party politics. Supported by the U.S. dollar, Prince William Lunalilo made a landmark decision. He called for a vote of the people, claiming that all the people should have a voice. So popular was his proclamation that he gained quick favor among the people, and on January 8, 1873, he became the first king voted into office by an overwhelming majority (Kuykendall, 1967).

The U.S. business faction was clever in its political maneuvers. Lunalilo endorsed a liberal government and was pro-United States and, therefore, nonthreatening to their economic objectives. Although Lunalilo was a representative of the people, he made no attempt to reestablish monarchical autonomous rule, but was quick to appoint four people from the United States to his cabinet: C. R. Bishop, Foreign Affairs; E. O. Hall, Interior; R. Stirling, Finance; and A. F. Judd, Attorney General. Lili'uokalani (1964) wrote in her memoirs that his reign was heavily influenced by U.S. interests:

> The policy of the new cabinet was distinctively American, in opposition to that which may properly called Hawaiian; the latter looking to the prosperity and progress of the nation as an independent sovereignty the former seeking to render the Islands a mere dependency, either openly or under sufficient disguise, on the government of the United States. (pp. 37–38)[8]

Unfortunately, Lunalilo's short one-year reign saw devastating economic depression, the result of the end of the Civil War which found the United States not needing island commodities. With no treaty of reciprocity, there was no ensured market for Hawai'i's goods. The need for quick income led Lunalilo to offer Pearl Harbor to the United States to encourage them to sign a reciprocity treaty. Unsuccessful in his efforts, new outcries from the U.S. element for annexation again began to fill the talk of high society; however, Lunalilo was not able to address these protests due to illness and his untimely death in 1874.

THE IMPACT OF MISSIONARY CONTROL ON HAWAI'I'S SCHOOLS

While education from the 1830s through the 1890s was dominated primarily by the influence of Protestant missionaries, with the impact of annexation and municipal reform in the United States and in Hawai'i, educational policymaking was controlled by strong professional educators. These school leaders formed a decision-making elite who implemented broad social policies aimed at controlling minorities. Marshall et al. (1989) suggested that if one studies the educational policy process through those who govern schools, the results will be greater understanding of core values embedded in policy decisions. They wrote that "The world of state education policy is populated with elites who were elected or appointed to maintain a certain cultural view—a preferred way of structuring schooling to achieve a preferred set of values" (p. 16). These primary policy actors are a part of the powerful governing inner circle, which defines values and initiates activity. This powerful position is afforded the leaders of the educational system because, unlike other elites, the head of education spends the most time and energy specifically on education over an extended period of time.[9]

Between 1840 and 1900, policy decisions were in fact made by the Minister of Public Administration, who would be later replaced by the President of the Board of Education and his Inspector General. The practices of this office were thoughtful and systematic, fully translating the values of the ruling elite into school policy and school-related activities. Logan (1897) wrote:

> The interest of the leading men of Hawai'i and of the Government as such in the cause of popular education has not been at all of a spasmodic or fitful kind, but has represented a settled policy, pursued systematically and persistently for over half a century. (p. 2)

As Logan continued:

> It was a fortunate thing for the cause of education in these Islands that so large a proportion of the earlier white settlers came from the most intelligent and substantial class of English speaking people. Many of these men identified themselves thoroughly with their adopted country and took active and leading parts in guiding the infant state on its course from barbarism to civilization, and in devising a civil policy and social order to replace the aboriginal feudal despotism. In nothing is the wise foresight and breadth of view of these men more manifest than in their having made early, and, in proportion to the limited resources of the country at the time, liberal provision for education; the education, not of a small class or a favored few, but of the whole people. (Logan, 1897, p. 20)[10]

The President of the Board of Education was a key member of Hawai'i's governing inner circle. Because representatives from the American Missionary Party and lucrative businesses defined Hawai'i's social, political, and economic activity, the schools reflected their social values and goals. Wist (1940) also echoed the effects of these policymakers. In his description of the Minister of Public Administration's many duties, he illustrated the power this one position had over all educational governance:

> . . . assigned to him were the following (1) to furnish superintendents with books and stationery as needed; (2) in collaboration with the Minister of the Interior, to set aside public lands for school purposes; (3) to inspect schools; (4) to hold examinations; (5) to bestow certificates of honor upon teachers and scholars, and to designate those individuals to be exempted from taxation; (6) to draft rules and regulations for the conduct of schools, and to present these for approval of the king and privy council; (7) to prepare, for the approval of the king, circulars of directions to teachers; (8) in collaboration with the Board of Finance, to prepare the annual school budget; (9) to serve as the agent of the king in chartering private and select schools; (10) to act as principal of the Royal School; and (11) to keep the Attorney General posted as to breaches of the educational laws. (p. 56)

To best understand the implications of educational policy on Native Hawaiians, we must examine the values of the early leaders who presided over the public schools, in particular Reverend Richard Armstrong and Charles R. Bishop. These early education system leaders had strong ties to the religious hierarchy in Hawai'i and understood its hold on the prevailing political tenor of the islands. Schools, then, heeded the values and beliefs of this dominant religious force. The implications of a foreign-constructed religion on a native people would create tensions that would almost devastate Native culture.[11]

Reverend Richard Armstrong, Father of Hawai'i's Public School System

During the years preceding Reverend Richard Armstrong's term (1848–1860), there was no substantial move to organize the administration of Hawai'i's schools. Although the government had appointed Mr. W. Richards (formerly Reverend Richards) as the first Minister of the Department of Public Instruction, formal educational objectives and purposes were ill defined. Schools were dominated by either the Protestants or the Catholics. Initial attempts to develop more formal education for students were an English-speaking school for the children of the missionaries, opened in 1841, and the Royal School, established in 1850, for the young chiefs of Hawai'i.

The Organic Acts of Kingdom of Hawai'i, 1845–1846, raised education's formal status to an executive function of government by creating the Department of Public Instruction with the Minister becoming a member of the King's cabinet. In effect, this legislation centralized the administration of education. This action further legitimized education's role in the social and political structure of Hawai'i. The laws created a system of universalizing education; however, they did not establish an administrative or economic support base to adequately pay teacher salaries, build and maintain school buildings and facilities, or provide for school supplies. Because the purpose of the school was not clearly defined in the Organic Acts or by Richardson, school activity was left to the whim of the teacher.

Reverend Richard Armstrong changed all this. Arriving in Hawai'i with the fifth missionary party in 1832, he was appointed as the second Minister of Education in 1848, a position he held until his death in 1860. Armstrong, a supporter of Horace Mann's ideals, believed strongly in universal education and, during his term as Minister of Education and President of the Board of Education, helped Hawai'i step closer to that goal. Armstrong's accomplishments included abolishing sectarian schools in 1854, establishing an independent Board of Education in 1855, laying the foundation for vocational education, seeing tax-supported public education, and raising the quality of teaching. His efforts to organize formal schools were identical to movements occurring in the contiguous United States.

This change was quite a feat, because Armstrong inherited a school system that employed teachers with very little training and knowledge and utilized a curriculum that provided only rudimentary skills in reading, writing, elementary geography, arithmetic, and lessons in the New Testament (Wist, 1940). School texts were unimpressive and minimal in content, as they were provided by either the Protestant or Catholic press. School facilities were ill equipped and in ill repair because schools were supported by local community monies. Because most communities were poor, the schools reflected this poverty. Attendance at most schools was inconsistent, as parents tended not to send their children to school. Moreover, there were no supporting structures through which policies such as mandatory attendance could be implemented, monitored, enforced, and evaluated.[12]

Armstrong's first move to realize his goal of a universal educational system was to ensure the efficient operation of the schools. He spent the first 7 years of his tenure reorganizing school governance, accounting for finances, building and maintaining school facilities, and providing schools with needed supplies. These changes were further reflected in school laws established between 1848 and 1855. Three important laws furthered the financial support of schools, the abolition of sectarian public schools, and the centralized governance of schools. By 1850, a School Tax Law was passed by the legislature that made support of schools compulsory (Kingdom of Hawai'i, 1850), and, in 1851, the first appropriation was made to support public education for a total of $22,000. In 1854, under Armstrong's strong insistence, sectarian public schools were abolished. This move clearly mirrored a continental move toward separation of state and church in governmental action and school policy.

Endeavors to move Hawai'i's schools toward more efficient governance by a select group of professionals resulted in another major legislative mandate, the Reorganization Act of 1855 (Kingdom of Hawai'i, 1855). This act replaced the Minister of Public Education with a Board of Education consisting of a President and two Directors, all appointed by the King. This board took charge of all activity of the Department of Public Instruction, which, after reorganization, came under the Minister of the Interior. Removing control of education from a cabinet post gave the impression that education was not a political activity. However, three interesting features of these laws reflected educational reformers' goals across the United States. First, the laws created a lay board, although numbering only three members, that foreshadowed the United States' school governing structure of having a lay group of professionals dictate policy and manage schools as a result of municipal reform. Second, the laws provided for the maintenance of a centralized control of the schools with a small group of professionals. Finally, the members of the board were linked to the Kingdom's inner governing circle, suggesting the consolidation of power for school policymaking within this small governing elite. This first board included Armstrong as President, Lot Kamehameha who was brother to the King, and E. H. Allen, who later became a Chief Justice and Minister to the United States.

The fact that Armstrong encountered very little, if any political opposition, reveals that education was defined by the values, intentions, and behaviors of Hawai'i's governing elite. Armstrong's ties to the King's cabinet and members of the majority party in the legislature served his objectives favorably. Indeed, his hiring of like-minded people further institutionalized schools' conformity to external social and political values. Armstrong's last 5 years as President of the Board of Education were devoted to curriculum development and teacher education. Believing strongly that teachers were the key elements in a child's education, he was determined to improve the quality of the classroom by instituting teacher conventions and in-service training. Consistent with broader social and cultural values, he stressed vocational and agricultural education for Native youths and education of girls in the skills of homemaking and motherhood (Wist, 1940). His work, however, was hindered by a lack of texts written in the Hawaiian language and a large population of teachers who were unskilled. In his *Biennial Report of 1856,* Armstrong wrote:

> One subject I have endeavored not to forget in my daily intercourse with the people during these tours, and that is the importance of industry, es-

> pecially in the way of agriculture, to the well-being of the native race. Being personally and specially charged by His Majesty to keep this subject prominently before the people wherever I went—I have not failed to do so, when addressing them on the subject of public morals; for the greatest source of our immorality is idleness. (as cited in Townsend, 1899, p. 45)[13]

Armstrong's 12-year effort to move Hawai'i's schools toward efficient governance and quality curriculum and teaching with the goal to maintain a stable socioeconomic order was consistent with Mann's views that the common school would keep the rich in power; however, the rhetoric to the poor suggested schooling would eliminate social class and poverty.[14] Traveling to the United States in 1857, Armstrong conferred with Mann, whose influence was seen in *Hawai'i's Codified Laws of 1859* (Kingdom of Hawai'i, 1859). The laws brought together previous school policies established in 1840, 1841, 1842, 1845–1846, and 1855. In the area of school governance, the laws maintained the school organization set in 1855, but removed it from under the auspices of the Minister of the Interior and gave the board and department their own identities. Both, however, answered to the legislature. Further, the laws gave complete control of the select schools (later to become the public schools) to the board and required complete financing of the schools by the government. Continuing to support the financial needs of education, the laws set a specific $2.00 school tax per working male.

For the first time, the laws stated specific curriculum requirements, thereby making the curriculum an option of legislative fiat. The laws also established English-language schools for Native Hawaiians, because many Natives and Asians were moving from common schools toward select schools where instruction was conducted in English. Although this could be construed as a choice for Hawaiians, that is, of either going to the Hawaiian-language common schools or to the English-language select schools, in reality, the quality of education provided was not the same. Most of the teacher professional development was conducted only for English-speaking education, and many of the texts and materials brought from the United States were not translated for usage in the common schools. Because Hawaiians recognized the need to acquire this new knowledge in order to live in their changing islands, they naturally attempted to enter the select schools. According to Mann's ideals regarding secondary education, Hawai'i law established secondary schools at Lahainaluna on Maui and designated the Royal School in Honolulu as a normal and preparatory school. Lastly, the laws set a 40-week minimum school year and provided a means to enforce mandatory school attendance.

Richard Armstrong has been called the Father of Hawai'i's Public School System (Wist, 1940), because he rallied his energy to mold the once fledgling school system into an efficiently run department that provided educational opportunity for all children. In his *Biennial Report of 1899*, Henry S. Townsend wrote about Armstrong:

> Some persons are too cautious for positions requiring action. They are so much afraid of making mistakes that they make the fatal mistake of doing nothing. Nobody ever accused Mr. Armstrong of being a man of this character. He worked intensely through hardships and difficulties of which present educators in Hawai'i can have but a faint conception. In the midst of all this it would be strange indeed if he had always pleased everybody and had been always in the right. But it is only stating an historical fact to say that out of a chaos of educational forces he organized an efficient and admirable system of public schools and that more than any other man we owe our present educational system to Richard Armstrong and to John Ricord, whose legislation gave him his opportunity. (p. 48)

Armstrong's efforts to create an efficient educational system in Hawai'i can be viewed as part of a larger effort to reduce diversity across the United States through the socialization process of formal education. While history books might laud Armstrong's effort in the Hawaiian Islands, the character and intent of his ideology and the larger intention to assimilate those with diverse cultural backgrounds is further reflected in the efforts of his son Samuel Chapman Armstrong. Born in Hawai'i in 1839, Samuel spent his formative years in missionary schools under the shadow and influence of his father. In 1860, Samuel was sent to Williams College, where he graduated in 1862. In April of 1868, after several years fighting as an abolitionist, Samuel co-founded and assumed the role of principal of the Hampton Institute.

The school, at its start, was co-sponsored by the American Missionary Association (AMA). The spirit and thrust of Hampton reflected the assimilation ideology Samuel Armstrong embraced. The curriculum did not empower the newly freed African American slaves, but it fit the needs of the Southern dominant class under the guise of universal education. Armstrong's argument, widely publicized as the "Hampton idea, essentially called for the effective removal of black voters and politicians from southern political life, the relegation of black workers to the lowest forms of labor in the southern economy, and the establishment of a general southern racial hierarchy" (Anderson, 1988, p. 36). Armstrong believed, in much the same way his father thought of the Native Hawaiian, that the former slaves did not have the right morals to govern. Therefore, a school curriculum would have to consist of hard work, political socialization, and discipline. James D. Anderson (1988) wrote about Armstrong's beliefs:

> He fell heir to a particular theory of racial subordination while growing up as the son of a missionary in the Hawaiian Islands. . . . Samuel Armstrong

> was told that his father's missionary career was "Noble work for the savage race." This missionary inheritance was reinforced and consolidated in the milieu of the postwar South. The Hampton principal easily shifted his missionary views from the Polynesian to the black southerners. Indeed, he observed that "there was worked out in the Hawaiian Islands the problem of emancipation, and civilization of the dark-skinned Polynesian people in many respects like the Negro race." In both instances, Armstrong maintained that it was the duty of the superior white race to rule over the weaker dark-skinned races until they were appropriately civilized. This civilization process, in Armstrong's estimation, would require several generations of moral and religious development. (p. 38)

The impact of this legacy would also extend to Native American education. Richard Henry Pratt's brief partnership with Armstrong at Hampton Institute, where he had brought a small group of young Native Americans, convinced Pratt of the value of manual labor and off-reservation schooling. In 1879, Pratt opened the Carlisle Indian Industrial School in Pennsylvania. Michael C. Coleman (1993) wrote about Carlisle, "The fundamental goal was to 'individualize' the pupil by separating him or her from other Indian children—and to 'lift him up' by total and solitary immersion in white life" (pp. 128–129). As these examples illustrate, the extermination of the African American, Native American, and Native Hawaiian soul was clearly institutionalized as Americanization into the curriculum and instruction of schools. Through consistent policy that maintained the superior status of European descendents, while denigrating all other cultures, Americanization fundamentally drove schooling.

Charles R. Bishop: Industrial Education and Americanization

Another key implementer of widely endorsed cultural values was Charles R. Bishop. A member of the Board of Education since 1869, Bishop was appointed President in 1874 by King Lunalilo. He retained this position through 1893 with a brief five-year absence between 1883–1887 due to political reasons.[15] Under Bishop's leadership, along with that of his inspector generals, Hawai'i's schools were further defined to provide education that stratified students socially and economically. Bishop is described by Wist (1940) as:

> . . . a man imbued with ideals of service, possessed faith in Hawai'i and in public education as a means of promoting its social and economic welfare. He held the confidence of both the native Hawaiian and the leading industrialists. While not belonging to the missionary group, he was in no way inimical to its purposes. (p. 78)

Although a man of business interests, Bishop had strong opinions and concerns about education. Similar to the work of Samuel C. Armstrong and Richard H. Pratt, Bishop leaned toward developing stronger industrial education programs valuing the dignity of hard work. He was also concerned about poor school attendance, lack of parental support of schools, and the incompetence of the teaching staff. In contrast to some of his predecessors, Bishop sought to educate the Native within his own environment and in partnership with the schooling of White children. In a speech delivered at the 40th anniversary of O'ahu College, Bishop expressed this philosophy toward education:

> No considerable proportion of the youth of a nation can be educated in boarding schools, or away from their parents or friends; and it is not reasonable to expect that they should be. The masses must work up together, gradually; and the character of the masses, (not the favored few) will be the character of the nation. In a field of cane there are large hills and towering stalks scattered here and there, but the crop depends upon the average of the field and the good cultivation of the whole.
>
> It is not probable that a majority of the children of foreign blood now in our schools will spend the most of their days on these islands? If so here will be their field of duty and labor; and here their influence will be felt. Should they not be taught in common with the youth of the aboriginal stock to look upon this country as their home and their country and upon themselves as Hawaiians? (as cited in Kent, 1965, p. 244)

In his biography of Bishop, Kent (1965) wrote that Bishop's ideology toward education was not so much egalitarian, but had more "practical sentiments" (p. 244). Consistent with other educational reformers' views at the time, Bishop recognized and supported the paradox of Hawai'i's educational philosophy that called for a universal education geared to the masses and an elite cadre of boarding or independent schools for the chosen few. His comments also encouraged non-Hawaiians to believe that they too had rightful claim to Hawai'i as their homeland. In one sense, Bishop's leadership can be seen as contributing to the sorting function of schooling in contributing to the socioeconomic status quo. On the other hand, Bishop's presidency has been credited with giving Hawai'i's schools their truly public nature, a nonsectarian thrust, fully tax-supported status, marked improvement in teaching, and Americanization of school programs. As the unpaid President of the Board, who was not expected to spend his days laboring over school activities, Bishop's strength was in his leadership ability that linked the King's cabinet, the Legislature, and educational objectives. Held in high esteem by many in government office, Bishop's philanthropic contributions improved many school facilities.

In 1870, while Bishop was a member of the Board of Education, the *Statute Laws* relating to the Bureau of Public Instruction outlined five essential school policies. The first, concerning the composition of the board, maintained the five-member board appointed by the King and directed by the privy council but also gave the board its nonsectarian direction, ". . . no person in holy orders or a minister of religion shall be appointed to fill the office of President" (section II). The second policy addressed the objectives of the curriculum, "The object of the Common Schools, supported by the Government, is to instruct the children of the nation in good morals, and in the rudiments of reading, writing, geography, arithmetic, and of other kindred elementary branches . . ." (section VII). This maintained legislative authority over school programs. Four sections, section 14 through section 17, focused on the supervisory responsibilities of the school agent, specifying the care of facilities. The laws continued to support the work of the independent boarding schools (elite private academies) for boys and girls and, more significantly, made financial appropriations for these schools to teach the English language. Finally, the laws directed that school revenue would come from a combination of legislative appropriated school funds, rent of school lands, the school tax, and accrued interest on these monies (section XIX).[16]

THE FALL OF HAWAI'I NEI

By the latter 1800s, many U.S. residents of Hawai'i, descendants of U.S. Missionaries and early businessmen, had become wealthy by acquiring land titles and controlling commercial and industrial businesses that supported the Kingdom's treasury. When Kalākaua assumed the crown in 1874, he posed a threat to the stability of U.S. holdings and profit. Kalākaua wanted absolute power and a return to *wā kahiko* (ancient home or old Hawai'i's lifestyle). He spent inordinate amounts of the treasury on lavish Hawaiian celebrations, travels abroad, and the building of 'Iolani palace. His outward defiance of the U.S.-dominated legislature and cabinet gained him wide support from the Native Hawaiian people and from a handful of United States- and Britain-born advisors. Because the Missionary Party (the name given to the wealthy U.S. aristocrats) had been in control of social, political, and economic institutions since the early 1880s, its supporters would not see the end of their personal benefit. Calling Kalākaua to a public meeting, advisors, cabinet members, and legislative committees coerced the King into signing a new constitution that took all power away from the monarch and vested it squarely in the U.S.-dominated legislature. This new set of laws, called the Bayonet Constitution of 1887, marked the end of the Hawaiian Monarchy and the restriction of Native Hawaiian voice in governance.

King Kalākaua's death in 1891 brought to the throne his sister Lili'uokalani. Lili'u Kamaka'eha (her name at birth) was *hānai* (adopted) to Konia, the granddaughter of Kamehameha I and her husband (Paki). At the age of four, Lili'u attended the Chiefs School (later to become the Royal School) which was run by Mr. and Mrs. Amos Cooke, American missionaries from New England. It is of interest to note that Kamehameha III (Kauikeaouli) began this school so that the *ali'i* children could learn how to deal with foreigners. Here, Lili'u became proficient in reading and writing English as well as learning Christian ways. Although she was a good student, Lili'u longed to return to her *hānai* parents and to the traditions and lifestyle of *wā kahiko*. When Lili'uokalani (Lili'u) took the throne on January 29, 1891, her goal was to give Hawai'i a new constitution that restored the monarchical power and limited the influence of U.S. institutions. Her people voiced their wish for a new constitution and her advisors were supportive of such a move.

While Lili'uokalani worked to rewrite Hawai'i's constitution, the pro-United States coalition, first known as the Annexation Committee and then the Committee of Safety, worked quickly for annexation to the United States. Their members had two concerns. The first concern was that the McKinley Tariff, which allowed the importation of all foreign sugar into the United States without taxation (an advantage previously reserved only for Hawai'i's sugar growers), had severely depressed Hawai'i's economy. Second, they feared that large private tracts of land and profitable businesses owned by U.S. businessmen would be lost if the monarchy gained control. Annexation to the United States would protect sugar profits and sustain the Missionary Party's position and lifestyle in the islands.

In January of 1893, before the release of Hawai'i's new constitution, the Committee of Safety appointed Sanford B. Dole as its leader. Dole was born in Hawai'i in 1844, four years after his parents arrived from Maine. His father was in charge of Punahou College. Dole attended law school in the United States and returned to Hawai'i, where he engaged in private practice and politics. He was appointed to the Supreme Court bench in 1886. With the support of the Committee of Safety and the United States Minister in Hawai'i, J. Stevens, Dole led a quiet but efficient revolution on a quiet morning, January 17, 1893. Protected by the United States Marines, Dole and members of the Committee of Safety entered Ali'iolani Hale (the government seat). The only person present was the head clerk of the Interior Department, who handed over the government offices. Dole declared that the Hawaiian monarchy had ended and that a Provisional Government would be established.

The Provisional Government was a short-lived interim administration, lasting only from 1893 to 1894. Nevertheless, it provided annexationists time to parade their issues through the United States legislature, thereby giving permanence to a Western-controlled governing structure. It also served to further alienate Native Hawaiians. Although there were at least three vocal special interests groups who fought for Hawaiian rights (i.e., Hui Aloha 'Āina, Hui Kala'āina, Women's Patriotic League), they were kept on the fringes of government by the controlling European descended businessmen, professionals, and politicians.

The Queen heard about the overthrow through her advisors, but she did not surrender to the Provisional Government. Instead, she temporarily abdicated her rule to the United States of America. She asked that the United States government study the facts of the overthrow and restore her Kingdom. President Grover Cleveland sent Commissioner J. Blount to investigate. Blount arrived in March of 1893 and ordered the U.S. flag taken down and all United States Marines back to their ships. His final report to Cleveland concluded that the United States Minister, J. Stevens, had assisted wrongfully in the illegal overthrow of the Hawaiian Kingdom and that the Kingdom should be restored to Lili'uokalani. Although Cleveland did not support the overthrow or the annexation of Hawai'i to the United States, only the House of Representatives agreed with the decision:

> President Grover Cleveland To Congress, December 18, 1893:
>
> The unlawful government of Hawai'i was overthrown without the drawing of a sword, or the firing of a shot by a process every step of which, it may safely be asserted, is directly traceable to and dependent for its success upon the agency of the United States acting through its diplomatic and navel representatives. But for the notorious predilections of the United States Minister for annexation, the Committee of Safety, which could be called the Committee of Annexation, would never have existed. But for the landing of the United States forces upon false pretexts respecting the danger to life and property, the committee would never have exposed themselves to the pains and penalties of treason by undertaking the subversion of the Queen's government. (cited in Blount's Report, 1894, p. iii)

Fearing reprisals would be taken by the Hawaiian monarchs toward the revolutionaries (most of whom were United States citizens), the United States Senate conducted its own investigation and concluded that, in the best interest of United States citizens in Hawai'i, the overthrow was necessary. In the end, Hawaiians lost their Kingdom and their *'āina* (land).

In the meantime, the leaders of the Provisional Government, often referred to by historians as the Sugar Oligarchy,[17] were not waiting for the possibility of a Royalty uprising or possible restoration of the monarchy. Knowing that annexation would not come soon, sugar owners sought a more formalized government in which to ground their control and assure their own political and economic lives. On July 4, 1894, the Provisional Government formally became the Republic of Hawai'i. Sanford B. Dole became its President; Francis Hatch, Minister of Foreign Affairs; James A. King, Minister of Interior; Samuel M. Damon, Minister of Finance; and W. O. Smith, Attorney General. The Constitutional Convention held in early 1894 reflects institutional structures that mimicked the values, intentions, and the behaviors of United States' social, political, and economic ideals. Privatization of conflict was an underlying objective of governance, as well as a blatant attitude of Teutonic superiority. To prohibit Native participation in the creation of the Republic's Constitution, the requirements for elected delegates included allegiance to the Provisional Government and land ownership (Russ, 1961). Kuykendall (1967) wrote:

> When the provisional government on March 15, 1894, called a convention to draft a constitution for the proposed "Republic of Hawai'i," they made certain that the revolutionary leaders would retain control. There would be thirty-seven members in the convention. Automatically named to the convention were the president and members of the executive and advisory councils of the provisional government. They numbered nineteen—a clear majority of one. The voters were then privileged to choose the minority of eighteen. But the oligarchy did not stop there. Even to allow the franchise to those who had voted before the revolution, under the limitations imposed by the Constitution of 1887, was considered dangerous. Therefore, those who were allowed to vote for a minority of the convention, besides possessing a certain amount of wealth, had to take an oath of allegiance to the provisional government and to oppose any attempt to re-establish the monarchy. In the finished constitution the qualifications for voting and holding office were so stringent that comparatively few natives, and no Orientals, could vote. Fewer still were eligible to serve in either house of the legislature. (p. 649)

Control of who participated ensured that the principles advocated by the Provisional Government would be maintained. Castle (1981) illuminated the motivations behind these exclusionary policies in the presentation of letters between Dole and Burgess.[18] Castle described John William Burgess as a Professor of Political Science at Columbia University who was raised in Germany and was a student of Kant, Hegel, Treitshke, and Griest. Burgess believed that political structures were determined along racial lines, seeing the Teutonic (German superiority) political structure as the best. In essence, only those who were Teutons (e.g., German,

Scandinavian, Dutch, English) or could be effectively socialized were capable of governing. In one letter, Dole commented on non-White voters:

> . . . under the monarchy, there were two classes of legislatures who sat together and who were elected by voters having different qualifications. There are many natives and Portuguese who had the vote hitherto, who are comparatively ignorant of the principles of government, and whose vote from its numerical strength as well as from the ignorance referred to will be a menace to good government. (as cited in Castle, 1981, p. 27)

Dole's racist attitudes were reflected in strict voter qualifications which resulted in keeping the undesirables out of office. Burgess' reply to Dole's letters reaffirmed the thinking that only Teutons should control Hawai'i. He urged the Constitutional Convention to be conservative, to establish a strong executive branch, to include electorate standards of age, education, and property, and to allow only those of Teutonic bloodlines to fill judiciary seats. The constitution fulfilled all his suggestions, and, to further exclude the Native Hawaiian, a voting requirement of reading and writing in the English language and the ability to explain the constitution in English were added. Although many Hawaiians could read and write, they could do so only in the Hawaiian language.

Even after the establishment of new leaders, the Queen still claimed her right to the throne and that of her heir, Princess Ka'iulani. For a short time there were several Royalist uprisings that sought to remove non-Hawaiians from government seats. In fear for the lives of her Native people, Lili'uokalani abdicated her throne on January 24, 1895. This closed the door on Native Hawaiian sovereignty.

Queen Lili'uokalani wrote a powerful and prophetic observation during one of her journeys to the United States:

> There was nothing lacking in this great, rich country save the people to settle upon it, and develop its wealth. And yet this great and powerful nation must go across two thousand miles of sea, and take from the poor Hawaiians their little spots in the broad Pacific, must covet our islands of Hawai'i Nei, and extinguish the nationality of my poor people, many of whom have now not a foot of land which can be called their own. And for what? In order that another race-problem shall be injected into the social and political perplexities with which the United States in the great experiment of popular government is already struggling? In order that a novel and inconsistent foreign and colonial policy shall be grafted upon its hitherto impregnable diplomacy? Or in order that a friendly and generous, yet proud-spirited and sensitive race, a race admittedly capable and worthy of receiving the best opportunities for material and moral progress, shall be crushed under the might of a social order and prejudice with which even

> another century of preparation would hardly fit it to cope? (Lili'uokalani, 1964, pp. 309–310)

TRANSLATING POLITICAL VALUES INTO EDUCATIONAL POLICY

It is during this period of political overthrow of the Hawaiian monarchy that a significant movement toward bureaucratization and centralization of decisionmaking evolved. These structures resulted from the growing importance of business interests and the far-reaching political and economic significance of the small island chain. Since 1820, schools had functioned to socialize the populace toward Western ways of thinking and behaving while degrading much of what was the Hawaiian way of life. Changes in the structure of education reflected dominant social and political norms, thereby moving toward greater centralization and professionalism.

English-Only Education

Moreover, these changes resulted in the formal institutionalization of English-only language policy in the schools under the leadership of Superintendent Baldwin further dispossessing Native Hawaiians of their cultural heritage. This is not to say that Native Hawaiians did not speak their mother tongue. Many continued, but in private, personal, and family communications. The 1890s did see the development of a pidgin (Hawaiian, Creole, English or HCE) oral language. Instead of standard American English, many Native Hawaiians (including Chinese, Japanese, Portuguese, Filipino immigrants) spoke HCE. This dialect had its origins among the working class laborers which served to further marginalize its speakers, many of whom were Native Hawaiians. Regardless, school policymakers forged an English-only policy, which would eventually prevent Native Hawaiians from attending the better public schools (see chapter 4). Townsend (1899) commented:

> . . . it was Mr. Baldwin's good fortune to stand at the beginning of our era of greater things. Every argument which had hitherto existed in favor of English education for Hawaiians was now doubled in value. . . . The immigration of relatively large numbers of English-speaking persons and their distribution through all the principal districts made it more and more a language of common communication. . . . The old argument of the poverty of the government and the great cost of such education practically disappeared in this era of prosperity. (p. 55)

The growing sugar industry and Hawai'i's reciprocity treaty with the United States rejuvenated the school budget and cleared the way for schools to better assimilate their students into U.S. cultural life. The first step occurred when two major teacher educational facilities, Lahainaluna and Hilo Boarding School, substituted the English language for the Hawaiian language. Of course, Americanizing the school programs began long before Baldwin was appointed superintendent in 1877. In a letter from Minister Henry A. Pierce in 1871 to United States Secretary Hamilton Fish, Pierce wrote, ". . . favorite songs and airs are American. Sherman's 'Marching Through Georgia' and 'John Brown's Soul Is Marching On' are daily heard in the streets and in their schoolhouses" (as cited in Russ, 1959, p. 5). However, with the political fervor of the day and the availability of funds, Baldwin was able to further develop the select school system or English day schools.

Many debates flourished that favored English-only education over education taught in the Hawaiian mother tongue. The common schools, taught in Hawaiian, were often referred to as inferior and the students incapable. Teachers of the select schools commented that students transferring from the common school to the select school were ill prepared to read, write, and think in English. Logan (1897) wrote about the common school that "the pupils had learned to read and write Hawaiian and acquired some knowledge of arithmetic, geography, etc., but they had also acquired a habit of not only reading and writing, but of thinking in their native language" (p. 3). This belief that "thinking Hawaiian" was an inferior way to think eventually led to many Hawaiians believing themselves to be stupid.

The eradication of ceremony, identity, culture, and language that led to the dysfunctional character of Native Hawaiians would also be the same journey that Native Americans traveled. The driving ideology was to replace Native thinking with Western thinking. In this way, the Native would come to see the White man as kind, just, and civilized and would recognize in himself his own debasement and savagery. Working hard and speaking English would be the Native road to civilization.

In support of this ideology, political pressure encouraged English-only instruction in the schools, employing the argument that, in order for Hawai'i to be a democracy patterned after the United States, it must have an educated and civilized citizenry. In an article written for the *Hawaiian Gazette* entitled "The Hawaiian Public School System," C. M. Hyde commented that "without good education Constitutional government is impossible" (1885, p. 2). This attitude that English was best was reflected in the growing number of select schools, increased attendance in these schools, lack of support for common schools (Kittleson, 1981), and the use of U.S. texts in the classroom. Much like the tactics used in Native

American schools, Native Hawaiian children were often sharply punished, ridiculed, and embarrassed if they were caught speaking their native tongue.

Because the aim of school-related activities was to Americanize students, thereby creating industrious citizens with no ties to the previously sovereign Hawaiian monarchy, an increasing number of U.S. English-speaking teachers were employed. One troubling comparison of the nationalities of Hawai'i's teachers between 1892 and 1897 (Table 3.2) reveals the steady growth of U.S. influence in teacher demographics. In 1892, 77 U.S. teachers comprised 35% of the employed teachers; however, by 1897, their number nearly doubled to 134 teachers or 45%. The number of Hawaiian and Part-Hawaiian teachers showed very little growth within the same 5-year period. Although Hawaiians had dominated the teaching field, representing 41% (91 teachers) of the total in 1892, by 1897 they represented only 33% with 97 teachers.

It is not surprising that Hawaiians were disproportionately underrepresented. Hawai'i's common schools, which employed Native and Part-Hawaiian teachers and where instruction was in the Native Hawaiian language, were fast becoming obsolete. The 1882 Biennial Report recorded nearly 550 pupils leaving the common schools to attend the government select schools, which employed primarily U.S., Western-trained, English-speaking teachers who were given financial incentives to teach (Bishop, 1882). The following table (Table 3.3) details teacher salary, revealing that the highest paid ($2,700 per year) teacher was from the United States, whereas the lowest paid ($120 per year) teacher was Hawaiian. Additionally, of the 43 teachers that comprised the $1,000+ annual salary range,

TABLE 3.2
Nationalities of Hawai'i's Public School Teachers Between 1892 and 1897

Ethnicity	*1892*	*1894*	*1895*	*1896*	*1897*
Hawaiian	50 (22.6%)	52 (22.7%)	53 (20.6%)	53 (18.9%)	49 (16.4%)
Part-Haw.	41 (18.5%)	50 (21.8%)	48 (18.6%)	49 (17.5%)	48 (16.1%)
American	77 (34.8%)	77 (33.6%)	95 (36.9%)	105 (37.5%)	134 (44.9%)
British	39 (17.6%)	36 (15.7%)	44 (17.1%)	52 (18.5%)	42 (14.0%)
German	4 (1.8%)	1 (.4%)	2 (.7%)	2 (.7%)	2 (6.0%)
Portuguese	5 (2.2%)	6 (2.6%)	3 (1.1%)	5 (1.7%)	6 (2.0%)
Scandinav.	4 (1.8%)	6 (2.6%)	3 (1.1%)	5 (1.7%)	6 (2.0%)
French	1 (.4%)	1 (.4%)	1 (.3%)	1 (.3%)	1 (.3%)
Chinese			1 (.3%)	1 (.3%)	1 (.3%)
Belgian			1 (.3%)	1 (.3%)	1 (.3%)
Japanese					
Other					2 (.6%)
Total	221	229	257	280	298

Source: *The Biennial Report of 1897* (Townsend, 1897, p. 83).

TABLE 3.3
Teacher Nationality and Yearly Salary,[a] 1897

	Yearly Salary Range							
Ethnicities	*$120*	*$180*	*$240*	*$300*	*$360*	*$1,000*	*$2,400*	*$2,700*
Hawaiian	1	2	5	8	10	2		
Part-Haw.			1	7	8	2		
American				1		37		1
British					2		1	
Portuguese				1	1			
Total	1	2	6	17	21	41	1	1

[a]This information reflects the salaries of teachers on the island of O'ahu as was extrapolated from an overview of salary data reported in *The Biennial Report of 1897* (Townsend, 1897).

only 2 were Hawaiian and 2 Part-Hawaiian; and all 4 were at the bottom of this category. Finally, at the lower end of the salary range, 26 Hawaiians and 18 Part-Hawaiians comprised 89% of teachers paid between $120 and $360 per year. It would seem that being from the United States in Hawai'i's teaching force was a financially rewarding vocation.

Free Schooling at English-Only Institutions

Although the use of the English language as the primary tool of public school instruction was a predictable eventuality given the political, social, and economic changes of the time, an actual mandate was not instituted until the 1900s. Another effort to acculturate large numbers of children to U.S. ideals was to make all public English schools tuition free. This move began two important currents in Hawai'i's education: an interest in adult education and government support of secondary education (Wist, 1940).

One can speculate about the part education may have played in the overthrow of Hawai'i and its subsequent annexation to the United States. After all, since Armstrong's tenure as superintendent, the schools leaned toward the Americanization of the Hawaiian populace. The values and beliefs about democracy were reflected in textbooks, teacher education, and curriculum requirements. Wist (1940) concluded:

> The extent to which public education played a part in the events leading up to this climax will, of course, never be precisely known. That it was an influential factor can readily be inferred. Public education was a foster child of the American missionaries; and its growing success only increased the efforts of the opponents of Americanism in Hawai'i. Public education had contributed to the general adoption of the English language in the Islands—

> a factor of some significance in the American decision favoring annexation. (p. 123)

During the years of Lili'uokalani's government and the brief interim authority of the Provisional Government which led to the Republic, the activity of the schools remained unchanged. The Inspector General, A. T. Atkinson (appointed in 1887), supported the growth of English education, a U.S. curriculum, teacher efficiency in instruction, and quality of character. Moreover, during his tenure, governmental funding of the independent private schools ended.[19]

In the *Biennial Report of 1894*, Atkinson (1894) discussed the qualifications of teachers, suggesting that the first requisite was a good moral character and the second was ability. He noted that "It is the intention to require of every teacher that, like Caesar's wife, he should be not only innocent but above suspicion" (p. 8). Although it was not the job of the schools to teach religion, because the population of the schools consisted of non-White children, it was expected that the teachers by example and tone would also teach temperance and morality—essentially, how to be good U.S. citizens. Coupled with these lessons, the teachers were also expected to teach the Hawaiian, Oriental, and Portuguese who made up the majority of students in attendance how to read, write, and think in English as well as to believe that the right way was the U.S. way.

The Impact of Act 57 and Progressive Education

In June of 1896, *Act 57* (Republic of Hawai'i, 1896) reorganized the school system. This act embodied the social and political values that permeated every institution of Hawai'i's governance. *Act 57*, much like movements occurring on the continental United States, sought to convince the public that centralized control of schools would take politics out of education. More devastating to the Native Hawaiian, *Act 57* devalued ethnic cultures, instead seeking a unitary, melting pot community in which everyone had a similar set of values and perceived opportunity. Finally, this act further gave the exclusive power of school governance to a very select group of U.S. professionals.

We summarize some of the key sections of the Act. The first 12 regulations returned the administration of schools to an executive-level status as the Department of Public Instruction. Section 8 provided the Department with policymaking power:

> The Department may adopt rules and regulations not contrary to existing laws, for the government of all teachers and pupils, and its officers, agents and servants, and for the carrying out the general scheme of education and for the transaction of its business, which, when approved by the Executive

> Council and published, shall have the force and effect of law. (Republic of Hawai'i, 1896, Section VIII)

The Board of Education consisted of the Minister of the Interior, who served as its head and sat on the King's cabinet, and six appointed commissioners. This arrangement maintained centralized control of public education by the executive branch of government. In a supervisory capacity, the position and responsibilities of the Inspector General were retained (sections 13 and 14). Section 13 of the Act continued to separate the church and state through the appointment of an inspector, by mandating that "no person in holy orders or a minister of religion, shall be eligible to fill such office." Besides ascribing administrative positions, the Act recognized two classes of schools—the public and the private: "All schools established and maintained by the Department in accordance with law, are public schools. All other schools are private schools." It further defined the Department's responsibility to manage all public school activities:

> The Department shall have entire charge and control, and be responsible for the conduct of all affairs appertaining to public instruction. The Department is authorized to establish and maintain schools for secular instruction, at such places and for such terms as in its discretion it may deem advisable and the funds at its disposal may permit. The Department shall regulate the course of study to be pursued in all grades of public schools, and classify them by such methods as it shall deem proper. (Republic of Hawai'i, 1896, Section XX)

Other section laws included details concerning attendance, property, supplies, teacher responsibilities, parental responsibilities, finances, and private school regulations. Public schools were kept free except in such situations where the Board deemed tuition was necessary (Section XXIII).

Perhaps the most important law required English-only instruction in all public schools, which brought a swift end to valuing diversity and the beginning of the unitary community belief:

> The English language shall be the medium and basis of instruction at all public and private schools, provided that where it is desired that another language shall be taught in addition to the English language, such instruction may be authorized by the Department. . . . Any schools that shall not conform to the provisions of this Section shall not be recognized by the Department. (Republic of Hawai'i, 1896, Section XXX)

The education of teachers became an essential endeavor of which the laws accordingly approved:

> The Department may establish and maintain one or more Teachers' Conventions or Institutes, or it may authorize and permit their establishment by and among its teachers, and may direct and authorize the attendance of teachers there at, as a part of their duties, and may permit the closing of schools at specified limited times, in order to permit their attendance at such conventions or institutions. (Republic of Hawai'i, 1896, Section XXXI)

Under the guidance of Superintendent H. S. Townsend, a champion of progressive education, an island-wide teacher association was established, summer teacher workshops were instituted, and every teacher received a copy of the periodical *Progressive Educator*. In fact, Townsend was even able to bring to Hawai'i both Colonel Francis W. Parker of the University of Chicago and, in 1899, the guru of progressive education, John Dewey. Laying a foundation for liberal and progressive education, Townsend "provided for the schools the first systematized course of study for general use, outlining the materials to be taught and listing the textual materials to be followed" (Wist, 1940, p. 138). He also stressed the importance of variety in vocational education.

His efforts to create better educational opportunity for all students, patterned after the ideals of John Dewey, however, became the root of his undoing. Much like other progressive movements on the United States continent, the precepts of Dewey's philosophy that Townsend supported were not aligned with broader social, political, and economic values. Equity threatened the well-being of elites as well as jeopardized the legitimacy of the existing schools. The belief in providing equal opportunity in the schools was in opposition to the existing socially supported two-class system consisting of the foreigner in the superior position and the Hawaiians and Asians (i.e., non-White) in the inferior position. The commonly held belief among agriculturists and businessmen in Hawai'i that educational funds should not be wasted on common laborers and second-class citizens led to the release of Townsend as the Superintendent of Public Instruction. Nevertheless, his values of parity and individual growth had struck a deep chord in Hawai'i's public schools. Try as the Republican Board did in the following years to arrest this egalitarian ideal, educational opportunity would eventually find its champions.

Values in School Policy

Because school activity was aligned with the political ideals of the day, centralization of the school structure gave control of teacher education, program definition, finances, supplies, and construction and maintenance of buildings to the Department of Public Instruction. Despite Townsend's move toward progressive education, the school organization had become deeply entrenched in values of efficiency and control. Centralization resulted in a hierarchy of control that effectively governed the schools and many other social and economic institutions.

This unique situation required that policy not only describe the governing structure of schools but also control all aspects of education. For example, regulations which sought to check adherence to laws were an integral component of policy as was program definition, curriculum development, and especially teacher education. Table 3.4 presents a content analysis of values embedded in *Act 57* of the Republic's Constitution (Republic of Hawai'i, 1896). The analysis consists of a tally of how each section law falls under the policy values of choice, efficiency, equity, and quality and examines the operational domains in which these values appear.

Table 3.4 indicates that educational policies reflected efficient means to attain a standard of quality education. These regulations reveal that efficiency was to be maintained through centralized control of school governance (Sections 1–15, 40), finance (Sections 27–29, 32, 36, 37), and programs (Sections 17, 18, 20, 30, 31). The regulations define the Department of Public Instruction as an executive department controlled by a Minister who sat on the President's cabinet. The responsibilities of the departments would encompass all areas of policymaking from control of finances, to certification of teachers, to regulation of school curriculum.

TABLE 3.4
Distribution of Values and State Policy Mechanisms (SPM) in Act 57

SPM	*Quality*	*Efficiency*	*Equity*	*Choice*	*Total*
Finance		7			7
Personnel	2	2			4
Testing					0
Program	1	1			2
Governance	2	24		1	27
Curriculum materials	1	1			2
Bldg. & facilities		1			1
Total	6[a]	36[b]	0[c]	1[d]	43

[a]Two sections of Act 57, 14 and 17, accounted for under quality could also be adequately placed under efficiency. Both establish governing positions, but more importantly, outline program as well as teacher and principal responsibility. [b]Sections 21 and 23, the regulation and licensing of private schools, and section 34, the enforcement of corporal punishment, were accounted for under Efficiency. [c]Section 39 gave grievance power to the parents, which could be construed as equal participation in governance; however, because the grievance procedure was used to hold teachers accountable, it was placed under the value of quality. [d]Two sections proved difficult to code. Section 19 recognized the public and private school as educational alternatives. Although this could be translated as a choice for students, in actuality, it served only to maintain the social hierarchy, thus, it was placed under efficiency-governance. Section 41, listed as the one policy under choice, provided limited choice in school district attendance. (See Republic of Hawai'i, *Act 57*, Republic of Hawai'i.)

Further, the centralized authority wielded by the Department stretches to the appointed Inspector General (Section 14) and all appointed district School Agents (Sections 16, 38).

More efficient governance of schools, accomplished in Hawai'i's case through centralized control, was believed to provide for better accountability and acculturation of Hawai'i's youth. With this understanding, the laws mandated free public education in English-speaking schools throughout the Republic (Section 30). To insure that Native Hawaiian children were socialized to Western values, the regulations established attendance laws with accountability mechanisms and enforcement procedures (Sections 24, 25, 33, 41, 43). Further, the goal to assimilate diverse students required getting the job accomplished with the least amount of capital. To assure that schools were kept to a conservative financial ledger, *Act 57's* regulations (Republic of Hawai'i, 1896) gave authority over money, supplies, and property management to only a few people. Moreover, discontinuing financial support of private schools with the exception of providing texts (section 35) relieved the Department's over-extended treasury and further separated church (religious private schools) and state functions.

The policy value of quality was reflected in regulations focusing on teachers and curriculum. Laws regulating the hiring and certification of teachers addressed the need for quality by supporting teacher conventions (section 31). Not surprisingly, the policy value of choice was limited to 1 policy, and equity did not appear in any of the 43 policies analyzed. Among the 43 sections, only 1 regulation provided parents with a choice of public schools, however limited (section 41), and only 1 gave parent grievance rights, again within prescribed restrictions (section 39).

The universal movement toward education for all did not mean equal opportunity for all, as equity was not supported by any of the school regulations. The school laws indicate the policy values found most desirable, as 41 out of 43 sections addressed the factors of cost-effective schooling, quality teaching force, and efficiency of centralized control. This combination of quality and efficiency as defined by the political culture led to policies which sought to Americanize the vast number of Native Hawaiians and Asians. The laws degraded anything that was Hawaiian.

The data in Table 3.4 also reveal the high priority given to the organization and governance of the schools, which aptly reflect the centralization and bureaucratization occurring throughout other governing institutions. Next, regulations regarding financial interests suggest policymakers' concern for holding schools accountable for limited funds. Although both policy areas of school personnel training and certification and school program definition each have only two policies listed, they both fall under the values of efficiency and quality. Both grant authority to the Department of Education to define the underlying attitude of what schools should teach and how teachers should teach.

In the end, under the direction of a well-propagandized movement to provide universal education for all, schools were thought to offer Native Hawaiian children the opportunity to improve their ability to live and compete in the Western world. In reality, the culminating effect of *Act 57* (Republic of Hawai'i, 1896) was that it legitimized centralized control of all educational activity, prevented culturally sensitive activities, restricted involvement of the public in the schools, and drove the curriculum toward teaching students how to think and behave in appropriate, Western ways.

THE IMPACT OF EDUCATIONAL POLICIES AND PRACTICES ON NATIVE HAWAIIANS

To say that educational policy alone impacted negatively on Native Hawaiians' academic, economic, and social standing would be naive; however, the public schools played an integral role. The oppressive ideals of Manifest Destiny, played out in social currents, denigrated the Native Hawaiian and glorified the Euro-American. Subsequently, every political, economic, and social objective pushed Hawai'i closer to being Americanized, forcing other cultures to accept new beliefs. Therefore, socializing Hawai'i's children to U.S. beliefs and ways of thinking became the primary objective of Hawai'i's public schools.

Educational policy and school activities embodied commonly held beliefs across the United States that valued economic self-sufficiency, hard work, moral uprightness, and citizenship and allegiance to Euro-American-led governance. Together, these formed the Protestant ethic, a core value of U.S. lifestyle (Adams, 1995). Students were taught to think in English, not Hawaiian, and to act like moral U.S. citizens, not like "heathen Hawaiians!" This process of socialization in the public and independent schools, coupled with the political turmoil of the latter 1800s in which Hawaiians' lost their sovereignty, their queen, and their land, created deep-seated resentment among the Native Hawaiians toward the *haole* (Makanani interviews, 1991–1992). This psychological barrier toward participation in any activity that was Western resulted in a Native Hawaiian population that was less capable of competing in Hawai'i's new economy, social and political structures, and academic institutions.

Cultural Difference: Defining Learning and Knowing

The introduction of a Western school system in Hawai'i brought new knowledge which added to the Native Hawaiians' view of the world. However, because there were fundamental differences between Western education and Hawaiian education that were never reconciled, conflicting values created an educational atmosphere pitting the new against the traditional. These conflicting values added to the difficulties Hawaiian children had in adapting to Western schooling. The Native Hawaiian embraced the spiritual and supernatural that connected the land and people. With the introduction of scientific knowledge that sought to objectify this relationship, the very fiber of native knowing was contested. Unfortunately for the Native Hawaiian, traditions that sought harmony, respect, and reciprocity with nature passed down from ancient times were increasingly replaced by new beliefs including individualism, private ownership, and economic exploitation of the land and people. There were at least six key differences between Western and Hawaiian ideas toward education.

First, there were dissimilarities between how each culture approached educating the child. The Western school structure placed children in grade levels according to their age and required that certain tasks be taught at different times. Lessons were taught through repetitive recitation and rote memorization, with lessons often times not repeated. This was in opposition to Hawaiian belief that what a child was taught was determined by his or her ability, not age or some prescribed curriculum that every child endured. Further, Native children were taught tasks as complex as astronomy through observation (*I ka nānā no a 'ike*) and activity (*I ka hana no a 'ike*), not through abstraction. Finally, students were taught one step at a time, thereby learning to do one thing well before moving on (Pukui et al., 1972).

The Hawaiian attribute of *mana*, defined by Pukui et al. (1972) as an "ultimate personal possession" (p. 296), is another tenet which differentiates the two cultures. Difficult to explain in words of any language, it is a talent or spiritual gift that obligates each person to always work toward excellence.[20] How this belief translated to traditional Hawaiian education had positive connotations, as students became accomplished in many Native skills. However, *mana* could not be communicated in Western schools because the idea of *mana* meant that Hawaiians needed immediate, tangible gratification which checked their skill. Therefore, they could not understand the long-term value of Western education, because it gave no immediate feedback of a person's work. How could they judge whether or not they were fulfilling the obligation of their *mana*? The Hawaiian had been taught that the power of one's *mana* was judged in relation to one's personal progress in tangible ways (Pukui et al., 1972). The abstract grading system used by the Western schools did not have *mana* or meaning, as it was difficult for a native to understand how an *A* grade showed skill just as a well-made canoe did.

A third contrasting value addresses the student's interaction and relationship with the teacher. Hawaiian children were always taught to avoid eye contact with their elders. Pukui et al. (1972) called this *nānā i lalo* (to look downward) and noted that students were never to be *maha'oi* (bold) by asking questions of the adults. On the other hand, forward and inquisitive behavior in the Western school was a sign of thinking and intelligence, and eye contact showed confidence and self-esteem. When Hawaiian children did not ask questions in class nor make eye contact with the teacher, they were often harshly reprimanded or labeled as dumb. It was quite unfortunate for the Native child whose act of respect was interpreted as misbehavior (Pukui et al., 1972).

Perhaps the greatest cultural change initiated by the Western schools was that they took learning away from the *'ōhana* (extended family unit). Education to the Native Hawaiian had been integrally tied to the *kūpuna* (grandparents and people of that generation) and *mākua* (parents and people of that generation). Pukui et al. (1972) wrote, ". . . eventually, parents and grandparents would no longer be his teachers. The child's world would, in time cease to be bounded by *'ōhana* (extended family); he would have another personal universe within the four walls of the school house" (p. 60).

The *'ōhana* was an important component of Hawaiian life, as it provided unlimited *aloha* (love), *malama pono 'ia* (care), *'ihi* (reverence or respect), and rules that every family member adhered to and honored (Pukui et al., 1972). As the power that had once belonged to the *'ōhana* was replaced by external agencies like the schools, the *'ōhana* structure was replaced by the Euro-American's civil laws.

Competition, the fifth theme, was highly valued by both the foreigner and the Native Hawaiian. For the Native Hawaiian, competition in areas of skill was evident in everything from *lei*-making to canoe construction to athleticism. Mastery of skill was seen as important to the survival of the whole community, not only to the select few. Competition was a healthy activity that stimulated excellence and achievement. The difference between the Hawaiian sense of competition and the Western perspective was that the latter saw competition as a profitable exercise that benefited the individual first. Furthermore, competitions among Whites were seen as healthy and natural; however, competition with the second-rate Hawaiian was an unsavory thought. The Hawaiian who attended the public school was unable to grasp the importance of competition for individual gain. When the Hawaiian did compete with his White counterpart, however, he was often reprimanded and, in the end, found it undesirable to compete in the Western world. Hawaiian children looked to sharing and fellowship amongst themselves, which inevitably distanced them from the activity of individual competition inherent in the foreign classroom.

A final theme illustrates differences in definitions of work and leisure. Both the Native Hawaiian and the White believed in hard work and a job well done. The difference was in the amount of time spent on work and on play. To the turn-of-the-century Euro-American, work comprised a good deal of one's waking hours—10 hours a day, 6 days a week. For the Hawaiian, however, the value of *ukupau*, or "get the work done, then play" (Pukui et al., 1972, p. 309), meant that one would get the job done in as much time as it required and then relax. Native Hawaiians traditionally lived their lives providing only what was needed and spent a good deal of their time in social leisure. Placing Hawaiian children in school for a minimum of 40 weeks and in a structured classroom that was dictated by the clock was contrary to their traditional lifestyle. Play and leisure were replaced with toil and drudgery.

The educational policies implemented in the schools of Hawai'i were never sensitive to these cultural differences. Nothing was done to recognize, appreciate, or incorporate the traditional beliefs the Native child brought to the formal schoolroom. In essence, those who sat at the head of the public school's hierarchical structure mandated the death of the Native culture.

Academic and Social Impact

Despite cultural differences in learning styles between Hawaiian culture and the formal school, the academic impact of formal schooling resulted in a gradual reduction of illiteracy, a trend that continued well into the 1930s (Table 3.5). This is a remarkable achievement given the cultural mismatch between the home and school.

Of course, these early statistics must be reviewed with caution because there were no standardized recording procedures. Although Hawaiians

TABLE 3.5
Illiteracy in Hawai'i Between 1853–1930

Year	*Age (in years)*	*No. Illiterate*[a]	*% of Population*
1853[a]	16 and over	NA	25.0
1884[a]	6 and over	31,372	44.6
1890[a]	6 and over	40,191	51.2
1896[b]	6 and over	33,567	36.1
1900	15 and over	41,949	35.2
1910	15 and over	39,465	29.2
1920	15 and over	35,083	21.2
1930	15 and over	41,018	17.5

[a]Figures for 1853, 1884, & 1890 are based on a person's ability to read and write in Hawaiian, English, and/or other European language. [b]Figures for 1896–1930 are based on literacy in any language.

Source: *Historical Statistics of Hawai'i* (p. 229) by Robert C. Schmitt, 1977, Honolulu: University of Hawai'i Press. Copyright 1977 by University of Hawai'i Press. Adapted by permission.

TABLE 3.6
Attendance Records, 1888–1896

Nationality	*1888*	*1890*	*1892*	*1894*	*1896*
Hawaiian	5,320	5,599	5,353	5,177	5,207
Part-Hawaiian	1,247	1,578	1,866	2,103	2,198
Euro-American	253	259	371	285	386
British	163	139	131	184	200
German	176	199	197	208	253
Portuguese	1,335	1,813	2,253	2,551	3,186
Norwegian	40	56	71	83	96
French	0	1	5	5	8
Japanese	54	39	60	113	261
Chinese	147	262	353	529	740
South Sea Isl.	16	42	36	35	29
Other Foreign	19	24	16	34	52
Total	8,770	10,006	10,712	11,307	12,616

Source: Townsend, H. S. (1896). *Biennial Report of the President of the Board of Education to the legislative assembly of 1896.* Republic of Hawai'i: Department of Public Instruction.

comprised the majority in school attendance (Table 3.6), their cultural background was never recognized as essential to formal education. What it might have suggested is that the schools had quite a task ahead to assimilate this 59% Hawaiian and Part-Hawaiian population into U.S. society as effectively as possible. In fact, Native Hawaiian children began attending English-speaking schools in 1854, and in 1884 Native Hawaiian attendance at select schools surpassed common school attendance (see Schmitt, 1977). Over this period, attendance by U.S. children grew by 53%, Portuguese attendance shot up 138%, and numbers for Asian students quickly increased (i.e., Japanese, 383%; Chinese, 203%). Native Hawaiian attendance, however, decreased by 2% due to intermarriages. Correspondingly, Part-Hawaiians increased by 76%. By 1896, Native Hawaiians comprised only 41% of the children attending Hawai'i's schools. Together with Part-Hawaiians, however, they represented 59% of the school population. The Portuguese were next with 25% of the school population, followed by the Euro-Americans with 7%.

During the last two decades of the 1800s, attendance at Hawaiian-language common schools decreased while attendance at the English-language select schools grew. This brought about a severe separation between the Hawaiian people and their Hawaiian traditions. Hawaiians felt shame conversing in their own language because of social pressures and changes of the time. Needless to say, students were lost without their mother tongue that expressed customs and beliefs and linked the people to their ancestral foundations. There were, however, Native Hawaiians educated in Hawai'i's schools who were successful living in both cultures and were leaders in education, professional occupations, and politics. For example, Josia M. Nae'ole became the first and only Hawaiian principal at Hilo Boarding School; J. W. Keli'iko, educated at Keauhou Common, served in the 1901 legislature; Charles E. King, educated at Waiahole English, served in the legislature from 1919 to 1921 and is noted as one of Hawai'i's greatest composers; Joseph Nawahi, educated at Hilo Boarding, served in Hawai'i's legislature and was appointed Minister of Foreign Affairs between 1892 and 1893; and Robert W. Wilcox, educated at Ulupalakua English, was Hawai'i's first Territorial Delegate to the United States Congress in 1900. This is a short list, not by design, but simply because there were very few Native Hawaiians who prospered in the new Western ways and structures of this time.

Certainly, many of the Biennial Reports during this period suggest that, because the schools were in poor shape and many teachers were still unskilled and ill equipped, the achievement of students was less than desirable. It is no wonder that many natives did not excel in the Western common and select schools. Biennial Reports refer to the excellent work of independent (private) schools, in that their students showed progress in thinking like Euro-Americans and becoming industrious citizens. However, such acknowledgment was not made about the common or select schools of the period. One can only speculate that the majority of Native Hawaiians in public schools had difficulties being successful at reading, writing, and thinking like Euro-Americans as well as learning to be industrious participants in the new hierarchical social structure.

The demographics in Table 3.5 also reveal the slow decline of the full-blood Native Hawaiian population and an increase in Part-Hawaiian and foreign children in the schools. A rapidly decreasing Hawaiian populace was yet another factor which played negatively on Native self-esteem. Although the schools were not the direct cause for the dwindling Native population, their pedantic and moralistic approach to learning certainly did not help. Decreasing population numbers were primarily due to disease and intermarriages; in fact, as early as Kalākaua's reign it was believed that the Hawaiian would someday completely disappear. Daws (1969) recounted a conversation between Armstrong and Kalākaua during which Armstrong observed, "Your people are dying out and will soon be extinct" (p. 292). The King responded simply, "Well, if they are, I've read lots of times that great races died out, and new ones took their places; my people are like the rest. I think the best thing is to let us be" (p. 292).

This comment was sadly prophetic. As Daws (1969) concluded, it was not in the interest of the United States "to let the Hawaiians be" (p. 292). The psychological influence of the foreign element on the Native Hawaiian and the overwhelming growth of foreigners in Hawai'i stripped away the customs and beliefs that made the Native culture unique. Table 3.7, compiled by Schmitt (1968), provides more evidence of this decrease in the Native Hawaiian populace.

The pure Hawaiian population was definitely on the decline (from 70,000 in 1853 to 31,000 in 1896). Whereas Native, pure Hawaiians comprised roughly 96% of the total population in 1853, they comprised only 28.5% by 1896. One can also read in Table 3.7 that this decline was only partially offset by intermarriage, as in 1853 there were less than 1,000 Part-Hawaiians reported in the Islands. By 1896, the number of Part-Hawaiians was still well under 10,000, representing only 7.8% of the total population in the kingdom. By 1896, therefore, pure and Part-Hawaiians comprised only about 36% of the total population in the new U.S. territory.

Over time, receding numbers, lack of political representation, and didactic indoctrination in schools combined to deteriorate Native Hawaiian culture and self-esteem. With U.S. customs and beliefs becoming more accepted among the growing numbers of Part-Hawaiians and Hawaiians, knowledge and practice of old traditions were lost. Pukui et al. (1972) wrote, "What was remembered would be recalled with increasing distortion. For when a specific practice was discarded or forgotten, there went with it the enduring, often wise concept from which the practice evolved" (p. 303). Gradually, the fragmented and often distorted knowledge of Hawaiian customs and foreign reminders that maintaining and practicing Hawaiian culture identified one as lower class produced shame, denial, and resentment about being Hawaiian.

This low cultural esteem led Hawaiians to feel inferior to the white and soon led to inequitable relations with Asian immigrants, in particular

TABLE 3.7
Native Hawaiian and Part-Hawaiian Population: 1853–1896

	Native Hawaiian		*Part-Hawaiian*		
Census	*N*	*% of Total Population*	*N*	*% of Total Population*	*Total Population*
1853	70,036	95.8	983	1.3	73,138
1860	67,084[a]	96.1[a]	[a]	[a]	69,800
1866	57,125	90.7	1,640	2.6	62,959
1872	49,044	86.2	2,487	4.4	56,897
1878	44,088	76.0	3,420	5.9	57,985
1884	40,014	49.7	4,218	5.2	80,578
1890	34,436	38.3	6,186	6.9	89,990
1896	31,019	28.5	8,486	7.8	109,020

[a]For this year, 1860, the demographics for Hawaiian and Part-Hawaiian were reported together.

Source: *Demographic Statistics of Hawai'i* (p. 74) by Robert C. Schmitt, 1968, Honolulu: University of Hawai'i Press. Copyright 1968 by the University of Hawai'i Press. Adapted by permission.

Japanese and Chinese. One Native Hawaiian quoted in Pukui's work suggested, "My in-laws [non-Hawaiian] think I'm just a stupid Hawaiian." Another Hawaiian remarked, "Yeah, I got promoted. I got the raise. Must be the *haole* in me." A young girl voicing the attitude of her generation admitted, "Even if we don't like the Japanese, we—my girl friends and me—we'd marry one to make us better!" (Pukui et al., 1972, p. 308).

Consistent reinforcement of low social status by the government, by the schools, by the teachers, and by the plantation bosses that Hawaiians were lazy, stupid, and low class resulted in destructive social behavior. For example, although Hawaiians only represented 28.5% of the total population in 1896 (see Table 3.7), they comprised the majority (66.6%) of children in reformatory schools in 1897 (see Table 3.8). They were the majority of offenders of truancy (20 children, 74%), larceny (17 children, 62.9%), and vagrancy (2 children, 100%). With the additional number of Part-Hawaiians, they comprised 100% (3) of all offenders who were disobedient to their parents.

The Hawaiian had become affected by the *'alamihi* (common black crab) complex, a well-known analogy of the Hawaiian social condition. Simply, when put into a bucket, *'alamihi* begin to climb on top of each other trying to get out by stepping on and pulling down on the rest of the crabs. Very few Native Hawaiians made it out of the bucket, as most were pulled down or perhaps pushed back by the crabber. Another example of Hawaiians' diminished social status was revealed in the few numbers of Hawaiian men represented in professional occupations. The *Native Hawaiian Educational Assessment Project* (Kamehameha Schools/Bishop Estate, 1983) provides information (see Table 3.9) that documents the lack of Hawaiian representation in upper level employment. Few Native men were professionals such as doctors, lawyers, businessmen, and government officials. Table 3.9 reveals only a 0.2% increase in Native Hawaiian men employed in professional occupations between 1896 and 1910. Additionally, the data reveal that, although the number of Part-Hawaiian men increased, their representation in professional occupations decreased by 0.9% between 1896 and 1910.

Whereas Native Hawaiians were underrepresented in the professional fields, they were overrepresented in labor and service occupations. Table 3.10 presents data compiled by Schmitt (1968) that, although not disaggregated by ethnicity, suggest that many employment opportunities for Hawaiians were more likely in agriculture and other labor areas. Utilizing the numbers from Table 3.10, we can calculate the number of Hawaiians and Part-Hawaiians in professional occupations. There were 942 male professional workers in 1896 (see Table 3.10) of which 186 were Hawaiian or Part-Hawaiian (from Table 3.9), representing 19.7% of the total professional jobs. When one considers that Hawaiians and Part-Hawaiians com-

TABLE 3.8
Attendance at Reform Schools, 1897

	Island				Nationality							
Violation	*Oahu*	*Haw*	*Maui*	*Kau*	*Haw*	*Am*	*Eng*	*Ger*	*Fre*	*Port*	*Chin*	*PtH*
Truancy	23	4			20	1				3		3
Disobey parents	3				1							2
Larceny	16	7	4		17			1		5	2	2
Assault & battery		1			1							
Obscenity & profanity		1								1		
House-breaking				1				1				
Vagrancy		2			2							
Attempt to assault		1			1							
Total	42	16	4	1	42	1		2		9	2	7

[a]The following lists the Nationality abbreviations used in this table: Haw(aiian), Am(erican), Eng(lish), Ger(man), Fre(nch), Port(uguese), Chin(ese), PtH(awaiian).

Source: Townsend, H. S. (1897). *Biennial Report of the President of the Board of Education to the Legislative Assembly of 1897.* Republic of Hawai'i: Department of Public Instruction.

TABLE 3.9
Gainfully Employed Men in a Professional Occupation: 1896 and 1910

	1896		1910	
Ethnicity	*Number Employed*	*% of all Hawaiian or Part-Haw. men*	*Number Employed*	*% of all Hawaiian of Part-Haw. men*
Hawaiian	132	1.4	126	1.6
Part-Haw.	54	4.0	71	3.1

Source: *Native Hawaiian Educational Assessment Project* (p. 30) by the Kamehameha Schools/Bishop Estate, 1983, Honolulu: Kamehameha Schools/Bishop Estate. Copyright 1983 by Kamehameha Schools/Bishop Estate. Adapted by permission.

prised over 36% of the population in 1896 (see Table 3.7), one sees that they were still considerably underrepresented. Schmitt's data (see Table 3.10) further illustrate that, in both 1890 and 1896, male employment, regardless of ethnicity, was generally limited to agricultural and labor fields with only a small number of men represented in professional fields.

TABLE 3.10
Occupations in Hawai'i: 1866–1896

Census Year	*Total*[a]	*Total % over 15 yrs.*	*Agri.*[b]	*Labor*[c]	*Mech.*	*Profes.*[d]	*Other*
			Both sexes				
1866			8,258	5,025	1,146	512	
1872			9,670	4,772	2,115	582	
1878	24,795	59.4	8,763	7,871	2,606	5,555	e
1884	39,541	68.1	10,968	12,351	3,919	12,303	e
1890	41,073	61.8	5,377	25,466	2,802	638	6,790
1896	55,294	70.2	7,570	34,438	2,265	1,224	9,797
			Male				
1890	38,930	83.6	5,280	23,863	2,690	483	6,614
1896	51,705	91.0	7,435	32,027	2,265	942	9,036

[a]This number may also include those under the age of 15. [b]Falling under this heading includes: farmers, planters, ranchers, rice planters, and coffee planters. [c]Laborers was a general heading for 1866, 1890, and 1896; in 1872 the term referred to plantation laborers; and in 1878 and 1884 to contract laborers. [d]In 1866 the term applied to anyone in an occupation other than agriculturists or laborer; by 1872 it included clergymen, teacher, licensed physicians, and lawyers. [e]Number for this year was combined with professional workers.

Source: *Demographic Statistics of Hawai'i* (p. 76) by Robert C. Schmitt, 1968, Honolulu: University of Hawai'i Press. Copyright 1968 by the University of Hawai'i Press. Reprinted by permission.

Abbreviations: Agri., Agriculture; Mech., Mechanics; Profes., Professional.

The statistics presented support the conclusion that the degradation of Hawaiians and Hawaiian traditions institutionalized in government policy and school activity, coupled with a dwindling Hawaiian population, resulted in increasing Native Hawaiian social alienation. This alienation is reflected in socially dysfunctional behavior as seen in reformatory figures and in a lack of representation in professional occupations. The following section discusses this alienation also evident in Natives' abject poverty levels.

Economic Impact

Because no income data were provided in either the 1890 or 1896 Census, the best measure by which to understand the economic condition of Hawaiians would be to look at the economic unit by which profitability was measured, that is, land ownership. The land laws of the *Māhele* and subsequent regulations were foreign concepts to the Hawaiian, thereby leading to grievous inequities in land divisions. An example of this disparity in land ownership was described by Sahlins and Kirch (1992; see Table 3.11) who noted that many of the Hawaiian land patents were given to a *hui*, a group or partnership of Hawaiians, whereas patents to foreigners were mostly given to individual patentees. The data in Table 3.11 illustrate that there were many more patents given to Hawaiians than to foreigners; however, the average acreage patent for Hawaiians was a mere 52.8 acres. Foreigners, on the other hand, were given on average 263.66 acres per patent. In other words, for every one acre that the Hawaiian got, the foreigner received *five*! Although this example represents just the

TABLE 3.11
Recipients of Royal Patents from Government Lands *on O'ahu*, 1845–1860

	Patents to Hawaiians			*Patents to Foreigners*		
Place	*No.*	*Total Acres*	*Acres per Patent*	*No.*	*Total Acres*	*Acres per Patent*
Waialua Area						
Kamamanui	232	8,784.87	37.87	22	7,179.92	144.42
Wahiawa to Kaena	58	3,730.8	64.32	19	7,143.2	375.96
Subtotal	290	12,515.67	43.16	41	10,323.12	251.78
Ewa, Wai'anae, Ko'olauloa, Ko'olaupoko	60	3,751.44	62.52	37	10,086.18	272.6
All O'ahu	350	16,267.11	46.47	78	20,409.3	261.66

Source: Royal Patent Grants/Index, 1916. *Note.* Reprinted in Sahlins, M., & Kirch, P. V. (1992). *Anahulu the anthropology of history in the Kingdom of Hawai'i* (Vol. I). Chicago: University of Chicago Press (p. 169). Reprinted by permission.

island of O'ahu, it reflects the general attitude of land distribution across all islands.

Quoting MacKenzie (1991), "By 1864, 213 Westerners had purchased more than 320,000 acres of Government Land. By 1893, 613,233 acres of land had been sold by the kingdom at an average price of 92 cents per acre" (p. 10). In fact, by 1893 the island lands were controlled by the foreigner (Russ, 1961). According to Schmitt (1977), the Republic of Hawai'i took control of all Government lands and crown lands, giving no compensation to the monarch. This totaled between 42.5% and 44.2% of all surface lands. The majority of the rest of the lands not taken by the government were held by Euro-American private ownership or in *ali'i* trusts (e.g., Bishop Estate and Lunalilo Trust).

It is imperative to understand that, since the days before Kamehameha I, power in Hawai'i came from possession of land. This deep-rooted belief was held by Native Hawaiians since the days of antiquity and remained a fact of life throughout the years of the Hawaiian Kingdom and through the time of the Republic of Hawai'i. Not coincidentally, land ownership remains at the center of efforts to reclaim sovereignty even to the present day. At first, the Hawaiian kings and chiefs owned the land, at least until the middle of the 18th century. Land became the economic foundation of Hawai'i; therefore, it established the direction the Kingdom would follow. As the foreigners, mostly from the United States, began to rapidly purchase the land, their power and influence grew. Their way of life was seen as superior, and their schools housed their beliefs. Eventually, the Hawaiians had very little or no land at all. Dispossessed of their land, they had no power to govern or to guide the people's future in Hawai'i.

CONCLUSION

> *Malihini no nā keiki o ka la kou 'āina pono'i iho.*
> The children of the land are strangers in their own land.
>
> —*'Ōlelo No'eau*

Understanding the educational policy process in Hawai'i is a complex task, as it is elsewhere in the United States. In every state, educational policy analysis is linked to a larger institutional, social, and political framework of which only a small portion is actually visible, and much more is embedded in a web of complex values, traditions, and activities. Despite local differences, however, an analysis of educational policy in Hawai'i from both political and institutional perspectives reveals the similarities between Hawai'i's past and national political trends. Although

Hawai'i may be miles away from the United States continent, its political action has been similar.

Schattschneider (1960) suggested that Thomas Jefferson's definition of democracy as "government by consent of the governed" (p. 133) adequately described political action in the United States. This idea implies that because "nobody knows enough to run the government" (Schattschneider, 1960, p. 133), people allow the professionals to govern; thus, democracy becomes "a form of collaboration of ignorant people and experts" (p. 134). Essentially, this group of leaders is able to work with very little intervention from the public during periods of quiescence. However, if the people become dissatisfied with the manner or the course taken by their entrusted leaders, conflict in ideas creates turbulence, which inevitably stimulates change. To avoid turbulence, the leaders employ political mechanisms (e.g., allocation of resources) to contain conflict and competition, thereby maintaining control. Conflict between the governing elite and some faction of the governed is the central idea of Schattschneider's dynamic political theory.[21]

As we have indicated, differing opinions concerning how Hawai'i should be governed created political turbulence during the 1880s, which presented an opportunity for the U.S. businessmen to take control of Hawai'i's governance. An elite group of professionals and industrialists, believing that they had every right to govern the heathen Kingdom, seized the opportunity to formalize U.S. control of Hawai'i. After successfully taking control of Hawai'i's government, the U.S. businessmen then quickly privatized conflict through imposing restrictive laws that allowed only members of a White-elite group to participate in governing activities. These actions quickly reduced the scope of conflict over governance issues. Iannaccone (1977) suggested that privatizing conflict "not only helps the advantaged but also further detaches their sphere of government from the rest of the political order" (p. 271).

Iannaccone and Lutz (1970) further posited that, as government changes to fit the needs of the governing elite, the scope of conflict (whether privatized or socialized) redefines political values and has a direct impact on social and, therefore, educational policies.[22] Iannaccone (1977) termed major changes in educational politics as revolutions and suggested that the first revolution in U.S. education was the Municipal Reform Movement around the turn of the 20th century. Essentially, this movement sought to privatize conflict by taking away local control of the schools, which empowered the lower, ignorant classes,[23] and formally giving control to a small, centralized board of professionals. The result of this revolution in local governance was the institutionalization of the belief in a unitary Western community based on Protestant values, the control of education by professional elites, and the separation of education from local politics (Iannaccone, 1977; Tyack, 1974).

Parallel to the events of the Municipal Reform Movement in the cities of the United States, Hawai'i also experienced a move toward governance by an elite group of professionals who faced similar social and economic problems caused by a growing population of non-Whites and heavy agricultural competition. In an effort to minimize conflict between the business elite and the Hawaiian Monarchy and to assure that the many non-White groups were kept in their place at the bottom of the social-economic structure, Hawai'i's governance revolution centralized power in the hands of a governing elite including legislators and school superintendents. This process resulted in the exploitation of popular sovereignty, thereby disenfranchising the Native Hawaiian, and, as Schattschneider (1960) observed, "the people are powerless if the political enterprise is not competitive" (p. 137).

Beyond the local political turmoil created by colonialism, however, was a more far-reaching coherent social policy aimed at silencing cultural differences among United States citizens of different ethnicities. Within this political and social context of submerging issues and limiting participation in governance, Hawai'i's educational policies and subsequent curriculum soon mirrored Americanization policies found across the United States. The motives for acculturating the diverse ethnic population of Hawai'i was identical to the motives of the Municipal Reformers. Iannaccone (1977) explained these motives succinctly, quoting David Tyack's point that:

> . . . underlying much of the reform movement was an elitist assumption that prosperous, native born Protestant Anglo-Saxons were superior to other groups, and thus should determine the curriculum and the allocation of jobs. It was the mission of schools to imbue children of the immigrants and the poor with uniformly WASP ideals. (p. 276)[24]

In essence, the themes of efficient control and quality social programs, which maintain the privatization of conflict, could aptly characterize the political culture of the Municipal Reform Movement on the continent.[25] The dominant values were reflected in the centralization of schools under the control of professionals. Likewise, revolutionary events in Hawai'i during the latter 1800s reflected an identical movement, thereby providing further empirical substance to Schattschneider's (1960) dynamic theory of political evolution and offering a conceptual framework through which to view the local political processes and their impact on educational policy in Hawai'i during this turbulent to quiescent era.

As political conflict provides a theory for understanding events surrounding the overthrow and subsequent change in governance structure in Hawai'i, institutional theory provides a rationale for why these Americanization policies became institutionalized in the schools. Americanization policies were consistent with efforts elsewhere to establish control over a variety of voluntary and nonvoluntary minorities in the United States. The aim was to create the myth of a unitary (melting pot) society in order to ensure their quiet assimilation into U.S. society. As we have shown, schools played an essential role in this socialization of immigrants and conquered cultures.

While the effects of colonialism on indigenous groups are well known, what must not be ignored is how this rhetoric was established. Here, the early educational policymakers and school superintendents played a major role in institutionalizing social policy. We conclude that the political events of the period institutionalized elite governance (e.g., the Board of Education, the Presidents of the Board of Education and their respective Inspector Generals of Schools) whose leaders pursued educational policies that kept Native Hawaiians at the bottom of the social and economic hierarchy. Examination of actual school laws revealed that the core values embedded in the political and economic institutions (e.g., efficiency) dominated educational policy and practice.

Policy rhetoric suggests that centralized governance of schools was a means of ensuring opportunity for all, but, in reality, racist policies undergirded the separatism of the dual-school system (the common vs. English and the independent vs. public schools) and the overt denigration of Native culture and language. The institutionalization of bureaucratic controls and professional educational leadership ensure that the allocation resources for school activities was consistent with what the governing elite defined as the primary purpose of schools—to maintain a stable labor force and instill patriotism for the United States. The goal was the successful acculturation of many ethnic minorities to join the U.S. progress parade.

At the same time, however, opposing agendas to elite preferences were also a part of the educational policy process. For example, Townsend's move for change in the 1890s attempted to introduce progressive education norms with the underlying belief that equity and choice should be valued. At first, he achieved positive results, garnering resources which financed visitations of his U.S. supporters, his teacher conventions, and his progressive journals. However, Townsend's push for change came at a time in which Hawai'i was seeking to take choice away from the majority and maintain a stratified social system. Thus, his endeavors were halted when he was replaced by a more conservative member of the elite governing circle.

Despite the efforts of a few like Townsend, schooling proved to be an effective means of subjugating Native Hawaiians to a politicized set of moral standards that made it acceptable to dispossess the natives of their land, eliminate their mother tongue, and dash a rich cultural heritage from memory. The result of this centralized and socially stratified governing system was successful control of the Native and Asian population. Through its social and educational policies, the goal of Americanization was well underway, as young Hawaiians were taught to accept, in fact embrace, Western structures as their salvation. Indeed, a new civilized Hawaiian would pledge allegiance to the United States' flag, sing the Star Spangled Banner, celebrate U.S. holidays, worship at Christian altars, and look to the United States as the fount of information and direction. Although there were some cries from Native Hawaiians (e.g., Home Rule party that challenged the early Republican party in Hawai'i) for sovereignty, they were almost always a temporary voice.

This wave of reform is reflected in the changing concept of *'āina* (land). To the Hawaiian the *'āina* could not be sold or bought, just as human life could not be sold or possessed by another. With the arrival of the Thaddeus in 1820, colonialism, because it measured the worth of a man by the property he owned, supported new institutional structures that valued profit and economy over the human soul. Social, economic, and political institutions coerced the Hawaiians, often in covert ways, to give up their homelands. As Queen Lili'uokalani struggled to regain the Kingdom's self-determination, the might of colonialism, which was now institutionalized into law and social practice, overpowered her efforts on the behalf of Native Hawaiians. The desperate attempts of the Annexation Club found a tiny island archipelago struggling for legitimacy by mimicking the structures and actions of the United States. In its wake, the oppression created by colonialism threatened Hawaiian culture, ridiculed Hawaiian spiritual rituals, nearly obliterated the Hawaiian language, and took away Hawaiian lands.[26]

It is a wonder that, during her unjust imprisonment, Queen Lili'uokalani, the last reigning monarch of Hawai'i, wrote the hauntingly beautiful *mele* (song), The Queen's Prayer (Elbert & Mahoe, 1970, pp. 88–89):

The Queen's Prayer

'O kou aloha nō Aia i ka lani, A'o kou 'oiā 'i'o Hemolele ho'i.	Your love Is in heaven, And your truth So perfect.
Ko'u noho mihi 'ana A pa'ahao 'ia, 'O 'oe ku'u lama Kou nani, ko'u ko'o.	I live in sorrow Imprisoned, You are my light Your glory my support.

Mai nānā 'ino'ino	Behold not with malevolence
Nā hewa o kānaka,	The sins of man,
Akā e huikala	But forgive
A ma'ema'e no.	And cleanse.
Nō laila e ka Haku	And so, o Lord,
Ma lalo o kou 'ēheu,	Beneath your wings,
Kō mākou maluhia	Be our peace
A mau aku nō.	Forever more.

ENDNOTES

1. The deep influence of the U.S. Christian missionary is evident in a variety of symbols. Perhaps the most compelling is the State's motto, *"Ua mau ke ea o ka 'āina I ka pono"*—"The life of the land is preserved by righteousness." These words, attributed to several speeches made by King Kamehameha III in 1843, have certain Biblical references. For example, the words and concepts of "righteousness" and "righteousness preserves life" stem from Proverbs 11:30, "The fruit of the righteous is a tree of life"; Proverbs 12:28, "In the ways of righteousness *is* life, and in the pathway *thereof there is no death*" (italics in original biblical text); and Proverbs 14:32, "Righteousness exaltheth a nation; but sin is a reproach to any people." Further parallels can be made with Deuteronomy, Ezekiel, and Isaiah.
2. Interview with Russell Kawika Makanani, 1991–1992.
3. Marshall Sahlins and Patrick Kirch's recent ethnography (1992) focuses on social and economic conditions of Native Hawaiians.
4. For further information documenting the *Māhele* and subsequent land laws refer to Kame'eleihiwa (1992), MacKenzie (1991), and Sahlins and Kirch (1992).
5. See *The Polynesian* (June 26, September 4, and October 9, 1847). Newspapers are essential tools of the historian. Although not cited in this work, a number of newspapers were referenced; they include: *The Star, The Pacific Commercial Advertiser, The Friend, Review of Reviews,* and *Holomua.*
6. Thomas G. Thrum (1900) provided ample information about Hawai'i in the yearly almanacs, which are consolidated in *A Hawaiian Almanac and Annual 1896–1900 A Handbook of Information.*
7. This text provides a perspective which favored the activities of the United States in Hawai'i.
8. This work, written by Queen Lydia Lili'uokalani, records her perspective of Hawai'i's politics and history.
9. Note that Aida Negron De Montilla's (1971) study regarding the impact of the United States on Puerto Rican school policy and school-related activity is also grounded in the values and works of appointed educational commissioners.
10. Daniel Logan, "Education in the Hawaiian Islands," *The North American Review* 165 (July 1897) 20–25. Logan's article provides primary data that records the history of Hawai'i's public schools as well as documents school activities during the 1890s.
11. We are aware that highlighting the contribution of white males appears to overestimate their contribution to the educational history of Hawai'i, especially because others were excluded. These early leaders were the implementers of elite domination. It is interesting to note that their efforts to silence Native voices are a stark contrast to the current efforts of many strong Hawaiian woman and men who are leading the way to re-establishing

the Native voice through their sovereignty efforts and through the Hawaiian Immersion program (see chapter 6).

12. Richard Armstrong, "Journal of a Tour-Around the Windward Islands, Hawai'i, Maui and Moloka'i, in the Months of September, October, November, 1848," filed at the Hawai'i State Archives dated November 1848. This report describes school activities, school governance, and evaluates Hawai'i's public schools during the 1840s.
13. Nine Biennial reports were used to draw information regarding school policy, school governance, school activity, and demographic data. The Inspector of Schools was required to include in the reports a variety of demographic data as well. *The Biennial Report of the President of the Board of Education to the Legislative Assembly, for the Years 1881, 1882, 1884, 1890, 1892, 1894, 1895, 1897, 1899* (Honolulu: Dept. of Public Instruction). Townsend, H. S. (1897). *Biennial report of the President of the Board of Education to the Legislative Assembly of 1897.* Republic of Hawai'i: Department of Public Instruction.
14. For further information concerning Horace Mann's ideals, refer to the following materials: Horace Mann, *American Pedagogy: Education, the School, and the Teacher in American Literature (2nd ed.)* (Hartford, CT: Brown & Gross, 1876); Horace Mann, *Horace Mann on the Crisis in Education* (Yellow Springs, OH: Antioch Press, 1965); and Horace Mann, *The Republic and the School; The Education of Free Men* (New York: Teachers College, Columbia University, 1957).
15. The connection between education and politics had never been a hidden fact, and, in 1883, it was no secret that Bishop, along with three other members of the board, all U.S. supporters, were forced to resign by Kalākaua's privy council. He was replaced by W. M. Gibson, whose extensive political responsibilities offered little time for school board activity. In fact, shortly after Gibson's appointment, in 1885, Baldwin resigned as Inspector and was not replaced. Attention to school activities declined until Bishop was reappointed to the board's presidency in 1887.
16. For more detailed information regarding Hawai'i's School Superintendents and leadership see: Maenette Benham, "Political and Cultural Determinants of Educational Policymaking: Their Effects on Native Hawaiian," unpublished doctoral dissertation, University of Hawai'i-Mānoa (1993).
17. Russ attempted to present an unbiased account of historic events in his two works employed as primary historic sources, although, reading his texts does seem to favor the U.S. perspective. See: William Adam Russ, Jr., *The Hawaiian Revolution 1893–1894* (Selinsgrove, PA: Susquehana University Press, 1959), and William Adam Russ, Jr., *The Hawaiian Republic 1894–1898 And Its Struggle to Win Annexation* (Selinsgrove, PA: Susquehana University Press, 1961).
18. Castle's article was a significant source as it describes the political values held by the governing elite, specifically Dole's perspective.
19. With the impending political turmoil of 1893 and because of his failing health, Bishop resigned his post as President of the Board of Education. W. R. Castle replaced Bishop for a short period of time and was followed by Professor W. D. Alexander. Atkinson remained Inspector General until his resignation in 1895.
20. We realize that we have presented a limited definition of a Native Hawaiian value that has much deeper significance and meaning. It reflects mystical power "charisma or authority" (Pukui et al., 1972, p. 44). For more information regarding *mana* please see Pukui, M. K., Haertig, E. W., Lee, C. A. (1972). *Nānā i ke Kumu* (Look to the source) (Vols. 1 & 2). Honolulu: Hui Hanai.
21. To understand the dynamics of this process one needs to define the scope of the conflict, the visibility of the conflict, the intensity of the conflict, and the direction of the conflict. See Schattschneider, *The Semisovereign People* (1960).
22. Several of Iannaccone's works were referred to in developing this study, they include: author *Politics in Education* (New York: Center for Applied Research in Education, 1967);

Laurence Iannaccone & Frank Lutz, *Politics, Power and Policy: The Governing of Local School Districts* (Columbus, OH: Charles E. Merrill, 1970); Laurence Iannaccone & Frank Lutz, (Eds.), *Public Participation in School Decision-Making* (Lexington, MA: Lexington, 1978); and Laurence Iannaccone, *Three Views of Change In Educational Politics* (Chicago, IL: The National Society for the Study of Education, 1977).

23. Iannaccone, op. cit., (1977), p. 276, quoted Samuel P. Hays, "The Politics of Reform in Municipal Government in the Progressive Era," *Pacific Northwest Quarterly* 55 (Oct. 1964) 163.
24. Iannaccone, op. cit., (1977), p. 276. He referred to and quoted David B. Tyack, "Needed: The Reform of a Reform," *New Dimensions of School Board Leadership* (Evanston, IL: National School Board Association, 1969), p. 35.
25. The goals of the Municipal Reform Movement can be summarized simply as: establishing a unitary community, separating politics and education, and setting out the neutral competence of the school administrator.
26. At the time of the overthrow, the crown lands was estimated to include approximately 911,888 acres. All this was seized by the provisional government.

Queen Lili'uokalani. Photo courtesy of the Hawai'i State Archives.

Queen Lili'uokalani's Staff: From left (standing) Col. J. H. Boyd, Col. H. F. Bertelman, Col. J. D. Holt; (sitting front) J. W. Robertson-Chamberlain. Photo courtesy of the Hawai'i State Archives.

"Proclamation establishing the Republic of Hawai'i, 1894." Photo courtesy of the Hawai'i State Archives.

'EHĀ

The Americanization of the Native Hawaiian, 1930s–1960s

Toward the end of his life Lorin Thurston reviewed the accomplishments of the "mission boys," and found, unsurprisingly, that they were a "splendid body of men. . . ."

—Daws, 1969 (p. 293)

HA'AWINA NO'ONO'O

Growing up in Hawai'i, I remember that many of my Part-Hawaiian friends were ashamed of being Hawaiian. Instead, they identified themselves as hapa-haole (half white) or Japanese. I have always identified myself as Hawaiian, partly because I do not look haole, and I do not look Japanese. In fact, I often heard older Hawaiian girls say that they would marry-up to a haole or Japanese boy. Marrying a Hawaiian boy was like marrying a janitor or airline porter. Many local girls, in order to avoid being called a stupid Hawaiian, read U.S. books and magazines, attempted to dye or streak their hair blonde, and wore fashions seen on U.S. television programs.

For the most part, we were all fairly successful at acting haole. I was especially good because I spoke standard English without a trace of pidgin. As a youngster I grew up speaking several languages—German, English, and Hawaiian. Living in Germany in the late 1950s, my parents believed German and English were important, but moving to Hawai'i in the early 1960s, my kūpuna (grandparents) believed I should speak Hawaiian. So, I spoke English with my parents and at school, Hawaiian with my kūpuna, and eventually lost the German.

It was not until I hit junior high school that the duality of my life became evident. On one hand I was very haole—very Americanized. I did well in school because of my excellent speaking ability, hard work, and respect for teachers and school administrators. Yet, there was a longing to enjoy the freedom of the Ka'a'awa countryside. This was old Hawai'i—where I spoke Hawaiian, worked the land and the ocean, sang and danced, climbed trees and mountains, and swam in fresh water streams and in the salty, blue ocean. Returning to Honolulu from the country I often heard people say, "Ah! Back to civilization!" I wanted to be successful in the U.S. Hawai'i, the newest and 50th state, yet, I longed for the fish and poi nourishment of my kūpuna in the country.

My mother, who has had a great influence on my own education, graduated from Roosevelt High School in Honolulu. It was, at that time, an English Standard School. These schools were established in the 1920s as select public schools (forerunner of today's schools of choice) for primarily haole attendance.[1] *In fact, the opening of the English Standard Schools marked the first time in Hawai'i's school history that haoles attended public schools in large numbers. The select schools were designed for the middle and upper class children of U.S. businessmen, sugar barons, professionals, and politicians. Because this group controlled most of Hawai'i's businesses, which made up most of Hawai'i's tax base, and for the most part sent their children to private schools, policymakers had to find a way to increase the financial support for education.*[2] *The English Standard School, which was thought to be comparable to an education in the continental United States, was the answer. Despite efforts to exclude local minority students through a variety of entrance requirements, by the late 1930s and early 1940s the composition of the English-Standard students shifted from primarily haole to Japanese, Chinese, Part-Hawaiian, and other ethnic minorities. This was due, in part, to the onset of World War II, which resulted in large numbers of haole children being evacuated to the United States.*

I recall the very different school stories shared by my mother, father, aunts, and uncles. My mother, a graduate of an English Standard School, was intelligent, capable, and well read. Her school experiences were challenging and informative and provided her an opportunity to attend college where she earned a B.A. and an M.A. in education, one of the few Native Hawaiian women in the late 1940s to do so. My mother became a school teacher for the Department of Defense School system overseas. On the other hand, my father graduated from a regular public high school in Honolulu, which he admits prepared him well to join the Army. He retired after 25 years of service and was later employed by the Federal Government. My uncle attended the elite, private Hawaiian Kamehameha Schools where, he says, he learned manners and how to be a productive United States citizen. He retired from public service in 1993. My aunts on the maternal side of my family all attended English Standard Schools and thus were employed in professional occupations with the State of Hawai'i or City of Honolulu government offices. My aunts and uncles on the paternal side of my family, like my father, attended regular public high schools. Most of them took service or entertainment jobs, if they worked at all.

It became obvious to me that, if I wanted to get ahead in the changing island culture, I needed to attend the right schools. I began my secondary school education at Kamehameha Schools, part of an elite Hawaiian core. As a way of maintaining my roots in Hawaiiana, I took 3 years of Hawaiian language while the rest of my friends were counseled to take Japanese, French, or Spanish. To illustrate the temporal effect of devaluating the Hawaiian language through English-only instruction, even in an exclusive Hawaiian-only private school, in my senior year (1974), there were only two students in advanced Hawaiian Language class. I also sought every opportunity to learn the culture and dances of wā kahiko (old Hawai'i) while the rest of my friends learned housekeeping, cooking, and sewing. At the same time, I excelled in academics, graduating in the top 5% of my class and winning many speaking awards and scholarships. As my mother was the first to earn a master's degree, I am the first in our family to earn a doctorate.

Throughout my life, I lived in the gray areas of what it means to be Hawaiian. At times, my heart fills with quiet rebellion, ready to strike out at the indifference of a Western society toward Hawaiian needs. Other times, I am alienated by my own people who say I am an object manipulated by the haole; they call me a coconut—brown on the outside, white on the inside. Regardless, I know that the island persists in me. In a recent speech, I shared my thoughts about Hawai'i:

> *My daily meditations take me to a center where the rhythmic flow of tides and predictable morning showers feed my spirit. My heart touches the soft melodies of Hawaiian style music and the honest tongue of my mother language. This land of towering peaks, green valleys, warm beaches, and mighty ocean embraces and comforts me. . . . Wherever I might be, my heart and commitment is to the 'āina of my kūpuna.*

INSTITUTIONALIZING U.S. VALUES IN HAWAI'I

As we have argued in the previous chapters, the missionaries' pursuit of a Christian kingdom, a general acceptance of the savage-civilization paradigm and the inherent inequity implied in this belief among early policymakers, and the desire to obtain native lands through any means in exchange for civilization combined to produce several institutionalized values in the colonial social and educational systems of Hawai'i. After the overthrow of the monarchy in 1893, political manipulation enhanced by economic power became the most effective means of assuring the stability of the *haole* on Hawaiian lands. Elite control and centralized authority controlled all aspects of government and defined the type and quality of social programs, such as the introduction and maintenance of English Standard schooling.

This chapter focuses on the relatively quiet period after the turmoil of revolution, from the early 1900s to 1960. We examine in greater detail how the Republican Oligarchy was able to maintain political, social, and economic stability and thereby perpetuate a colonial lifestyle in the territory. Toward the end of this period, however, several key events combined to produce social and political changes in Hawai'i's politics leading to statehood. In particular, three pivotal events appeared to drive this change: (a) a national shift from Republican Party domination to Democratic Party control, first in the United States Congress and culminating with the election of Franklin D. Roosevelt; (b) a similar state-level party shift in Hawai'i, due in part to upheaval and diversity in local Hawaiian businesses and ethnic population growth during World War II; and (c) the impact of the Nisei in Hawai'i, a growing younger class of United States born, well-educated Japanese, many of whom were returning war heroes.

Although these events resulted in a change in the political actors, institutional values of the past were maintained. The era is perhaps best characterized by the action politics[3] or politics of protest which dominated the United States in the late 1940s and 1950s. At this time, competition to control Hawai'i resulted from strong party politics and a growing number of citizens joining special interest groups in united fronts that challenged the established Republican Oligarchy. After describing these changing governance processes, we examine the implications of this governance on the development of educational policy and its impact on Native Hawaiians during the 20th century. The resultant policies of this era are best characterized by the institutionalization of "Americanization" in the schools. Instruction focused on assimilation and the *melting pot* view of U.S. society in preparation for Hawai'i's eventual statehood.

A TIME OF POLITICAL CHANGE

Shortly after the overthrow of the monarchy, Hawai'i officially became a part of the United States in 1898, and, with the passage of *The Organic Act for the Territory of Hawai'i* on June 14, 1900, the U.S. belief in one-man, one-vote was established in Hawai'i. This, of course, was an upsetting decision in economic circles, as it meant that all people who were citizens of the Republic of Hawai'i in 1898 could vote. There were no property or income stipulations that had previously kept the unwanted Natives out of political office. After temporary setbacks due to divided political power among several fledgling political parties, the Republican Party rallied behind Prince Jonah Kuhio Kalanianaole, a popular young Native Hawaiian who had been named heir (along with his brother Prince David

Kawananakoa) by Queen Lili'uokalani and who had become a Republican. His popularity proved favorable for the Republican Party, who regained its control of all aspects of Territorial governance in 1902—a domination that would continue until 1954.

Samuel Crowningburg-Amalu, in his book *Jack Burns: A Portrait in Transition* (1974),[4] observed that the Republicans literally set up an antediluvian social structure that placed at its head the old family-owned sugar companies and their supporting business and banks that held Hawai'i in unilateral control. In essence, there were five companies (and so the term The Big Five) who held the Territory's purse strings. They included Castle and Cooke, Alexander and Baldwin, Theo. H. Davis and Company, C. Brewer and Company, and American Factor. So powerful were these five companies that, by 1910, they controlled 75% of all island crops and, by 1933, increased their control to 96% of island agriculture (Daws, 1969). Daws wrote that these five companies took control of ". . . every business associated with sugar; banking; insurance; utilities; wholesale and retail merchandising; railroad transportation in the islands; shipping between islands and between the islands and California" (1969, p. 312). Recognition of economic strength and government's compliance to industry's demands suggested the need for a governing structure consisting of a business-dominated elite striving for efficiency.

The meritocratic values of Hawai'i's evolving political culture, efficient governance in the hands of professionals and social policies that reflected business demands, became so entrenched in Hawai'i's political organization that it was difficult to separate the governing leaders of the Territory from the leading agriculturists and businessmen. Commenting on this centralized authority of governance and economics in 1903, Attorney General of Hawai'i, Edward P. Dole (a relative of Sanford Dole), said, "There is a government in this Territory which is centralized to an extent unknown in the United States, and probably almost as much centralized as it was in France under Louis XIV" (as cited in Daws, 1969, p. 313). Daws further commented that representatives from the Big Five were ". . . on governmental boards that dealt with tax appraisals, land leases, and other items of interest" (p. 313).

As we have suggested, the governing elite was comprised of White men who respected and upheld Republican ideals of Teutonic control of government and economics. Centralizing the governing organization enabled this small minority to establish and implement efficiently new social programs that satisfied their special interests and maintained their control of Hawai'i's economic base. Further, centralization of social institutions such as the public schools allowed insiders in government to dictate (e.g., through the appointment of school superintendents) what were appropriate beliefs and activities of the people through defining school structure and curriculum. The head of this elite structure, which brought together strong government and cohesive industry, was the appointed governor of the Territory. Coffman, in his book *Catch a Wave* (1973),[5] described this position as a high stakes job that had no comparison in any other state of the union. He wrote that "the governor sets the tone for Island life. He is not only the first creator of policy, but also the foremost creator of values" (p. 5). The extent of the governor's control over institutions, even to this day, is perhaps unique to the State of Hawai'i. The power of the governorship was supported in the Territory's Organic Law, ratified by Hawai'i's *Constitution of 1950*, and reaffirmed by Hawai'i's *Constitution of 1968*. It should be emphasized that, from the early years, the setting of policy was largely a function of the governor's office through both direct (e.g., through line-item veto) as well as indirect (e.g., by making political appointments) efforts.

Although annexation to the United States promised the people of Hawai'i equity through government including guaranteed voting rights, equal representation, and equal rights under the law, in reality, however, it created only a false sense of parity and fostered growing racism. As Tamura (1994) noted, this racism was shown in several attempts from the 1920s through 1940s to legislate loyalty to the United States from the growing Asian population. Some of these laws took the form of charging high school tuition for students who were not citizens or had not given proof of their sole allegiance to the United States, requiring instructors in Japanese-language schools to obtain permits demonstrating their knowledge of U.S. ideals, and limiting the amount of instruction in these schools to 6 hours per week.

More overtly racist was the structuring of a segregated, English Standard school system in 1924. As others have noted, such efforts corresponded with a larger agenda to stamp out cultural and ideological diversity in the early decades of the 20th century across the United States (Tamura, 1994; Tyack & Cuban, 1995). These policies represented attempts to institutionalize the "Americanization" of immigrants and Native people within the country's extended political borders.

The Impact of World War II: Burns and the Democratic Party

The social agenda in Hawai'i from the overthrow of the monarchy in 1893 through the World War II years was set by the Republican Party. At this time, Hawai'i's political scene could be described as a relatively quiescent period; that is, the majority of Hawai'i's populace remained silent, thereby presenting the rulers with an unwritten mandate to exercise greater control. Prewar life centered around the production of sugar and pineapple on plantations controlled by Whites. As a result of Roosevelt's terms in the White House, however, the 1930s and 1940s began to encourage a new liberalism through Democratic-appointed territorial governors. Moreover, growing unionism in the Territory led to several strikes. Although the oligarchy was able to curb democratic intentions for some period of time, over the long run it could not isolate the islands from national social trends or political change.

During the early years of the war, rulers exercised much control with a type of hysteria toward the local population. This was brought on by fears of disloyalty and spying. For example, Japanese immigrants and U.S.-born Japanese people were rounded up and detained on Sand Island (a small peninsula in Honolulu) or shipped off to the detention centers on the West Coast of the United States. Additionally, many Euro-American families sent their young children to live with relatives on the United States continent. The end of World War II was an important turning point in Hawai'i's political history, however, as it brought home the Japanese-American war hero—the Nisei (second generation) who were born and educated in Hawai'i—all of whom were determined not to be seen as un-American. Armed with the GI Bill, many of the young Nisei soldiers eventually returned to Hawai'i well educated, with a proven record of loyalty to the United States, and with the attitude that they should be able to enjoy the rights of U.S. citizens—rights they had been denied. This belief that they were not going to accept the status quo, coupled with mandates that enabled the Chinese and Filipino (1946) followed by the Japanese, Korean, and Samoan (1952) to seek citizenship changed the structure of political power in Hawai'i. Throughout the late 1940s and 1950s a newly empowered set of leaders, including war veterans, labor leaders, and social activists, dissatisfied with the government and backed by political, economical, and educational achievement, began to push for change in the pre-war political, social, and economic structures. This created a period of political turbulence that removed the Republican Oligarchy from control.

Although the specific political players changed from Republican to Democratic party affiliations, we were surprised to find that the values, beliefs, and political actions they pursued were not much different from the colonial scripts that were written and enacted by previous leaders (Benham & Heck, 1994). This is perhaps partially explained by the desire among Japanese Americans to prove their loyalty to the United States by denouncing their heritage with Japan. For example, John Burns, who might be considered the icon of the Democratic Party movement, was a mainland *haole* who relocated to Hawai'i. During the war years he served as a police liaison in Honolulu with the Japanese community. His ties, developed with many Japanese families during this time, provided the honor and respect that were later needed to gain local political support. Moreover, Burns became the spokesperson for many returning soldiers and other ethnic youths looking for equity. These youthful and well-educated young men rallied behind Burns' political endeavor to unseat the Republicans. They were to become well-known in the 1950s as Hawai'i's Young Democrats or Young Guard.

The Young Guard consisted of second generation Japanese and Filipino youth who were born and educated in Hawai'i. Many had been educated at McKinley High, a progressive school that exemplified the philosophies of John Dewey. They worked toward equity in employment opportunity, a share of the wealth, and progress in Hawai'i. Their ideals were more progressive than the older members of the Democratic Party. They voiced the needs of the oppressed, with the Japanese being the largest group, which became the platform for a political party of racial inclusion. Behind John Burns stood men and women representing a variety of ethnic backgrounds and a more educated populace. Included among their rank and file, for example, were such local leaders as United States Senator Inouye (who still retains this position), and United States House of Representative members Matsunaga, Mink (currently United States Senator), Oshiro, and Mau. Using the growing power of pressure groups such as government employees, teachers, and small business owners, the Young Democrats won elections, one-by-one, gradually gaining momentum and increasing their numbers. Hawai'i's quiescent complacency was therefore disrupted by new political and social movements that sought to uproot the very foundation of the well-entrenched elite composed primarily of Euro-American male Republicans. For nearly 40 years, these new leaders and their protégés have been the backbone of Hawai'i's Democratic Party that has controlled the state politics.

The Democrats' political power at the voting polls across the state was supplemented by revolutionary economic changes in labor and in diversification of industry. In 1945, the Hawai'i Employment Relations Act was passed, affecting workers' abilities to organize and conduct union activities. This action was critical to the growing power of the Democratic Party, as it shattered the economic grip of the Republican Oligarchy over plantation workers. Although the National Labor Relations Act was passed in the United States Congress in 1935 and was ruled constitutional by the United States Supreme Court in 1937, in Hawai'i, the growth of unionization was met head-on by the Republican Oligarchy that fought tirelessly against union activity. With the passing of legislation in 1945, union activities in Hawai'i were given legal footing and, by the following year's end, the unions gained the support of laborers on the sugar and pineapple plantations and on the docks. The ability of the unions to strike and to vote in blocks became a serious threat to Hawai'i's status quo. In effect, the growth of unions severed industrial monopolies which, in turn, opened the doors to economic diversity, a growing tourism industry, and new business opportunities. It also gave voice to the non-White,[6] who acquired greater power in a united front to unseat the Republicans.

Voicing the needs of the oppressed minorities, between 1945 and 1954 the Democratic Party grew in membership and backing. By 1954, for the first time, the Young Democrats controlled the Territorial Legislature of Hawai'i, a political mechanism they continue to dominate to the present day. The Republicans never recovered after the Democrats' 1954 sweep. Although, in retrospect, the election years of 1960 and 1962 have been considered more open because neither party seemed to control the legislature (Bell, 1984), the two-party system in Hawai'i (which was short lived anyway) was by the 1960s nonexistent.[7]

The Road to Statehood

Hawai'i's road to statehood was a long one, spanning over 60 years from the time of annexation to the actual granting of statehood. Prior to the Democratic Party's success in Hawai'i's Territorial legislature, the Republicans pushed Hawai'i's case for statehood through the United States Congress. They argued that statehood would allow citizens of the Territory to have more voice in governance by allowing them to vote for the United States President, provide their delegate to Congress with voting power, and prevent the United States Federal Government from changing Hawai'i's Organic Laws at will.

On a national level, there were at least three arguments voiced at different times against statehood for Hawai'i. First, despite Democratic successes in government, the state was seen as a long-time Republican stronghold. By the 1930s, the United States Congress had become the playground for the Democratic majority. Interestingly, the Republican contention that Democrats in Congress were responsible for holding up statehood for Hawai'i was at least partially supported when Alaska, a Democratic state, was admitted before Hawai'i (Quinn, 1984).[8]

A second reason Hawai'i was not a desirable candidate for statehood, in some circles, was due to the unique mixed racial composition of the Territory. The dominant population of Japanese in Hawai'i became a thorn for many Southern representatives (Bell, 1972). Justus F. Paul (1975)[9] recorded the popular racist attitude of Congressional politicians toward Hawai'i: A Republican representative from Nebraska named Hugh Butler wrote to Mrs. A. Picard on August 8, 1947, "A lot of other people have asked me if I want to see two Japs in the United States Senate. No, I don't!" (p. 142). Because Hawai'i had given citizenship to Asian ethnic groups and had also begun to dismantle the segregated public school system, the state looked too liberal. This carried negative political implications because of the continued widespread segregation practices found among Southern states.

To the debates over party affiliation and ethnic composition was added a third plea against statehood—the purported threat of communism in Hawai'i. The Dies Committee on UnAmerican activities established in 1938 (the antecedent to McCarthyism) found strong supporters. Basically, any actions that opposed the political and social status quo could be labeled communist inspired. The political activity in Hawai'i became a prime arena for these beliefs because of the growth of labor unions coupled with overwhelming numbers of Japanese rising to higher political office. Communist scare tactics fostered the attitude that Hawai'i would be controlled "by militant left-wing, allegedly Communist-controlled labor unions" (Bell, 1984, p. 149). Senator Butler also used communism as a legitimate reason to block Hawai'i's statehood, writing in a letter to Stella Pettijohn on April 28, 1952, "Until the Communist situation is cleaned up in Hawai'i, I am against statehood" (as cited in Paul, 1975, p. 145). This debate did not include the voice of Native Hawaiians.

The Territory of Hawai'i, therefore, faced tough debate for and against statehood, which had been promised in the *Organic Law of 1900*. It fulfilled economic qualification with a treasury that supported both the state and federal government. Although the Territory had not fully assimilated its ethnic groups into the governing structure, it had successfully and efficiently Americanized the people. By 1950, Hawai'i's government had in place a variety of democratic institutions, such as the recently dismantled segregated English Standard school system, and had introduced political platforms that expressed beliefs such as employment opportunity for all, support of organized labor, and ethnic participation.

The 1950 Constitutional Convention prepared Hawai'i for Statehood. In 1949, Hawai'i's legislature adopted Act 334, section 1, which stated:

> In order that Hawai'i may be admitted in the Union on an equal footing with the original states, a convention for the purpose of forming a constitution and state government and otherwise preparing for such admission as a state shall be held, and the act of said convention shall be submitted for ratification by the people, as provided in the Act. (Session Laws of Hawai'i, 1949)

The constitution was ratified on November 7, 1950, preparing the smooth transition for Hawai'i from territorial governance to the independence and responsibility of state governance.

There were, however, some who opposed the constitution because such personal guarantees representing equal opportunity, citizen participation in governance, and choice were not well represented. In his article, "Hawai'i Drafts a Constitution," Lowrie (1951) observed:

> Some opposed the Constitution in the hope that a more liberal document might result. The only organized opposition came from the International Longshoremen's and Warehousemen's Union, and this union on May 1, 1950, reiterated it was on record in favor of "speedy enactment of statehood." The features objectional to the union in the Constitution as submitted were, lack of initiative, referendum and recall provisions, lack of provisions for free school books and supplies, the appointment of judges and departmental head, the apportionment section for selection of legislatures, and an article dealing with the Hawaiian Homes Commission. (p. 217)

Despite considerable debates in the United States Congress and on the home front over the next 10 years, Hawai'i was finally granted statehood in 1959. On March 18, 1959, President Eisenhower signed Hawai'i's statehood bill that went before the Hawai'i plebiscite on June 27, 1959. Bell recorded that 7,854 rejected the bill while 132,938 voted for statehood (1984, p. 277). Where did the Native Hawaiian stand? Bell continued, "In only one of the islands' 240 voting precincts did a majority vote against the provisions of the plebiscite. The unique exception was the small, privately owned, isolated island of Ni'ihau. It voted seventy to eighteen against statehood" (p. 277). This is a noteworthy revelation, as the vote on Ni'ihau was placed by pure-blood Native Hawaiians.

A little-known fact regarding Hawai'i's statehood would eventually lay the foundation for current movement toward Hawaiian self-determination. In 1946, United Nations Article 73 required the United States to report the status of its colonial-type arrangements with Hawai'i, American Samoa, Puerto Rico, Guam, Panama, and Alaska. Article 73, an attempt toward decolonization, stated that when these governments reached full self-governing capacity they would have to be given the opportunity to choose whether they would emerge: a sovereign independent state, a free state in association with an independent state, or a state fully integrated within an independent state. In 1953, Puerto Rico chose to be a commonwealth. Shortly thereafter, Alaska became the 49th state and Hawai'i would soon follow. The vote in Hawai'i does not record a choice between statehood or sovereign state! However, in 1959, the United States reported to the UN that Hawai'i had chosen to be fully integrated.

On July 28, 1959, Hawai'i elected its first governor and its first representatives who had a vote in the United States Senate and House of Representatives. Although the Republicans won the gubernatorial race, which went to Quinn, and also sent Long to the Senate and Fong to the House, the Democrats' young Daniel Inouye proved a formidable foe, winning the second seat in the House. The Democrats also won a majority of seats in Hawai'i's State Legislature; however, with the governorship allied with the Republican Party, their platforms were difficult to enact. This did not last. As a result of the 1962 elections, John Burns became governor, Daniel Inouye won the second seat in the United States Senate, and Democrats Spark M. Matsunaga and Patsy Takemoto Mink won in the House. The only Republican in this group was Hiram Fong, United States Senator from Hawai'i. With statehood in 1959 and the complete takeover of the Democratic Party by 1962, the Nisei had risen to full citizenship and the political turbulence of this period found its end.

The Democratic Machine Maintains Power

The annexationists who engineered the 1893 overthrow, having successfully gained power by selling the people on reform ideals, soon centralized their power to satisfy their own needs at the expense of their constituents. The liberal Democrats who replaced this Republican Oligarchy in the 1940s and 1950s proved to be little different from their predecessors. During the 1960s, the Democrats managed to privatize political conflict, successfully limiting government participation to the key players in Burns' political machine and aspiring AJAs American-born Japanese Americans who fit the elite image. In essence, the Democratic Party resembled the previous governing elite. Fred Rolfing, the Republican minority leader, aptly characterized the Democrats governing organization as "a new closed system ruled by an elite clique" (Coffman, 1973, p. 119). Perhaps one reason for this continued conservatism was the tremendous push for Japanese Americans to "be American," thereby retaining former organizational structures and political behaviors.

The Democratic Party, headed by the Burns' people, had become the status quo. The institutionalized colonial social system that they had fought to replace, in reality, remained largely intact. Only the players had changed. The Japanese Nisei now controlled governance, along with their White companions. One example of the Democrats' display of power and disregard for other ethnic groups surrounded the Land Reform Act in 1967. Aspiring for land ownership, the Japanese Nisei found that there was no land to be had. The major portions of surface land were controlled by the federal and state government as they had been taken from Hawaiians and ceded to the United States after the overthrow and subsequently returned to the state upon statehood. These lands were virtually impossible to touch. So, they went after the easiest target, the private land owners, most of whom were Hawaiian (e.g., Bishop Estate). In order to realize their dream of owning the land on which their home sat, they, like their Republican counterparts, chipped away at Native Hawaiian-owned land.

The centralized power of the Democratic Machine was again felt at the Constitutional Convention of 1968. Although its objective was to establish equity in voter representation (reapportionment), what came out of the convention merely maintained the status quo. Norman Meller, in his 1971 work *With an Understanding Heart: Constitution Making in Hawai'i,* wrote that:

> The product which emerged from the 1968 deliberations consequently could be expected to be more confirmatory than novel, more amendatory than revolutionary, and more concerned with the details of implementation than the broad sweep of philosophic formulation. (p. 84)

Perhaps the only highlights of the 1968 Constitution were more liberalized voter qualifications, changes in some legislative processes, and a provision allowing collective bargaining for public employees. For the most part, Hawai'i governance maintained a colonialist attitude and reaffirmed an oppressive demeanor toward Native Hawaiians.

The turbulence of the late 1940s and 1950s had been marked by militant ideals voicing the politics of the dispossessed and embracing all ethnic groups in an effort to force the Republicans out of office. Despite these calls for widespread social, economic, and political changes, however, the basic structure of Hawai'i's governance did not change. It remained a highly centralized, closed system composed of the Democratic elite (i.e., an Old Boys Club). Over the relative quiescent period of the late 1960s into the 1970s, the Democrats similarly managed to control every aspect of Hawai'i's governing institutions. Politically, this period is significant in that individuals in a lower class ethnic group, the Japanese, were able to utilize the political, social, and economic tenor of the day to catapult themselves into power. Indeed, the passing of the scepter from the Hawaiian Monarchy to the Sugar Oligarchy (later called the Republican Oligarchy), and then to the Democratic Machine was replete with kings and many merry men.

SCHOOL POLICY AND ACTIVITY: THE EARLY TERRITORIAL YEARS

As our discussion of politics suggests, the years from the overthrow of the monarchy in 1893 to the end of World War II were relatively stable. We now turn our attention to the effects of this stability on the pursuit of education policies in the state. The school's governing board in the early years of the Territory faced an excruciating problem with the growing ethnic population. The Asian population in Hawai'i, which had an unthreatening start with 816 Chinese in 1860, had grown to overwhelming proportions by 1920. In fact, statistics reveal that by 1920 there were 109,274 Japanese, 23,507 Chinese, 4,950 Koreans, and 21,031 Filipinos in Hawai'i (Lind, 1967).[10] Gay reported in his 1945 thesis that, by 1919, the Japanese comprised 38% of the public school population, the Chinese 8%, and the Koreans 1%, a total of 47% of the schools' population![11]

This burgeoning ethnic population was problematic for politicians, as children born in Hawai'i would have the privilege of casting votes. MacCaughey wrote in his 1909 article published in the *Paradise of the Pacific*:

> The next generation of voters will have a large proportion of Orientals. . . . As to the attitude which may be taken by these future voters on Territorial and National matters it is impossible to predict, but it is surely a National duty and a needed precaution to attempt to increase and diffuse patriotic ideals and conceptions of the duties of citizenship. (p. 34)

In much the same way that schools were viewed as the solution for the Indian problem on the United States continent, the purpose of schools in Hawai'i reflected a broad attitude of acculturation to colonial ideals, which often meant that students should accept their position in the socioeconomic hierarchy. Consistent with the municipal reform of local politics taking place across the United States which sought to replace lay governance of the schools (Tyack & Cuban, 1995), reformers in Hawai'i sought to replace immigrant participation in school governance by centralizing and placing the responsibility for governance in the hands of professionals, both as board members and as administrators in charge of implementing educational policies. The public schools' programs concentrated on creating an efficient labor force that spoke English and lived by U.S. moral standards. The uniqueness of individual ethnic cultures was not recognized, but rather devalued, in the process. MacCaughey (1909) described the goal of Hawai'i's Territorial Schools as:

> . . . the harmonious development of the individual, physically, mentally, and morally. This is the fundamental basis of all good citizenship, of all efficient living. . . . This development is attained through the following media: (a) The correct usage of the official mode of expression, which is the spoken and written English language; (b) The important facts concerning the immediate and more remote environment of the child, the great truths learned by the human race during past ages, the principles of mathematics; (c) Manual Training, which may later be developed into definite industrial efficiency; (d) Habits of right living and moral conduct, both individual, and as a member of the school society. (p. 33)

In all United States land holdings overseas, schools became a U.S. institution serving the needs of a political and economic elite. One notices efficiency addressed twice in the previous quote. Certainly, efficiency was a driving force behind school reform of this era. To illustrate this point, Aida Negron De Montilla (1971), quoting a 1902 annual school report regarding schooling in Puerto Rico, shared:

> . . . colonization carried forward by the armies of war is vastly more costly than that carried forward by the armies of peace, whose outpost and garrisons are the public schools of advancing nations. . . . five hundred thousand dollars for one year or even that sum for a series of years, would not support a very extensive campaign. But it would work such a change in Porto Rico [sic] as to put beyond the suspicion of a doubt the ultimate and splendid success of the engrafting of American institutions upon a Spanish American stock. (p. 62)

In order to realize the optimal socialization of the ethnic lower classes, the educational governance in Hawai'i, much like other United States territories, continued to be centralized and the content and instructional approaches mirrored U.S. standards.

Similar to other relatively large school districts across the United States at the turn of the century, Hawai'i's Territorial Board of Education was composed of a board of education (professionals appointed by the governor), a superintendent (appointed by the board of education), and six commissioners (all appointed by the governor and approved by the territorial senate). To imply that the organization was not influenced by political preference or that the schools' structure was anything but centralized would be misleading. Despite reform educators' rhetoric that the nation's schools should be separate from political infighting and governed by professional administrators who were neutral, schools were everything but apolitical (Iannaccone, 1977; Tyack & Cuban, 1995). In Hawai'i, every level of policy decisionmaking and implementation was defined by leadership that was tied to the broader governing values of the time. So effective and efficient was this school structure that an investigation by a federal commission made as early as 1898 concluded that:

> The present public school system of Hawai'i is very satisfactory and efficient. The conduct of the public schools and the tendency of the entire educational establishment of Hawai'i is in the highest degree advantageous to the United States. The laws of Hawai'i already provide that school attendance by all persons of school age shall be compulsory, and also that the English language shall be the universal language taught. The effect of these two enactments is the most beneficial and far-reaching in unifying the inhabitants which could be adopted. It operates to break up the racial antagonisms otherwise certain, to increase and to unite in the schoolroom the children of the Anglo-Saxons, the Hawaiians, the Latins, and the Mongolians in the rivalry for obtaining education. No system could be adopted

which would tend to Americanize the people more thoroughly than this. (as cited in Wist, 1940, p. 142)[12]

Certainly the idealism of this one best system, which couches its underlying message in nonracist rhetoric of equality and the righteous means of breaking up racial antagonisms to unite in the schoolroom for the purpose of Americanization, needs to be seen as a view of education serving the interests of the political culture of its leaders, not the various local ethnicities including Native Hawaiians. Centralization enhanced the quick ability of schools to disseminate directives as well as implement and monitor programs. This view is illustrated by a pamphlet written by Robert Littler published by the *Honolulu Star Bulletin* in 1927 about school management, which observes:

Control of education in Hawai'i is extremely concentrated. The superintendent in Honolulu and the board of education plan the courses of study, choose the textbooks, hire all the teachers, principals, and superintendents; they do, in fact, have complete control over the entire educational system—with one exception. All matters of construction and maintenance of buildings is in the hands of the counties. (p. 16)[13]

English-Only Policy

The work of school policymakers during this period was to maintain the traditional element of centralizing governance of the schools so that there could be control of the curriculum to enable efficient education and Americanization of children who were culturally diverse. The influx of middle-class *haoles* to Hawai'i created a need to provide their children with an education free from the influence of the local pidgin English dialect (e.g., words from several languages, different patterns of speech and voice inflection). By the early 1920s, the English problem was considered the most difficult of academic problems in Hawai'i (Tamura, 1994). Demands for the creation of English Standard Schools was a response to Euro-American disgust with pidgin (Hawaiian Creole English) spoken in public schools. School superintendent Givens (1924) commented that:

Most of the children come from non-English speaking homes. The first so-called English that they hear is the "pidgin" English of the cane fields, the ranches and the street, frequently mixed with profanity. This jargon is used when conversing with their playmates and improper speech habits are formed before the children attend school. Once these habits are formed the correction of them is not an easy problem. (p. 17)[14]

Under what was the best-for-the-majority policy, English Standard Schools were established as a means of transmitting middle-class U.S. values to any intellectually capable student.[15] Admission to the schools, determined by English proficiency, prohibited the attendance of most minority groups. This system of tracking students according to their ability to speak the English language, in reality, separated the students by racial lines. Lincoln Elementary School, the first English Standard School opened in 1924, had a student body composed of 572 White, 19 Japanese, and 27 Chinese.[16] Tracking by language ability created a dual-school system where the English Standard Schools received better financial support and better teachers, most from the continental United States.[17] In contrast, providing vocational and industrial education was further means for the schools to track ethnic students into occupations that would not jeopardize middle and upper management positions reserved for Whites.

In response to instruction in the public schools and in the effort to maintain their cultures, many groups turned to a growing number of foreign language schools. For example, as Tamura (1994) noted, 98% of the Japanese students attending public schools in 1920 also attended Japanese school. These schools were supported by the community and operated during nonschool hours. Moreover, Buddhism, which was often emphasized in these schools, was considered a threat to Christianity. The Asian community never assumed that policymakers would support these schools. The expectation was the maintenance of their culture (e.g., language and customs) within U.S. society. To block these efforts, policymakers acted to limit access to these schools by passing several laws aimed at limiting their effectiveness (by limiting instruction) or by placing them under the supervision of the Department of Public Instruction (Tamura, 1994). The various activities of these schools, therefore, were kept under the watchful eye of the appointed territorial governor, his appointed board of education, and school superintendent and his staff.

The priority of English-only policy became institutionalized across the United States and its territories as a useful tool to subjugate waves of immigrants. Gilbert G. Gonzalaez (1990) wrote about the Mexican-American (Chicano) experience in California:

> . . . Americanization placed valued judgements upon virtually all things Mexican. Thus, language, religion, dress, recreational activities, family traditions, and home life-style, constituted social as well as political problems that needed to be either eliminated or reconstructed upon a new foundation. (p. 158)

Similarly, to ensure an English-only policy in schools, Euro-American teachers were often hired to teach other children. In Hawai'i, the schools hired teachers from as far away as New York State and the Midwest.

Similar activity occurred in Puerto Rico where, as early as 1901, teachers were brought into the islands from the United States, most having recently taught on Native American reservations.

Superintendents' Roles in Legitimizing School Policy

As we observed in chapter 3, certainly, the early school superintendents in Hawai'i played a central role in the process of defining how schools socialized students. While we are mindful of over-emphasizing their efforts, they played a role in implementing dominant social policies in the schools through stressing efficiency and centralized control. Similar to municipal reform that consolidated control of school governance to a group of professional administrators, Hawai'i's school superintendents were the ones who translated the cultural values of the governing elite into actual school activities. Although the schools eventually became rather narrowly focused, this was not, however, the result of single-minded thought. Upon closer examination, we found that superintendents, themselves, varied considerably on their particular views of the educational system. This is aptly demonstrated by looking more closely at some of their activities from the early 1900s through the implementation of the English Standard Schools in 1924 and vocational education in the late 1920s and early 1930s.

As we noted in chapter 3, early leaders in the middle to late 1800s were aware of a strong Christian religious presence in Hawai'i. By the early 1900s, the role of the schools changed toward economic (as opposed to spiritual) ends. Superintendents in the early 1900s focused on students as raw material to be molded into a colonial labor force. Winifred Babbit (1907–1910) directed his efforts to the development of vocational education and citizenship. These efforts maintained the governing elite's desire for schools to produce an industrious labor force and easily consenting citizenry. Willis T. Pope, appointed in 1910, began the *Hawai'i Educational Review* in 1912 that quickly disseminated curricular information to teachers. Thomas H. Gibson, who followed Pope in 1913 and served for less than a year, maintained a laissez-faire approach to school management, believing that the schools should teach only rudimentary skills to ensure a docile labor force.

This attitude was changed by newspaper editor Henry Walsworth Kinney's (1914–1919) appointment as superintendent. A professional businessman and believer in scientific management, Kinney's focus was "economy in operation and business efficiency in administration" (Wist, 1940, p. 154). He was bent on holding the schools accountable to financial budgets, curriculum objectives, teacher qualifications, and student performance. Professionalizing the schools was a means of legitimizing the work of schools within a competitive economy. For example, teacher salaries were based on training, experience, and teacher evaluations that were determined by the number of students passing statewide tests (Wist, 1940). Accountability through student testing had never before been of concern in Hawai'i until Kinney. Testing was held at the end of every year for grades 1 through 4, and at the end of each term for grades 5 and 6. However well intentioned the testing process might have been, the 75% passing criteria led to cheating and many unhappy teachers who did not like the idea of being judged by the outcome of their students' test scores.

If Kinney was the conservative end of the superintendent spectrum, then Vaughan MacCaughey (1919–1923), appointed by Governor McCarthy, was the opposite. The teachers' choice for superintendent, he supported the ideals of the progressive movement. In contrast to his efficient predecessors, MacCaughey wanted teachers to create their own curriculum and to do away with the rigid testing routine of his predecessor. MacCaughey's term is significant in that his progressive educational views opposed restricting the intellectual growth of the ethnic minority. The aim of schooling was to produce a common culture that bound the classes and fostered a more knowledgeable populace. At the same time, education would train the individual to become a productive United States citizen through tracking, testing, Americanization, and curriculum differentiation.

Although MacCaughey's intentions of Americanizing the schools could not be viewed as inappropriate activity, the industrial base of Hawai'i was not fully satisfied by his attempts that placed the idea of social advancement into the minds of the ethnic laborers. In response to industrial demand and pressure from the growing *haole* population who could not afford to send their children to private schools but who disdained the public schools where pidgin (a mixed ethnic language) was spoken, Governor Wallace Farrington replaced MacCaughey with Willard E. Givens (1923–1925), former principal of Kamehameha Boys School.

By the early 1920s, Governor Farrington and Superintendent Givens faced a dilemma: the need to maintain an elite organization on one hand, and the need to uphold the ideals, or at least the rhetoric, of democratic parity on the other. Their policy reflected the struggle of these two opposing demands. Both men saw the purpose of schools as expanding Hawai'i's industrial base and, so, supported the opening of high schools to instruct the non-*haole* population in manual labor and agricultural industry. This would maintain a source of labor for the plantations. Americanization, specifically the proper use of Standard English, was a key focus. Givens worked hard to upgrade the use of the English language in the schools by establishing the English Standard School system. This dual-school system, in effect, reflected social relations embedded in

Hawai'i's social structure: the *haole* at the top and the locals and Asians at the bottom. Of course, Givens' efforts segregated the schools in Hawai'i and institutionalized the melting pot ideology that one-culture, the U.S. culture, was best (Tyack, 1974).

While the practice of social stratification was imperative to the maintenance of the system, the appearance of equal opportunity was just as important. Given this, Governor Farrington also supported the rhetoric of the progressive education movement by placing the influential Miles Carey[18] as principal of McKinley High School, the school that served local ethnicities. In addition, support was given to establish the Kawananakoa Experimental school, which studied progressive teaching methods and curriculum.

Will C. Crawford (1925–1934), school superintendent under both Governors Farrington and Judd, faced the tough economic times of 1929. As in all economically stringent times, the governing elite turned its attention to its social institutions, especially the activity of the schools. A 1920 report by the federal government had recommended that Hawai'i liberalize its system of school governance and improve the quality of its curriculum to provide more opportunity for its students. In response to the report and the growing progressive activity of teachers in the public school, Governor Judd appointed a commission to examine the schools.[19] This report, the *Prosser Report of 1930*, urged educators to realize the industrial needs of the Hawaiian community. This conclusion was an expected result, as the report was financed indirectly by the Chamber of Commerce. The committee members were also members of the industrial elite; in fact, Prosser worked closely with Cooke, the new President of Hawai'i's Sugar Planters Association.

Essentially, the report argued for a shift in thinking away from progressive reforms. Using the recommendations of the report, Crawford sought to replace the liberal attitudes of educators with limitations in high school enrollment, more vocational aims, and a cut in school expenditures. However, the social context was changing. With an increasing number of ethnic laborers having families and with technological advances on the plantation, something needed to be done about the surplus of young men and women in their teen years. High schools with a focus on industrial and agricultural education were seen as an appropriate place to send the youths.[20] Schools became more than a holding area to acculturate an industrial-based labor force.

No matter how the Republican Oligarchy fought education, however, it was a losing battle. The value of education was entrenched with its roots planted by the American Missionaries and its constant pruning by the influx of progressive educators from the continential United States. Education, therefore, posed a real dilemma for policymakers during this era who recognized its obvious centrality to larger cultural issues. On one hand, the democratic ideals of parity and individual competition were seen as a means of Americanizing Hawai'i's schools. In contrast, however, educational progress began to tear apart the ideals of a docile labor force and teutonic control. Like it or not, education had laid the seed for political changes and the oligarchy's grip on educational policy would be broken by individuals such as Miles Carey, who believed in the right to an outstanding education for Hawai'i's diverse ethnic groups.[21]

Education Policy: 1900–1930s

The transference of cultural values from the dominant political rulers into concrete educational policy is evident in two sets of school laws written in 1905 and 1924, and one set of educational policies developed in 1931. Table 4.1 illuminates the distribution of values in the *Revised School Laws of the Department of Public Instruction of the Territory of Hawai'i, 1905* (Territory of Hawai'i, 1905).[22] This reveals that the values of efficiency and quality far outnumbered the values of equity and choice.

The school laws of 1905 gave the Department of Education the power to mandate curriculum which reflected growing professional control over the educational process. For example, Section 207 gave the Department "entire charge and control and responsible for the conduct of all affairs appertaining to public instruction" (Territory of Hawai'i, 1905, p. 7). In addition, the statute clearly outlined governing procedures of the board, responsibilities of the superintendent and commissioners, and detailed instructions regarding school attendance, building maintenance, and financial matters. One section dealing with choice provided parents with a grievance procedure. Another section suggesting equity stated that no tuition would be charged for public school attendance. Other sections of note that were not accounted for in Table 4.1 included laws which dealt with private schools and reform schools.

TABLE 4.1
Distribution of Values and School Policy Mechanisms (SPM), 1905

SPM	*Quality*	*Efficiency*	*Equity*	*Choice*	*Total*
Finance		1	1		2
Personnel	1			1	2
Testing					0
Program	12	1			13
Governance		25			25
Curriculum materials		2			2
Bldg. & facilities		3			3
Total	13	32	1	1	47

TABLE 4.2
Distribution of Values and School Policy Mechanisms (SPM), 1924

SPM	*Quality*	*Efficiency*	*Equity*	*Choice*	*Total*
Finance		10			10
Personnel	4	3	1	2	10
Testing					0
Program		1			1
Governance		18			18
Curriculum materials		2			2
Bldg. & facilities		6			6
Total	4	40	1	2	47

The *School Laws and Laws Relating to Child Welfare* in 1924 (Territory of Hawai'i), presented in Table 4.2, also reflected the broader values of the elite policymakers. Focused on the need for efficient control of all aspects of school governance and school-related activities, content analysis of the laws revealed 40 statements (see Table 4.2) that held schools accountable to prescribed activity dominated by the domains of governance and finance, followed by 4 citations addressing the quality of the schools' personnel. The policy values of equity and choice were mentioned a total of three times.

Although the value of efficiency, unsurprisingly, appears to overwhelm the school laws during the 1920s, it is important to note that more emphasis was placed on teachers. For example, teachers' rights in addressing dismissal from the department and the introduction of teachers' pensions (a reflection of McCaughey's belief in teacher rights) received considerable attention in these laws. Also, qualification of teachers, teacher pay, teacher responsibilities, and overall financial concerns seem to reflect the work of Pinkham's administration under Kinney. Also occurring during this period (1931), the Territorial Normal School merged with the University of Hawai'i School of Education to create the Teacher's College. The criteria for admittance, the length of schooling, and the cost of the program was prohibitive for most Native Hawaiians.

Although we could not include all related laws in our analysis, we did discover policies concerning the Department's care of war time bonds, health vaccinations, mandate to display the United States' flag, private schools, and limiting the reach of foreign language schools. In general, the scope of this activity suggests a policymaking focus on maintaining control in response to growing ethnic diversity.

Political cultures that work to maintain traditional patterns of government, limiting control to an appropriate elite as well as favoring its economic needs, emphasize efficiency and quality in policymaking. Efficiency is promoted in its economic form, such as in the allocation of resources, as well as in the manner that ideas are implemented into laws and social programs. Quality, as defined by this specific organization, seeks the best in personnel and methods in order to realize those social programs deemed essential to attain the desired view of what society should be like. This activity, according to Easton (1965a, 1965b), describes politics as the authoritative allocation of values. A closer look at actual school policy reveals this political activity, specifically in defining who benefits from schools and who does not.

An analysis of the Department of Public Instruction's *Education Policy* of 1931[23] illustrates this very point. The policy manual is divided under five major headings. The first four areas address the need for quality programs. For example, under the subheading "Elementary and Intermediate Schools," the policy's objective is to ensure that the school curriculum reflects a U.S. attitude. The second subheading, "High Schools," defines the curriculum and attempts to restrict high school attendance to "all youth who have by habits of study, attitudes and intellectual ability demonstrated their fitness" (p. 28). The third subheading, "Vocational Education," addresses Hawai'i's industrial concerns of promoting a better labor force, and "The Curriculum," the fourth subheading, defines the principles on which curriculum should be established. The last heading, "Teaching," recognizes the importance of the teacher and sets out moral criteria that must be fulfilled.

All five policy statements reflect the single policy value of quality. More specific examination of the section regulations under each of the headings, however, reveals comprehensive directives to departmental personnel that outline efficient governance of programs, finance, curriculum materials, testing, personnel or teachers, and building and facilities. These regulations, which total 221 sections, are not printed under the five main topics they define, but are instead found in a separate addendum. Outside of the general public's view, it suggests that the rhetoric promoting educational quality to the public was far easier than the bottom-line, efficient financial approach. This enabled the centralized board of education and the superintendent to limit public participation and implement each of the policies according to their intentional design.

Of course, as we have suggested, the underlying theme of this policy was to Americanize the ethnic minority populace as well as remind them covertly of their place in the social hierarchy. This would ensure a labor force to meet industrial needs. The most prominent curriculum decisions implemented by this political thought were English-only instruction, separate schools primarily for Whites and curricular tracking emphasizing vocational education for local youths and academic preparation for whites. Through implementation of these types of policies, school leaders could allocate future social position. Students in Hawai'i's schools would learn from United States texts that did not reflect local affairs, culture, history, or knowledge. The United States' flag flew over every school, and students recited the Pledge of Allegiance and sang "The Star Spangled Banner" daily. Much like the other colonies such as Puerto Rico, students celebrated U.S. holidays and were expected to speak only English in school (Spring, 1993).

Although education's governing elite wanted to limit democratic participation in policymaking, its leaders could not escape the inevitable conflict over access to education among the islands' immigrant population and their desire for separate schooling. There were also isolated followers of progressive reforms. Perhaps the hallmark of progressive education during this period was McKinley High School. As Fuchs (1961) argued in *Hawai'i Pono*:

> Mckinley High School became a symbol. To some it was Tokyo High, where the children of Hawai'i's immigrants were filled with crazy ideas unsuited to island life. To thousands of school children on O'ahu, it was a symbol of hope. To mainland educators, it was a movement to the progressive ideas. (p. 290)

Under the inspiration of Principal Miles Carey, the curriculum at McKinley High School urged the students to think, challenge, impact, and change their environment. In 1930, he initiated the core curriculum which integrated English and Social Studies in a 2-hour block, focusing on current social and political issues. The popularity of this program is illustrated in sheer numbers, for within 3 years following its inception, the school's enrollment leaped to 3,000 students.

The importance of McKinley High School, Principal Carey, and its progressive teachers to future economic and political life in Hawai'i cannot be underplayed. If the worth of education is manifested in the achievements of its students, then McKinley graduates support the power of education. Its graduates are a "Who's Who of Notables" in the State of Hawai'i's early political, economic, and social environment. In government there was Senator Hiram Fong, Senator Daniel Inouye, Senator and Governor George Ariyoshi, Chief Justice Wilfred Tsukiyama, Associate Justice Masaji Marumoto, Governor Samuel Wilder King, and Attorney General Bert Kobayashi. Graduates entering the field of education included District Supervisor Richard Kosaki, Dr. Andrew In (Dean of the University of Hawai'i College of Education), Toma Tasaki, Dr. Dai Ho Chun (Director of the East–West Center), Dr. Chitoshi Yanaga (professor at Yale University), and Dr. Shiro Amioka (professor at the University of Hawai'i). Among the religious leaders were Reverend Abraham Akaka,

Charles Kuroch, Harry Komura, and Seid Ogawa. Business leaders included Chinn Ho, President of Capitol Investment, City Bank, and *Honolulu Star Bulletin*; Hung Wo Ching of Aloha Airlines; entrepreneur Q. C. Lum, who invented wireless telephones for cars; and W. Russell Starr of Matson Shipping. There were also artists, entertainers, military heroes, and Olympians.[24] Ironically, under a system of stability, Miles Carey's progressive ideals provided the future leaders who would successfully see the fall of the Republican Oligarchy and the rise of the Democratic Party.

The war years in Hawai'i resulted in the temporary closure of McKinley High School from December 7, 1941, to February 2, 1942. Education responded to the war effort. The school board mandated the opening of more kindergartens, so that parents were free to work in support of the war. The schools' curriculum was filled with lessons about U.S. beliefs and wartime patriotism. Despite questions about the loyalty of the Islands' citizens, the entire population became energized, identifying themselves with the war effort in every possible way. Young students joined the war effort digging trenches, sewing camouflage nets, and learning emergency medical skills. Respect for curfews, rationing, and martial law was taught alongside new U.S. citizenship classes, music classes that taught U.S. songs, and a heavy dose of U.S. history. So successful were the schools that, in 1947, a United States congressional report ". . . lauded Hawai'i for its outstanding efforts in its successful campaign to institute Americanization in its schools" (Bell, 1984, p. 104).

PRESSURE POLITICS: EDUCATION FROM 1945–1960

Against a pre-war society with stable socioeconomic institutions and a stable ruling party, the end of World War II brought sweeping political change to Hawai'i. The latter 1940s and early 1950s was a turbulent period. World War II focused attention on Hawai'i strategic importance as "The Crossroads of the Pacific" and turned its agricultural economy on its head. This resulted in a tide of business opportunities to support the growing military presence in the islands and a booming tourism industry. The growth of these businesses challenged the old-time plantationers' hold on Hawai'i's purse strings. In an effort to maintain their elite governance of Hawai'i, the leaders sought to limit the scope of issues, but the debates could not be restricted. Eventually, the Young Democrats of Hawai'i gradually took control of Hawai'i's Territorial legislature.

Coupled with the growth of new businesses came the expansion of the labor unions. Unions represented a majority of ethnic laborers who realized the power of their unified vote. Their influence was felt in many social and economic arenas including education. Political special interest groups in Hawai'i, therefore, began to make some significant inroads toward opening up the educational policy system during this period (Benham & Heck, 1994). Kitaguchi (1962) observed that the growing union presence in Hawai'i directly impacted education through a variety of activities including: a general publicity campaign aimed at the people, communication with the Department of Public Instruction, participation in Department of Public Instruction advisory councils and other school activities, labor publications made available for school use, student scholarships, attempts to organize school teachers, and lobbying and other political activities. Union efforts to define participation in educational policymaking resulted in several policies that established the Adult Education Division under the Department of Public Instruction in 1945 (Act 108), expanded the kindergarten program from 12 classes in 1943 to 29 classes in 1949, and increased vocational education programs in agriculture, homemaking, and business fields, while adding distributive education, industrial arts, and occupation information (Kitaguchi, 1962).

Despite such efforts to increase the types of educational opportunities for students and increase the professional voice of teachers, breaking the colonial dependency that had become deeply embedded in the social, political, and economic institutions of Hawai'i was much more difficult to accomplish. As Tyack and Cuban (1995) have argued, changes incorporated into existing educational institutions over the past century have tended to last if they were structural add-ons that did not disrupt too harshly the long-standing structures of the system. The challenge, which really began in the 1930s, was to bridge the sugar plantation business and the schoolroom in a way that would provide alternative economic options for students other than staying on the plantation. Gradually, reformers' efforts opened the doors to progressive ideals that sought to develop educational opportunity for all of Hawai'i's children.

The Fight Against English Standard Schools

Another key instance illustrating efforts to increase educational opportunity among the ethnically diverse groups in Hawai'i surrounds the efforts of political pressure groups to remove the segregated school system. Just as the labor unions sought to develop policies that would enhance students' educational opportunities, the Hawai'i Education Association (HEA) also became a powerful pressure group. Prior to its beginning in 1921, there were many teacher groups that worked to improve teaching conditions; however, because they acted individually, they were generally unsuccessful. Behind the Hilo Teachers' Union leadership of Fred Clowes and Eugene Capellas and the organizational skill of Willard E. Givens, a united group of teachers was achieved. The HEA was dominated by members of the Democratic Party, and their ideals of liberalism were evident in their beliefs of what education in Hawai'i should be. The focus of their efforts for Hawai'i's schools was dismantling the English Standard school system.

Accepted at a 1946 HEA meeting, the following resolution expressed outrage toward the dual-school system:

> Whereas, it is a questionable policy to segregate pupils on the basis of their ability to speak English, and whereas, in a democracy it is desirable and necessary that children of all races study and play together, and whereas, segregation hinders the rapid growth of good speech, therefore: Be it Resolved that the Hawai'i Education Association in convention assembled go on record as favoring the re-establishment of a single standard school system and the elimination of the dual system by June 1950. (p. 22)

Supported by the Parent Teacher's Association (PTA), the Draper–Hayden Curriculum Survey in 1944–1945, Commissioner Ruth E. Black, and several newspapers, HEA began its political battle to change the English Standard School policy. In 1947, HEA members passed another resolution that became the basis for the actual law abolishing the English Standard system. The resolution written in the minutes of the HEA 1947 convention states:

> Whereas, there is serious question regarding the consistency of the dual system of "English Standard" and "regular" public schools with the principle of democracy, and
>
> Whereas, there is a growing sentiment for elimination of English Standard Schools and the return to a single standard of public schools, and
>
> Whereas, it is undeniable that (granting the undemocratic implications of the dual system) unwholesome and disruptive tensions would be introduced into the community by the sudden abolition of the English Standard Schools. Therefore, Be it Resolved that the Hawaiian Education Association in convention assembled this 3rd day of April, 1947 reiterate its stand favoring the reestablishment of a single standard school system and the elimination of the dual system, but that the Association urges in the interest of community harmony, that legislation to this end provide for the gradual transition from the dual to the single standard, and that it recommend a system of redistricting for schools which would put all elementary schools on a single standard basis for the first grade only as of September, 1947; for the first and second grades as of September, 1948; for the first, second, and third grades as of September, 1949 and so on until at the end of a 12 year period all grades and all public schools would be established within the framework of a single standard schools system. (p. 12)

The momentum against the social injustices of the earlier territorial years soon peaked. On May 11, 1949, Act 227 (Territory of Hawai'i, 1949) was signed into law by Governor Stainback, which read:

> The Department of Public Instruction is hereby directed to raise the standards of all public schools to the level of the English Standard system starting in September 1949, and to continue these adjustments annually until all schools of the territory are raised to the level of a single standard system.

The banner of parity in educational policy was heralded in actions by both the PTA and the American Association of University Women (AAUW). The Parent Teacher Association successfully abolished the fee on textbooks in public schools and the AAUW pushed for equitable and consistent grading and promotion policies. Although there seemed to be more people becoming involved with educational issues, in actuality, it was only a few pressure groups with very specific platforms which forced the still centralized school board to mandate equitable programs for all children, consistent grading and promotion criteria, and improved courses in industrial education. It is noteworthy that this action put Hawai'i ahead of mainland policy in dealing with segregation in education, as the Brown Decision would not occur until 1954.

Hawai'i's School Policy: 1940s–1960s

Despite the ability of special interests to influence the policy system at this key moment in time over the segregated school issue, in general, past institutional practices focused on centralized structure, efficiency, and elite decision making dictated that school policy would still made by a small group. This trend can be noted in Tables 4.3 through 4.6, which present a content analysis of Hawai'i school policy or school laws between 1947 and 1969.

In May 1947, the three policies (see Table 4.3) that reflected quality in the area of programs mandated teacher neutrality toward controversial issues, directed a mandatory amount of time to be spent studying United States History, and restricted foreign language classes to students who were English proficient. In part, these policies reflect vestiges of Americanization and concern with the growing vocal power of teachers. Efficiency was observed in the handling of book rental fees, mandating that teachers vote, and outlining grievance procedures.

Reflecting the continued political demand toward wider participation in governing activities, the school laws of 1961 (see Table 4.4) provided for citizen election of community school advisory councils and greater representation of teachers in the desicionmaking process of job and salary classification. The focus of the laws was governance, however, and the

TABLE 4.3
Distribution of Values and School Policy Mechanisms (SPM), 1947

SPM	*Quality*	*Efficiency*	*Equity*	*Choice*	*Total*
Finance		1			1
Personnel		1			1
Testing					0
Program	3				3
Governance		1			1
Curriculum materials					0
Bldg. & facilities					0
Total	3	3	0	0	6

two laws reflecting efficiency reiterated the need for centralized administrative control through an appointed school board and superintendent.

As seen in Table 4.5, the Hawai'i School Laws of October 1966, Chapter 37 and Chapter 39 further illustrate the educational policy focus on efficient financing of public schools and school governance. It is of interest to note that a section under financing appropriated funds for the transportation of disabled children, suggesting a beginning awareness of special populations. As we suggest in the next chapter, however, Hawai'i policymakers were not quick to respond to the needs of special populations, despite the early decision to dismantle school segregation and this isolated policy on transportation of disabled students. As we have developed, this lack of attention to equity, despite policy rhetoric, is revealed directly by the content analysis of the actual mandates—which reflect more directly the actual beliefs of policymakers. Quality in programs addressed driver education and establishment of teacher in-service conferences. Although efficiency is highlighted in the 1966 law, for the first time choice is provided for the first elected board of education.

The assumption one might make, due to the public outcry for parity, is that the dominant values in Article IX in the January 1969 Hawai'i

TABLE 4.4
Distribution of Values and School Policy Mechanisms (SPM) in Act 182, Hawai'i Session Laws, 1961

SPM	*Quality*	*Efficiency*	*Equity*	*Choice*	*Total*
Finance					0
Personnel				1	1
Testing					0
Program	1				1
Governance		2		1	3
Curriculum materials					0
Bldg. & facilities					0
Total	1	2	0	2	5

TABLE 4.5
Distribution of Values and School Policy Mechanisms (SPM) in Hawai'i School Laws, 1966

SPM	*Quality*	*Efficiency*	*Equity*	*Choice*	*Total*
Finance		8			8
Personnel		1			1
Testing					0
Program	3				3
Governance		15		1	16
Curriculum materials					0
Bldg. & facilities					0
Total	3	24	0	1	28

Constitution would be equity and choice; however, Table 4.6 reveals otherwise. Three sections of the law clearly dictate the structure of command between the school board and superintendent, place the University of Hawai'i under the control of the state, and provide for a governor-appointed University Board of Regents. Again, despite actions that appear to provide some greater access to the policy system such as an elected board, these sections clearly indicate maintenance of a political elite in control of K–12 schools and higher education. Despite language giving people power to elect board of education representatives (i.e., one board for the whole State), the statute's directives also limited the board's control of schools (i.e., no financial power, no power to settle contracts) and eliminated the local voice of the community advisory councils. The board, therefore, to the present only holds broad policymaking power (e.g., approving curriculum, approving personnel issues).

The school curriculum still broadly reflected the larger institution of efficiently Americanizing the ethnic population. For example, Social Studies classes focused on United States History, U.S. Problems, Civics, and

TABLE 4.6
Distribution of Values and School Policy Mechanisms (SPM) in Article IX, Constitution of the State of Hawai'i, January 1969

SPM	*Quality*	*Efficiency*	*Equity*	*Choice*	*Total*
Finance					0
Personnel					0
Testing					0
Program					0
Governance		5			5
Curriculum materials					0
Bldg. & facilities					0
Total	0	5	0	0	5

Geography. Citizenship training carried over the war theme "Speak American, Think American, Act American." In fact, in 1955, citizenship training programs in the schools were heralded for their exemplary work. Observed in the governor's conference on education:

> . . . our students are learning and have learned the lessons in citizenship is evidenced by the many fine PTA groups throughout the Territory, most of which are led by people educated in our public school system. . . . A glance at the rosters of our service clubs, trade associations, and our City and County and Territorial governments will again point up the fact that our schools are capable of producing and do produce not only good citizens but outstanding citizens. (Governor's Office, 1955, p. 15)[25]

Many curriculum mechanisms in Hawai'i's schools standardized classroom activities in order to provide better U.S. instruction. Home economics became a comprehensive training program to ensure that students were able to achieve family well-being. Business education was expanded, and partnerships with local businesses put many students into part-time working positions. The 1947 Vocational Education Act put an agricultural teacher in every high school. Additionally, in response to the launch of Sputnik in 1957, Hawai'i too increased requirements in math and science.

As this discussion demonstrates, the policy system has remained relatively intact despite the occasional ability of special interests to force some incremental change. This supports Tyack and Cuban's (1995) thesis that, for all the policy talk, meaningful change occurs in small increments and in ways that are least disturbing to the continuation of the system.

IMPACT OF EDUCATIONAL POLICY ON NATIVE HAWAIIAN SOCIAL AND ECONOMIC STATUS, AND ACADEMIC ACHIEVEMENT

> *I maika'i no ke kalo i ka 'oha.*
> *(The goodness of the taro is judged by the fine young plants it produces.)*
> —*'Ōlelo No'eau*

We turn now to the impact of this policy culture on Native Hawaiians during this period. Beginning in the 1820s, the dominance of the beliefs held by the governing elite regarding what schools should teach had a cumulative effect on Native Hawaiians. So complete was this control over schools that programs tracking ethnic students into predetermined social classes were not only considered the norm, but were upheld as quality examples of what schools should be. The political pressure to devalue cultural plurality had been institutionalized in the public schools.

Colonialism and Manifest Destiny, as they had affected Native Americans, Mexican Americans, and Puerto Ricans, had also subjugated the

Native Hawaiian. This inflicted a disease of inferiority, inequality, and powerlessness so entrenched in Native Hawaiian minds that they had become accommodating to the White establishment over time. Giving up their power in the process of governance, instead of speaking against domination, they often found comfort in a subculture that opposed the ways of the Westerners, but which resulted in low social and economic status and academic achievement. More importantly, dominant institutional structure succeeded in keeping them marginalized through limiting them.

The Native Hawaiian: A Dying People

A cumulative effect resulting from contact with Western civilization was population decrease. A summary of such demographics for the period indicates that the Native and Part-Hawaiian population has steadily decreased since 1900 (see Table 4.7), their life expectancy at birth was lower than all other ethnic groups in Hawai'i (see Table 4.8), and Hawaiians died at substantially higher rates per 100,000 than any other resident in Hawai'i from 1940 to 1960 (see Fig. 4.1).

Even in the early 1900s (see Table 4.7), the Native Hawaiian had dropped in numbers below the influx of Japanese laborers and their families. By 1910, the Native Hawaiian and Part-Hawaiian comprised only 20.1% of the population, as opposed to the increasing percentage of Euro-Americans (23%) and Japanese (41.5%, see Table 4.7).

This demographic shift in majority to the Japanese and Euro-Americans in Hawai'i indicates Hawaiian and Part-Hawaiian represented only 17.3%

TABLE 4.7
Population in Hawai'i by Ethnicity,[a] 1900–1960

		Native Hawaiian		*Part-Hawaiian*		*White*		*Japanese*	
Year	*Total*	*N*	*%*	*N*	*%*	*N*	*%*	*N*	*%*
1900	154,001	29,799	19.3	7,857	5.1	28,819	18.7	61,111	39.7
1910	191,874	26,041	13.6	12,506	6.5	44,048	23.0	79,675	41.5
1920	255,881	23,723	9.3	18,027	7.0	54,742	21.4	109,274	42.7
1930	368,300	22,636	6.1	28,224	7.7	80,373	21.8	139,631	37.9
1940	422,770	14,375	3.4	49,935	11.8	112,087	26.5	157,905	37.3
1950	499,794	12,245	2.5	73,845	14.8	124,344	24.9	184,598	36.9
1960	632,772	11,294	1.8	91,109	14.4	202,230	32.0	203,455	32.2

[a]*Note.* This demographic table does not include Chinese, Filipino, Korean, African American, or other ethnic groups as comparison to these groups was not the purpose of displaying this data.

Source: From *Demographic Statistics of Hawai'i* (p. 115) by Robert C. Schmitt, Honolulu: University of Hawai'i Press. Copyright 1968 by University of Hawai'i Press. Reprinted by permission.

TABLE 4.8
Life Expectancy in Years, 1910–1970

Year	*White*	*Chinese*	*Filipino*	*Hawaiian & Part-Haw.*	*Japanese*	*Other*	*Total*	*Range*[a]
1910[b]	52.90	56.36	N/A	30.28	49.09	10.59	43.61	26.08
1920	57.02	54.75	32.95	35.03	51.22	28.95	46.91	24.07
1930	62.39	59.60	48.88	42.92	59.89	35.40	54.82	19.47
1940	64.91	65.05	62.92	52.35	67.46	53.99	62.84	15.11
1950	69.64	69.82	69.74	62.64	72.57	67.63	69.63	9.93
1960	72.78	73.83	71.64	64.94	75.55	62.72	72.32	10.61
1970	73.19	76.10	71.79	67.46	77.30	76.88	73.97	9.84
Male	70.68	74.78	70.21	65.05	75.71	75.25	72.03	10.66
Fem.	76.04	77.60	75.54	69.91	78.93	78.39	76.37	9.02

[a]The range takes into account the highest minus the lowest and excludes "Others." [b]The authors of the assessment report caution the reader to be skeptical of the 1910 data as a breakdown into ethnicities is speculative.

Source: From the *Native Hawaiian Education Assessment Project* (p. 43) by Kamehameha Schools/Bishop Estate, 1983, Honolulu: Kamehameha Press. Copyright 1983 by the Kamehameha School/Bishop Estate. Reprinted by permission.

of the population in 1950 and 16.2% of the population in 1960 (see Table 4.7). It is important to note, however, that this census is based on reported Native Hawaiian identity, during a time when being Hawaiian was not popular. Nevertheless, the statistical story is significant in that the numbers alone reflect an eventual confrontation between the two majority ethnic groups, the Euro-American and the Japanese, which would further alienate the Native Hawaiian from a voice in governing and their cultural identity.

The Native Hawaiian and Part-Hawaiian population not only made up the minority population in relation to Euro-Americans and Japanese, but also had the shortest life span between 1910 and 1970 (see Table 4.8) and the highest death rate (see Fig. 4.1). Hawaiians had become the minority in their homeland. The impact of this long-term trend was finally revealed when the United States Census (1960) determined that since the numbers of Native Hawaiians were so small and of no consequence, their data would be listed under "Other."

A dwindling population, coupled with social policies that emphasized a lack of cultural plurality, accounts for some of the reasons why Whites and then Japanese were able to gain governing power over the Native Hawaiian. Statistics reveal that in 1902 Native Hawaiian and Part Hawaiians comprised 68.8% of votes cast in local elections. However, by 1940, their dwindling numbers found their contributions to electoral votes a mere 14.7%.[26] This underscores the very idea that the Native Hawaiian had very little political voice by the 1930s.

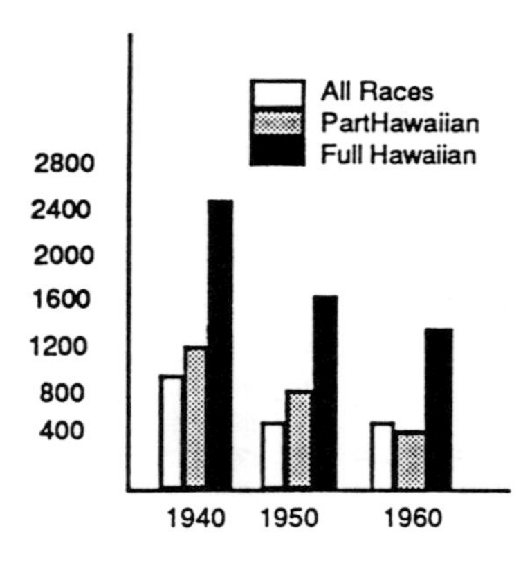

FIG. 4.1. Rates of death per 100,000 residents. From the Native Hawaiian Education Assessment Project (p. 43) by the Kamehameha Schools/Bishop Estate, 1983, Honolulu: Kamehameha Press, Copyright 1983 by the Kamehameha Schools/Bishop Estate. Reprinted by permission.

Economic Status of Native Hawaiians

Although Native Hawaiian and Part-Hawaiian voters comprised at least half of the voting population into the 1920s, their participation in politics at the turn of the century had been channeled by Republican domination in the voting polls of 1902 and the subsequent appointment of Republican Territorial Governors. The political strategy of using popular Native Hawaiians (e.g., Jonah Kuhio Kalanianaole) as figureheads for the Republican Party had successfully gained Native Hawaiian support for the Republicans. Over time, the effectiveness of the Republicans' political values, which were institutionalized in social programs such as the schools, fostered low Native Hawaiian representation in professional occupations and high representation in laborer classified employment and low-income brackets.

Table 4.9 illustrates that tracking Native Hawaiians and other ethnic groups into agricultural and industrial lines enabled the governing elite to maintain class and race separation through employment. Additionally, tracking and segregation in schools kept undesirables out of the professional arena.

An examination of Tables 4.9 and 4.10 reveals that only a small percentage of the population in 1950 was represented in gainfully employed professional positions (7.3%). Of this small percentage, Hawaiians and Part-Hawaiians were represented by 742 men, while Euro-Americans flooded the professions with 4,232 (48% of the total jobs), followed by the Japanese with 2,506 (about 30% of the total, see Table 4.10). Underrepresented in professional fields, Native and Part-Hawaiians, by 1950, were overrepresented in labor occupations. Table 4.9 illustrates that the majority of Hawaiians employed were represented in labor occupations in 1910 at 75.4%, in 1930 at 61.7%, and in 1950 at 54.6%. By 1977, only 10.6% of Hawaiians were employed as laborers, reflecting the general decrease in these types of jobs in the state (i.e., only 8.0%).

TABLE 4.9
Gainfully Employed Males—Laborers

	1910		*1930*		*1950*		*1977*	
Ethnicity	*N*	%[a]	*N*	%	*N*	%	*N*	%
Hawaiian & Part-Haw.	4,609	75.4	3,284	61.7	2,958	54.6	1,980	10.6
White	6,898	43.8	2,440	34.5	2,235	5.1	2,917	3.6
Chinese	6,680	48.6	2,088	24.4	431	5.3	40	.3
Japanese	33,871	76.8	12,754	35.9	7,482	16.3	3,433	5.2
Filipino	0		41,075	90.1	13,387	52.5	4,400	19.9
Korean	0		1,142	53.4	160	11.4	221	9.2
Puerto Rican	0		1,455	78.2	851	34.4	408	28.3
Other	5,355	89.7	173	81.2	787	21.2	1,683	9.4
Total	57,413	65.0	64,411	53.6	27,277	22.5	16,124	8.0

[a]% refers to Total % of the specific ethnic population.
Source: From *Hawai'i's People* 4th Ed. (p. 85) by Andrew W. Lind, 1980, Honolulu: University of Hawai'i Press. Copyright 1980 by the University of Hawai'i Press. Adapted by permission.

Table 4.10 reveals stark inequities—with only 6.9% (in 1977) of the Native Hawaiian population represented in professional occupations ahead of the Puerto Rican, Korean, and Filipino. Furthermore, supporting data continued to find Native and Part-Hawaiians excluded from top-managerial and middle-managerial positions.[27] Stark ethnic differences in employment reveal that Native Hawaiians comprised the majority of craftsman, foreman, operative, and service worker positions. In manage-

TABLE 4.10
Gainfully Employed Males—Professional

	1930		*1950*		*1977*	
Ethnicity	*N*	%[a]	*N*	%	*N*	%
Hawaiian & Part-Haw.	535	10.8	742	9.9	1,916	6.9
White	1,743	19.8	4,232	16.9	11,223	21.2
Chinese	259	3.0	876	10.7	1,344	19.8
Japanese	1,204	3.4	2,506	5.5	11,983	18.1
Filipino	268	.6	296	1.2	1,344	6.3
Korean	58	2.7	121	8.6	187	7.8
Puerto Rican	20	1.1	15	.9	59	4.1
Other	32	4.2	138	3.7	1,788	10.5
Total	4,119	3.4	8,829	7.3	30,851	15.3

[a]% refers to Total % of ethnic population.
Source: From *Hawai'i's People* 4th Ed. (p. 87) by Andrew W. Lind, 1980, Honolulu: University of Hawai'i Press. Copyright 1980 by the University of Hawai'i Press. Adapted

TABLE 4.11
Percentage Distribution of Male Income by Race, 1949

Ethnicity	*Under $1,000*	*$1,000–$4,999*	*$5,000–$9,999*	*$10,000 and up*	*Median Income*
Hawaiian	22.5	71.3	5.2	0.1	$2,368
White	9.7	71.0	15.6	3.7	$2,856
Chinese	17.6	68.0	10.9	3.5	$2,964
Japanese	18.6	74.8	5.1	1.5	$2,427
Filipino	18.7	80.2	0.1		$1,995
Total	16.6	71.6	10.0	1.8	$2,340

Source: From *Hawai'i's People* 4th Ed. (p. 106) by Andrew W. Lind, 1980, Honolulu: University of Hawai'i Press. Copyright 1980 by the University of Hawai'i Press. Adapted by permission.

rial positions, the Hawaiian was clearly ahead of only one other ethnic group, the Filipino. Tables 4.11 and 4.12 illustrate this high representation of Native and Part-Hawaiians in service and laborer occupations and lower-income brackets.

In both 1949 and 1977, a majority of Native Hawaiians fell into the low to middle income bracket. In 1949 (see Table 4.11), 93.8% of Native Hawaiians' income was less than $4,999 a year ($2,368 median income), and in 1977 (see Table 4.12) this trend continued, with 75.8% of the Native Hawaiian population earning an income of less than $19,000 (median $10,280).

In comparison with other ethnic groups in 1949 (see Table 4.11), Native Hawaiians were the highest group represented with incomes of less than

TABLE 4.12
Percentage of Families by Income, 1977

Ethnicity	*Under $5,000*	*$5,000–$9,999*	*$10,000–$19,999*	*$20,000–$24,999*	*$25,000 & Over*	*Median Income*
Hawaiian	10.5	28.3	37.0	11.0	13.4	$10,280
White	3.3	25.4	35.3	12.9	23.3	$15,140
Chinese	2.6	8.3	34.3	19.6	35.2	$21,237
Japanese	2.2	11.9	38.1	19.3	28.5	$19,475
Filipino	7.1	29.2	45.8	8.1	9.8	$12,401
Korean	4.8	15.8	31.5	28.9	19.0	$19,330
Puerto Rican	8.5	43.4	40.5	3.3	4.2	$ 9,774
African American	5.9	40.4	40.0	4.5	9.3	$10,838
Samoan	17.5	52.8	23.6	6.1	0	$ 8,093
Total	4.8	22.0	37.3	14.2	21.7	$15,837

Source: From *Hawai'i's People* 4th Ed. (p. 106) by Andrew W. Lind, 1980, Honolulu: University of Hawai'i Press. Copyright 1980 by the University of Hawai'i Press. Adapted by permission.

$1,000 and third highest with incomes between $1,000 and $4,999. Hawaiians were far behind the White and Chinese within the $5,000 or above categories. This trend is repeated into 1977 (see Table 4.12), with 10.5% of Hawaiians earning less than $5,000. The only other ethnic group with a higher percentage is the Samoan. Together, these figures begin to provide strong evidence that, over time, the various political, social, and economic programs of state leadership did nothing to enhance the economic standing of this group. This is an issue we will return to in the next chapter.

Academic Achievement: "Speak American, Think American, Act American"

By the time the Democratic Party took control in the middle 1950s and Hawai'i was declared a state in 1959, the foreign element had significantly stripped Native Hawaiians of their cultural integrity through depopulation, land control, and social directives instituted through the schools. Class divisions, evident in both occupational–income data and feelings of inferiority, compelled Hawaiians to reject the pride of their past and assimilate the negative stereotypes of the present.

Much like the Native Americans, Native Hawaiian children were considered to be stupid, lazy, and troublemakers. As it goes with many stereotypes, there were a number of Hawaiian children who did not try to excel in the U.S. schools. They may have been thought to be less capable than their Asian or White classmates. There were many Native Hawaiians who did succeed, but most did not identify themselves as Hawaiian. John Burns is quoted in Bell's (1984) text commenting on cultural identification:

> Now, even today, the thing to be is a Haole, you know what I mean? To acculimate [*sic*] yourself to our society is to act like a Haole and Haoles-so-called haoles-from the good old days when they were always the better bred people and so forth. . . . it was never good to be on the other side of the fence. (p. 115)

A similar story was unfolding on the continental United States and the Caribbean Sea. Education failed Native Hawaiians, Native Americans, Mexican Americans, and Puerto Ricans because policy and practice moved against the indigenous cultural patterns. Two divergent perspectives regarding education for nonEuro-American children emerged at this time. Progressive education grounded in U.S. ideology sought to build upon a child's capacity to assimilate the ideas of scientific knowledge and social progress. This movement, however, lacked attention to issues of race and cultural difference. The second stream of thought concluded that ethnicity limited learning. From this thinking came vocational education and IQ tests, which helped institutionalize segregation in schools. Regarding the

IQ test, Gonzalaez (1990) wrote that it "upholds the right of a minority to govern the majority not by virtue of free choice and election, but by virtue of natural selection" (p. 64).

Whether consciously or not, many Hawaiians avoided the competition and conservatism of the U.S. schools because participation meant relinquishing what little they had left of their heritage. It meant becoming a "coconut" (brown on the outside and white on the inside). Because of this separateness, the Native Hawaiian adult lacked the economic and political skills and integration necessary to achieve social change or economic stability. Nevertheless, Native Hawaiians had overall good attendance in schools through the 1950s and had a higher English literacy rate than other ethnic groups in Hawai'i through 1930 (see Table 4.13). For example, 1940 graduation rates for high school students was about 25% against 20% of Hawaiians (United States Census, 1940). College graduation rates, however, were different. In 1940, 4% graduated from college in the United States against 2% for Native Hawaiians (United States Census, 1940). This supports our thesis that Native Hawaiians were not only highly capable of intellectual work, but that families and values continued to encourage children to learn in Western schools despite often oppressive structures that marginalized them economically and culturally.

Although the early 1900s suggest a high literacy rate among Native Hawaiian and Part-Hawaiian youth, one needs to realize that most Chinese, Japanese, Korean, Filipino, and Puerto Rican youth were struggling with language differences and ability to attend school, as most worked or lived on the plantations. By this accounting, many ethnic minorities would not have been termed literate. However, many of the Asian-derived

TABLE 4.13
Percentage of Literate School-Age (10 years) or Older People, by Ethnicity, 1910–1930

Ethnicity	*1910*	*1920*	*1930*
Hawaiian	95.3	97.0	96.6
Part-Hawaiian	98.6	99.2	99.3
Portuguese	74.6	81.1	90.3
White	96.5	99.2	99.7
Chinese	67.7	79.0	84.3
Japanese	65.0	79.2	87.3
Korean	74.1	82.7	82.4
Filipino	66.4	53.3	61.5
Puerto Rican	26.8	53.3	68.0
Total Population	73.2	81.1	84.9

Source: From *Hawai'i's People* 4th Ed. (p. 94) by Andrew W. Lind, 1980, Honolulu: University of Hawai'i Press. Copyright 1980 by the University of Hawai'i Press. Adapted by permission.

populations, who valued education and saw it as a means for upward mobility, would soon take advantage of public schooling and excel at all levels of education.

Table 4.14 shows a large percentage of Hawaiian and Part-Hawaiian teens attending Hawai'i's public schools between 1910 and 1950. The low percentage of attendance among Whites is due to private and mainland school attendance. The data partly reveal the issue of continued school segregation in Hawai'i's schools. Although there is no clear ethnic majority, different ethnic groups have been traditionally concentrated in particular types of schools (e.g., public or private) and in particular geographic locations. With so many Hawaiian children in U.S. public schools, efficient acculturation became a relatively easy task as long as the curriculum was controlled. The instruction and course requirements, as have been described earlier, left much to be desired in the area of academic development. In fact, a Kamehameha Boys School alumnus wrote about the curriculum at this all-Hawaiian school:

> The assumption is made by the school authorities that the mind of the Hawaiian boy is capable of developing up to a certain stage only and no further. . . . The school authorities are making every effort to strengthen the industrial work of the pupils; that is very commendable; but the training of the hand must be accompanied by the proper training and development of the head. (Daws, 1969, p. 301)

Being U.S. citizens and speaking English were no guarantee that a Native Hawaiian would succeed. However, the schools were successfully teaching young Native Hawaiians the value of individual labor, private ownership, and individual responsibility for economic and spiri-

TABLE 4.14
Percentage of 16- and 17-Year-Olds Attending School by Ethnicity, 1910–1950

Ethnicity	*1910*	*1920*	*1930*	*1940*	*1950*
Haw./Part-Haw.	96.4	98.8	92.6	97.6	78.1
White	25.9	34.0	49.1	58.6	77.4
Chinese	57.3	69.1	76.7	88.9	94.1
Japanese	29.9	35.1	54.3	72.8	94.1
Filipino	21.7	17.6	24.2	50.2	81.8
Korean	53.1	65.4	68.0	NA	NA
Puerto Rican	8.4	9.3	15.2	NA	NA
Total Population	35.9	40.1	51.4	67.1	85.8

Source: From *Hawai'i's People* 4th Ed. (p. 96) by Andrew W. Lind, 1980, Honolulu: University of Hawai'i Press. Copyright 1980 by the University of Hawai'i Press. Reprinted by permission.

tual well-being. The long-held Native belief in community (*'ōhana*) and communal responsibility was giving way to a citizenry that asked, "How much can *I* accumulate?" Vocational skills, seen as the Native's promise to individual wealth and well-being, in reality, only limited access to social mobility and full participation in accruing economic and political benefits.

CONCLUSION: AMERICANIZATION AS AN INSTITUTIONALIZED VALUE

As we have developed in this chapter, the dominant institution that emerged during our analysis of this period was Americanization. This cultural value was translated into educational policies that had as their goal the acculturation of Native Hawaiians and other ethnic children into a social order demanding English speech, adherence to U.S. social and political ideals, and industrious labor in their assigned jobs. Students learned their social places, were taught to avoid confrontation and competition with the Euro-Americans, and to accept without protest the laws and regulations of the Territory of Hawai'i. In this, educational policy was successful. Other consequences were that Native Hawaiians were heavily represented in lower social classes, laborer or service occupations, middle to lower income brackets, and in non-English Standard Schools.

The paternalistic attitude of Hawai'i's early Territorial years resulted in a dual-school system which claimed that high standards in education would be met by an English Standard School system. In reality, however, this policy was merely a mask for continued racial stratification that placed the Euro-American at the top and all other ethnic groups at the bottom. The Americanized curriculum pushed efficiency in speaking standard English and stressed the qualities of industriousness, morality, and the notion of a passive and consenting citizenry. The notion of white superiority translated to actual classroom activity committed Native Hawaiian children to an education that denied them the opportunity to take pride in their Hawaiian heritage and become involved with the governance of their land.

With the influx of progressive teachers from the continental United States and a national sweep in political power by the Democratic Party in the 1930s, however, such beliefs as equal opportunity and wider participation in the scope of political and school governance found their way into the secondary school curriculum. What was occurring in the classroom is best expressed by Mitsuyuki Kido, one of the first teachers of Japanese descent:

> I identified myself as a Democrat—I was enamored of FDR and his idealism. I tried to point out to my students some of the inequalities in the Hawaiian society—the political, economic and social structure was so controlled by a small group that I felt that the American dream of a free, democratic society was the thing we should try to achieve in Hawai'i. (as cited in Bell, 1984, p. 104)

On the political scene and in the classroom, attitudes were gradually changing, but the events of World War II catapulted Hawai'i into the global movements of the 20th century. The war opened Hawai'i's window of economic opportunity, offering industrialists and entrepreneurs a home. It was a catalyst that promoted social and political change, beginning with growing union power that instilled the belief among the citizenry that their dissatisfaction could be successfully addressed through a united front. Coupled with the growing strength of the Nisei-backed Democratic Party, the Republican Oligarchy's grip on Hawai'i's politics was broken by 1962.

The Young Democrats' political protest against inequity resulted in the end of the dual-school system, textbook fees, and the election of a statewide school board. What were the overall results of this obvious political turmoil? Our findings suggest that, for all the talk which postulated a politics of protest against the overpowering control of the Republican Oligarchy, governance and decision-making processes remained largely unchanged. The values of parity and choice, which were the banners under which the Young Democrats fought, appeared to be rhetoric through which the public was persuaded to allow another elite group to govern. With the possibility of statehood looming, Hawai'i's school curriculum in the 1950s and into the 1960s was more heavily imbued with the fervor of Americanism then ever before. School reform was not defined as a change in school governance, but merely appeared in laws and policies that gave the appearance of allowing other groups to participate within the established system.

As we have grown to expect, therefore, despite turmoil surrounding the educational system brought on by periodic shifts in the public's perceptions over who should govern, schools remain remarkably resistant to social and political turmoil. In fact, this has been one of the hallmarks of the federalist system in the United States; that is, despite tension produced at its various levels (federal, state, local) or between its various branches (executive, legislative, judicial), the system itself has proved to be remarkably flexible in withstanding economic, social, and political turmoil (e.g., the Depression, Civil War, Civil Rights Movement).

The system of school governance, which mirrors the federalist system in its attachments to senior governments (Heck, 1991–1992; Iannaccone, 1977), also appears to mirror this flexibility. Despite turnover in policymakers apparent during this era of Hawaiian politics, schools were still managed by a professional bureaucracy through its centralized, single state-wide school district. Reform was more incremental, aimed at Americanization, and implemented through institutionalizing the curricular tracking, the control of teachers and the substance of the curriculum, and the maintenance of centralized financial control—while appearing to promote greater public input in decision making (e.g., through an elected board of education).

Table 4.15 presents a final compilation of school laws across the era (1905–1969) and highlights the domination of efficiency (106 of 138 actions) across the seven domains of school policy. In contrast, we can observe the conspicuous absence of policy activity reflecting equity. Thus, for all the Democratic Party rhetoric of equity for all races, there was not one mention of parity in any of the school laws between 1947 and 1969. The distribution of school policy mechanisms across the domains reveals the dominance of efficiency in governance and finance, and the value of quality is largely focused on the program domain, regardless of whether the Republican Oligarchy or the Democratic Machine dominated the policymaking elite. In contrast, actions reflecting values of choice and equity were due primarily to the efforts of special interest (pressure) groups such as the HEA.

Plank and colleagues (1996) argued that educational reforms adopted during this era in most large school systems in the United States were in response to an increase in the popular demand for schooling and the growing importance of industry and services. Moreover, the schools were an effective means of indoctrinating students of immigrants into the U.S. way of life. Educational changes to the curriculum were accompanied by shifts in governance and administration. More complex systems required an expanding professional staff. Because reformers were linked to a national network of like-minded experts (Tyack & Cuban, 1995), proposals

TABLE 4.15
Distribution of School Laws and Policies, 1905–1969

Year	*Quality*	*Efficiency*	*Equity*	*Choice*	*Total*
1905	13	32	1	1	47
1924	4	40	1	2	47
sub-total	17	72	2	3	94
1947	3	3	0	0	6
1960	1	2	0	2	5
1966	3	24	0	1	28
1969	0	5	0	0	5
sub-total	7	34	0	3	44
Total	24	106	2	6	138

for change were modeled on innovations adopted elsewhere. Thus, local figures had relatively limited impact on the reform agenda, and local politics had only a marginal impact on the character of educational change (Plank et al., 1996).

As Tyack and Cuban (1995) argued, because broader values do become institutionalized, especially if they have been added on to the existing structure without disturbing the system greatly, schools do change over time. Certainly, this is the case in our analysis of Hawai'i's educational past. Broad cultural values defined the development of English Standard Schools and, similarly, contributed to their demise. Eventually, with the end of World War II and the threat of the Cold War subsiding, the need for Americanization of immigrants gave way to an increasing spirit of diversity. As our analysis demonstrates, however, it would be a mistake to conclude that there is a close correspondence between broad institutions that define gradual changes in schools and the often sharp political rhetoric calling for reform in the schools. In fact, (as in other parts of the United States) despite the political rhetoric of the time, most school reforms in Hawai'i during the 1950s and early 1960s did not alter the structure or operation of the educational system. Despite reformers' good intentions, schools in the United States have remained relatively difficult to change in major ways (Tyack & Cuban, 1995). With the decline of feelings about Americanization, however, change is unfolding that is realizing some benefit for Native Hawaiians—an issue to which we turn our attention in the next chapter.

In my mind, as I reflect on my own experiences as well as those of my mother's and father's generation, I can understand the sense of powerlessness and hopelessness that characterized Native Hawaiians during the first half of the 20th century. Within the framework of broader social, political, and economic values, the schools emerged as a primary determinant of a Native youth's choices in life. Therefore, the welfare state ideology that swept the 48 contiguous states provided equality of opportunity within a centralized, bureaucratic hierarchy that measured success through U.S. standards of academic success. For the most part, Hawai'i was caught in this current of Americanization; if one wanted to be considered successful, one became "American." The mirror, however, would also reflect growing resistance movements by Native Americans, African Americans, Mexican Americans, and Asian Americans—groups that had been long marginalized by the policymaking system.

ENDNOTES

1. Other English Standard Schools included: Stevenson Junior High, Lincoln Elementary, and Lincoln Junior High (in Honolulu), Leilehua Elementary (in rural O'ahu), Standard Elementary of Maui (on Maui), and Hilo Standard Elementary (in Hilo).

2. Public schools in Hawai'i are directly funded through legislative action.
3. This concept is further developed in chapter 3, "Whose Game Do We Play," in E. E. Schattschneider, *The Semisovereign People* (Hindsdale, IL: The Dryden Press, 1960).
4. This text is slanted in favor of Burns and the Democratic Machine.
5. Coffman's political case study provides generous insight into the politics of the 1960s and early 1970s. Through an analysis of two major elections (1962 and 1970), Coffman examined the political mechanics of the Burns administration.
6. This included primarily Japanese, Chinese, Portuguese, Filipino, and Part-Hawaiian groups.
7. Information concerning the Young Democrats was retrieved from numerous sources, among them texts by Roger J. Bell, *Last Among Equals: Hawaiian Statehood and American Politics* (Honolulu: University of Hawai'i Press, 1984), Tom Coffman, *Catch a Wave: A Case Study of Hawai'i's New Politics* (Honolulu: University of Hawai'i Press, 1973), and Lawrence Fuchs, *Hawai'i Pono: A Social History* (New York: Harcourt Brace, 1961).
8. A number of sources were accessed for detailed information about Hawai'i's debate for statehood. Primary sources included: William F. Quinn, "The Politics of Statehood," an essay presented to the Social Sciences Association of Honolulu, printed in the *Hawaiian Journal of History* 18 (1984) 1–12; and Roger J. Bell, "Admission Delayed: The Influence of Sectional and Political Opposition in Congress on Statehood for Hawai'i," *Hawaiian Journal of History* 6 (1972) 45–68.
9. Justus F. Paul, "The Power of Seniority: Senator Hugh Butler and Statehood for Hawai'i," *Hawaiian Journal of History* 9 (1975) 140–147.
10. Statistical information for the Territorial Years seems to be more accurate than years prior to the turn of the century. Most demographic figures for the Asian population came from Andrew W. Lind, *Hawai'i's People* (Honolulu: University of Hawai'i Press, 1967).
11. Student work in the area of Hawai'i's schools and politics was accessed through the University of Hawai'i Library. The studies proved helpful with supportive descriptive and statistical information. One such work was Floy T. Gay, "A Study of the Development of the Senior High School," unpublished master's thesis, University of Hawai'i (1945).
12. Wist quoted *The Report of the Hawaiian Commission Appointed in Pursuance of the Joint Resolution for Annexing the Hawaiian Islands to the United States* (Washington, DC: Government Printing Office, 1898), pp. 132–133, 136.
13. Found in the State Archives of Hawai'i, the following pamphlet proved helpful in adding perspective to the management of Hawai'i schools. Robert Littler, *The Government of the Territory of Hawai'i* (Honolulu: Honolulu Star Bulletin, 1927).
14. See Willard Givens, "Elementary Schools," statement in the *Report of the Superintendent of the Department of Public Instruction for the Biennial Ending December 31st, 1924* (Honolulu: Dept. of Public Instruction, 1924), p. 17.
15. See David Livingston Crawford, "Statement of Policy," in the *Biennial Report of the Department of Public Instruction for the Years 1931–1932* (Honolulu: Dept. of Public Instruction, 1932). Many of the Inspectors added introductions to their biennial reports which provided insight into their belief of what purpose schooling had.
16. See Lawrence Fuchs, *Hawai'i Pono: A Social History* (New York: Harcourt Brace), p. 277.
17. See Phillip R. Brieske, "A Study of the Development of Public Elementary and Secondary Educations in the Territory of Hawai'i," unpublished doctoral dissertation, University of Washington.
18. Miles Carey, an advocate of progressive education, was principal of McKinley High School in Honolulu between 1924 and 1948 and initiated the core curriculum in 1930. He was known to be the spokesperson for the rights of the ethnically oppressed.

19. See Territory of Hawai'i, *Governor's Committee on Education: Survey of Schools and Industry* (Honolulu: The Printshop, 1931). This report is better known as the Prosser Report.
20. Phillip Richard Brieske, "A Study of the Development of Public Elementary and Secondary Educators in the Territory of Hawai'i," unpublished doctoral dissertation, University of Washington (1961). This dissertation provided excellent secondary data recording school activity, governance, problems, and movements during the Territorial years.
21. For more information on the Prosser Report see: Ralph Steuber, "Hawai'i: A Case Study in Development Education 1778–1960," unpublished doctoral dissertation, University of Wisconsin (Ann Arbor, MI: University Microfilms, 1964); and David Crawford, "Statement of Policy," *Biennial Report of the Department of Public Instruction, 1931–1932* (Territory of Hawai'i: Dept. of Public Instruction, 1932).
22. School laws cited were content analyzed in order to assess what values were embedded in them and to what extent the political culture effected the actual policy.
23. Department of Public Instruction for the Territory of Hawai'i, *Policy Handbook, Education Policy, 1931* (Territory of Hawai'i: Author, 1931). This is an unbound collection of memos that was put together with other archival data on Hawai'i's Territorial Schools found in the Hawai'i State Archives.
24. Information regarding McKinley High School can be found in Henry Y. K. Tom, L. Y. Furushima, & P. T. Yang, (eds.), *A Hundred Years: McKinley High School 1865–1965* (Honolulu: McKinley High School Press, 1965).
25. For more information see *A Report of the Governor's Conference on Education* (Honolulu: Territorial Department of Public Instruction, 1955).
26. Source: Andrew W. Lind, *Hawai'i's People, 4th Ed.* (Honolulu: University of Hawai'i Press, 1980, p. 102).
27. For further information refer to Andrew W. Lind, *Hawai'i's People, 4th Ed.* (Honolulu: University of Hawai'i Press, 1980).

Kindergarten Class, 1950s, students learning about George Washington and King Kamehameha I. Photo courtesy of the Hawai'i State Archives.

"The Democrats: President J. F. Kennedy, Governor J. Burns, and Senator D. Inouye." Photo courtesy of the Hawai'i State Archives.

'ELIMA

Toward a New Hawaiian Voice, 1970s–1990s

The cause of Hawai'i and independence is larger and deeper than the life of any man connected with it. Love of country is deep-seated in the breast of every Hawaiian, whatever his station.

—Queen Lili'uokalani (1964, p. 311)

HA'AWINA NO'ONO'O

Since the 1960s, Native Hawaiians—myself included—have been working for both a personal and collective sovereignty. My own professional journey these past 20 years has brought me to the writing of this book. This experience has pushed me to come to understand historical events from a Native Hawaiian perspective—not through colonized eyes. I believe I have claimed my voice as a Native Hawaiian warrior and will always advocate for a sovereign Hawaiian spirit. To understand this Native Hawaiian journey of sovereignty, we must look back to the late 1700s.

In the minds of Native Hawaiians, prior to the arrival of the haole, the ali'i (high chief) had ultimate authority. This position, however, was not translated as personal or individual power, but as authority that was channeled through the ali'i, by nā akua (gods), to the larger Native population. In short, the ali'i was the trustee of the 'āina (land), its resources, and its people. This ideology had been interwoven into the culture for over a thousand years through reciprocal rights and obligations—that is, while the maka'āinana (commoners) were obligated to work for the ali'i, the ali'i was charged to care for the maka'āinana, who could move about the 'āina (land) freely.

The arrival of the Whites in the latter 18th century brought the contrasting ideology of private ownership of land which, to Westerners, was a measure of authority, power, and economic success. This concept of land ownership was indeed a foreign idea to the Native Hawaiian. Common belief among the Whites was that the Natives had too much land for their individual needs. The land requirements for large-scale agriculture (e.g., sugar cane), however, required large tracts of land. Although Native Hawaiians fought to maintain their reciprocal relationship with the ali'i and the ability to move about freely, they were at a clear disadvantage. Through the process of 'aihue, or legalized theft of land, large corporate entities occupied what they claimed to be abandoned land—land not currently worked by Native Hawaiians.

Proving abandonment in Hawai'i's courts has always found the Whites winners. In 1898, 2 million acres of Hawai'i's land were ceded to the United States as part of annexation. When the islands were given statehood in 1959, the federal government retained 400,000 acres for military and national parks; 1.35 million acres was given to the newly formed state. Currently, the United States Federal government owns about 40% of the land in Hawai'i, and, of the remaining 60%, six land owners (Bishop Estate, Parker Ranch, Dole Foods, Samuel Damon Estate, Alexander and Baldwin, Inc., and C. Brewer and Co.) control 40% (State of Hawai'i, 1993). How to redistribute these lands to the people has been a source of continued debate.

The overthrow of the Hawaiian Monarchy which legalized the land-grabbing actions of foreigners stirred the pride of the Native Hawaiian. In 1993, on the 100th anniversary of the overthrow, the first elected Native Hawaiian Governor, John D. Waihe'e III, raised the Hawaiian flag over the State Capitol. The United States flag was not flown. This same year, the United States Legislature passed, and President Clinton signed, a formal apology to the Hawaiians for the overthrow of the Hawaiian Kingdom.

Although federal recognition is valuable, further redress is still due the Native Hawaiian, given that the move toward statehood was devoid of their voice. The plebiscite vote in 1959 presented two choices: statehood or continuation of territorial status. Because there was no option for sovereignty, this vote violated international law and Article 73 of the United States Charter under which Hawai'i was placed in 1945. Native Hawaiians could not participate in the vote unless they were citizens of the United States; few were. Military personnel stationed in the islands, however, could and did vote. In 1959, the vote records that statehood won.

Today's current movement toward Hawaiian sovereignty signals the distrust and anger of a populace who is tired of being pushed to the margins. Hawaiians, much like Native Americans, have suffered great injustices caused by intolerable social policies. They have garnered no social capital or cultural capital to define their futures, thereby failing miserably in schools and other social and political activity. As a renaissance of Hawaiian thought and language takes hold, we must embrace King Kamehameha I's law of the splintered paddle; that is, we must frame our policies, actions, and relationships around the common good—not the individual good. This requires a rethinking of the assumptions which have built our social, political, educational, and economic institutions. It means valuing community responsibility, respect for environment, and reciprocity.

THE PURSUIT OF GREATER SELF-DETERMINATION

The present period chronicles the changing dimensions of the impact of statehood on Native Hawaiians. We have suggested a variety of reasons why larger cultural values became institutionalized in schools across the United States, focusing particularly on education in Hawai'i because of its geographical and cultural uniqueness among the states. Political support for dominant cultural values came from powerful elites that first influenced and then dominated island politics. Educational policy in the previous periods resulted in stripping away, layer by layer, the cultural identity of Native Hawaiians through institutionalizing missionary values and then Americanizing the various ethnic minorities in the Territory. As we suggested, superintendents as supposedly neutral administrators often played a role in the implementation of educational policy.

Our last period of discussion focuses on the impact of an emerging Native Hawaiian voice in politics (e.g., pursuing national sovereignty) and, more specifically, in educational policy (e.g., resulting in Hawaiian studies and Hawaiian language immersion programs in public schools).[1] Of course, the results of this new activism in politics and educational policy have been uneven, and there is still much frustration among Native Hawaiian groups about the state's ability, and political parties' efforts, to address their needs. In contrast to the mostly singular educational voice of the past (e.g., White male superintendents), Hawaiian women have been especially prominent in framing the recent agenda for education and politics. We first look at the effects of a Hawaiian cultural re-awakening on efforts to gain political sovereignty. Next, we examine the general policy system's continued resistance to change with respect to education and, more specifically, Native Hawaiians. Finally, we discuss the effects of this cultural renaissance for educational policies and schooling that addresses the needs of Hawaiians. In particular, Hawaiian cultural awareness and emergent political power have produced curricular changes to infuse Hawaiian culture and language in the schools and, eventually, have led to the creation of several Hawaiian language immersion schools.

The emerging political influence of Native Hawaiians, similar to other minority and Native American efforts, has resulted at least in part from the national civil rights movement during the 1960s (Tyack & Cuban,

1995). Yet, Native American issues extend further than the guarantee of civil rights, including, for example, the definition of a democratic society and its ideals, the consent of the governed, and cultural survival (Chaudhuri, 1985). The thrust of early Native American policy was the dispossession of Natives from their lands, gradually evolving to policy focused on economic and social acculturation to the dominant social order. Over the past few decades, however, federal policy for Native Americans has become more consultative, democratic, and, hence, self-determining (Deloria, 1985).[2] The opening of the policy system to Native American issues, however, has not been without confrontations. Some of the most intense Native American protests occurred in the 1970s when the civil rights movement was waning (Chaudhuri, 1985). In Hawai'i, an increasing awareness and concern for Native Hawaiian issues was formally expressed during the state's Constitutional Convention of 1978 and the resulting new State Constitution.

While the Democratic Party in Hawai'i has continued to maintain almost complete executive and legislative control during the period following WW II and statehood in 1959, the ethnic composition of the governing body reflects a more diverse group of individuals—one that is more similar to the multiculturalism of the state's population (e.g., Japanese American, Hawaiian, Filipino, Euro-American). To illustrate, the 1986 election brought the first governor of Hawaiian ancestry to power. At the end of his terms in 1994, he was replaced by a Filipino governor, and a Japanese American woman was elected Lieutenant Governor.

Current indications suggest that this one-party control over the state's political agenda may be weakening somewhat. For example, the 1994 gubernatorial election produced a viable third-party candidate. The Democratic candidate won, but with only a bit over one third of the popular vote. Similarly, the November 1996 elections jolted the dominance of the Democratic Party, as it lost several seats in the State House and was presented with strong challenges in several other races, including one for the United States Senate seats (One-party dominance, 1996). Against a backdrop suggesting a political system that is somewhat more open than in past periods of our analysis, we explore Native Hawaiians' efforts to re-establish their cultural traditions.

DEVELOPING A NATIVE VOICE IN POLITICS

It is useful to understand educational policy to infuse Hawaiian culture into the public schools within a larger political movement to gain political sovereignty. Native Hawaiians perceive themselves as the least powerful group in Hawai'i politically and economically (Linnekin, 1983).[3] As Linnekin noted, a local saying states that the Japanese have the politics, the

Chinese have the money, the *haoles* have the land, and the Hawaiians, in the words of a song, "get plenty not too much of nutting [nothing]." Perhaps because of their relative standing socioeconomically, other groups in Hawai'i have not specifically organized to gain power and advantage. Hawaiians, therefore, have not really gained politically or economically by using the current political system. To illustrate, when the state elected a Native Hawaiian as governor in 1986, the results of his two terms in office achieved mainly marginal results for Native Hawaiians. As opposed to using the existing educational and political systems to achieve social mobilization and political power (e.g., like the Japanese in Hawai'i), the political models for Hawaiian nationalism (i.e., sovereignty), are other groups that have been colonized and dispossessed such as Native Americans and Puerto Ricans (Linnekin, 1983).

Efforts Toward Sovereignty

Civil rights movements, the search for cultural roots, and other struggles of minority people against colonialism have been central issues in national and international politics over the past few decades (Afaga & Lai, 1994; Deloria, 1985; Hastings, 1988). International governmental and nongovernmental organizations have been working to formulate human rights standards designed to protect indigenous peoples (O'Brien, 1985). In Hawai'i, these issues emerged gradually surrounding the overdevelopment of lands, the rebirth of Hawaiian culture, the preservation of the Hawaiian language, and the establishment of ethnic studies at the University of Hawai'i (Afaga & Lai, 1994).

Several episodes became early rallying points for the Hawaiian nationalist movement. One early focus on Hawaiian culture was the voyage of the *Hokulea* in 1976, where Native Hawaiians sailed a traditional canoe from Hawai'i to Tahiti. This voyage, led by Nainoa Thompson, became a mission of cultural revival for Hawaiians (Linnekin, 1983). The 1970s also saw growing interest in the dances and chants of *wā kahiko* (ancient times). Many *hula hālau* (house of hula instruction) joined in the rebirth of Hawaiian music, dance, and *oli* (chant). Additionally, the creative arts of *lei* making, weaving, carving, and quilting were shared with generations of children and young people. Much of the ancient arts and crafts had been continued in small pockets of the islands—out of the mainstream and far from the colonial shadow. Whereas the 1970s opened the gate for indigenous arts to take their place in the daily life of all Hawaiians, the 1980s saw full appreciation, practice, and respect for creativity and accomplishments of Native Hawaiian artisans and craftsmen.

Another political issue has been the restoration of Hawaiian lands taken during colonization. This was perhaps best exemplified by the unfolding situation concerning the island of Kaho'olawe. This 11-mile-long island was the subject of protests during the 1970s and 1980s, as it was used by the United States Military since 1941 for bombing practice. It was an apt rallying point, as it symbolized the blatant disregard for Hawaiian culture through the bombing of graves and Hawaiian homeland, water, fishing, and hunting rights. On January 3, 1976, the political activist group Protect Kaho'olawe 'Ōhana landed on the island. This was followed by several more occupations by Native Hawaiians. An archaeological survey of 14% of the island resulted in the location of 29 sites which were eligible for the National Register of Historic Places. Further occupations of the island led to arrests and the deaths of George Jarrett Helm, age 26, and James Kimo Mitchell, age 25, between the island of Kaho'olawe and Lāna'i.

Thus, Kaho'olawe became the archetype of Hawaiian land, in the sense that the colonists disregarded Native lands and culture by turning the traditional lands into plantation fields, by building hotels and other high rises, by constructing theme parks, and by bombing sacred cultural sites. Importantly, efforts to regain the land finally paid off. On May 7, 1994, 18 years after the first *'ōhana* landing, the federal government finally gave the 45-square mile island back to the state. Over the past few years, similar protests concerning Hawaiian land rights have centered on the building of a federal freeway through sacred lands to Pearl Harbor and the forceful removal of Hawaiians living in tents on state beaches.

Simultaneously, several Native Hawaiian groups (e.g., Ka Lāhui, Pu'uhonua, Ka Pākaukau, and the Institute for the Advancement of Hawaiian Affairs) have solidified efforts toward gaining political sovereignty, with the issue receiving increased media attention. At the center of the debate is whether the state or Native Hawaiians themselves should control the process of determining sovereignty. Many of the groups representing Native Hawaiians, however, have been splintered, which has hampered efforts to organize. In 1993, a Hawaiian Sovereignty Elections Council was set up by the legislature to oversee a vote on the issue of whether Hawaiians wish to elect delegates to propose a Native Hawaiian government.

The vote drew harsh criticism from *Kānaka Maoli* (indigenous people of Hawai'i) because it appeared to be a state government, rather than a Native Hawaiian, determined process. For example, the Hawai'i Sovereignty Elections Council (HSEC), which defined the voting process, was a governor-appointed board. The governor, while publicly supporting Native Hawaiian rights to self-determination, has also stated that he would not support an independent Hawaiian nation. Furthermore, the ballot presented only one option: "Shall the Hawaiian People elect delegates to propose a Native Hawaiian Government? *'Ae* (yes) *'A'ole* (no)." Native Hawaiian groups condemned this single issue ballot. The concern is that any state connection in the determination of Hawaiian sovereignty might jeopardize Native Hawaiian claims on lands that were ceded to the United States. Several other events cast an uneven shadow on the vote. Because there was a call by Native Hawaiian groups to boycott the vote, 2 weeks prior to the distribution of the ballots the state plebiscite law, which required a majority of qualified votes, was changed to a majority of ballots cast to approve a ballot question. Due to this, the Unrepresented Nations and Peoples Organization (UNPO), based at the Hague, urged the vote to be canceled, citing no real choice in question and insufficient safeguards against voter fraud.

In the fall of 1996 the vote took place. Court maneuvering followed, delaying the outcome of this vote. Mostly, these appeals concerned who in the state (i.e., Native Hawaiians or everyone) should have had the right to vote on the issue. As one Hawaiian attorney suggested, "Once again, history has been repeated. A federal agency has interfered with the emerging voice of the Native Hawaiian people" ("Delay Angers Backers," 1996). When the vote was finally announced, fewer than one half of 85,000 Hawaiians who were sent a ballot voted. A little over half (22,294) voted in favor of moving toward sovereignty.

As a result of this vote, the timeline indicates holding a constitutional convention to discuss options and a vote on a form of sovereignty within two years ("Delay Angers Backers," 1996). The future direction of the sovereignty issue appears in doubt at present, however, because of the lack of validity that the election had in the minds of key Hawaiian groups. They have challenged the vote by pointing out that only a small minority of the 300,000 identified Native Hawaiians (most are of Part-Hawaiian ancestry) around the world were sent ballots. In addition, of those who were asked to vote, a large majority either boycotted or voted "no." The plebiscite law defined by the state legislature, however, validates the minority vote.

At the core of the debate is whether the state or Native Hawaiians themselves should control the self-determination process. There is a long-standing tradition of skepticism regarding the state's efforts to provide open access to services for Native Hawaiians. From the Native Hawaiian perspective, most efforts have been aimed at controlling or isolating them (e.g., through language and separate schooling) or have been half-hearted attempts to redress previous wrongs.

Given this, the fear of Native Hawaiians is that colonial power in the islands will produce a puppet government much like past Hopi arrangements with the United States. In short, the Hopi boycotted a vote, much like the Hawaiians, to reorganize its governing structure, yet the Board of Indian Affairs still imposed a United States defined organizational structure. Native Hawaiians also fear that a governing contingency with alliances to the United States will not act in the interest of Native people, much like the Navajo Grand Council. In 1923, the United States Interior selected representatives as the legitimate governing group for the Navajo. This led to a deal struck between the Navajo and Standard Oil Company which allowed drilling for oil on Navajo land.

This fear is not ungrounded. A little known event prior to the vote has, in fact, delimited a broader definition of self-determination. In 1995, two federal bills (HR671 and S479; see Indian Affairs, 1995a, 1995b) were introduced in the United States Congress. In essence, the bills recognize Native Hawaiians as an "Indian tribe." As we suggested in chapter 1, Hawaiians do not necessarily consider themselves Native Americans. Members of the *Kānaka Maoli* argue that the 1993 Apology Resolution (Public Law 103-150; see Apology, 1993) recognizes Hawaiians as inherently sovereign yet currently deprived by the United States of their right to self-determination (Blaisdell, 1997). They believe that the statehood movement was also fraudulent, suggesting that Hawaiians should pursue sovereignty under international law. This labeling suggests that any form of self-determination other than a nation within a nation could not exist in Hawai'i.

Acceptance of status as Native American limits groups to being wards of the government with only internal autonomy. This means that Native Hawaiians, like Native Americans, will continue to be attached to the colonizing power. History has repeated itself. Native policy continues to be constructed according to the values of policymakers who will seek validation among some contingency of natives.

Hawaiian Homelands

As we developed in earlier chapters, a key aspect of U.S. policy toward native groups during westward expansion and foreign colonialism was the acquisition of needed lands for economic exploitation. The frustration of Native Hawaiians' political efforts to gain social programs to meet their needs is perhaps best demonstrated in the issue of attempting to regain their lands in some small measure. The Hawaiian Homelands Program (also known as the Hawai'i Rehabilitation Act, 1921) has a long history in the State. The program began in 1921 with the intent of parceling out 203,500 acres to Native Hawaiians. Prince Kuhio pushed the act through Congress as a means of saving Hawaiians from urban poverty. The State's largest landowners, however, convinced Territory politicians to do away with general homesteading on Hawai'i's prime lands and, instead, limited awards to 200,000 unwanted acres (Barrett, 1996). In the process, they secured the prime property for themselves. The land was to be drawn from ceded lands (2 million acres that belonged to the Hawaiian crown) turned over to the federal government without compensation to Native Hawaiians when Hawai'i was annexed in 1898. Except for acres set aside for homesteads, most of the remaining ceded lands were eventually returned to the state in 1959.

Historically, a variety of problems and manipulations plagued the program, however. The homestead land consistently turned out to be of very poor quality. Applications were lost, utilities were missing—suggesting that perhaps as much as 2 billion dollars would be needed to create infrastructure for the lands (Barrett, 1996). Moreover, most of the homestead land that has been leased to date has been leased to businesses, with most of these companies owned by nonHawaiians. This practice was started from the beginning of the Hawai'i Rehabilitation Act's implementation. Since 1978, however, the preference has been toward Hawaiian-owned businesses.

While the program has been in existence for 75 years, in that time just 6,379 homestead leases to Native Hawaiians have been awarded (Barrett, 1996). Leases were originally intended to give poor Hawaiians a place where they could make a living off the land. Through the years, as demand rose, however, lot size shrunk correspondingly; from 2 acres, to 1 acre, to 10,000 square feet, to as small as 5,000 square feet today (Barrett, 1996). A recent complaint is that, in the residential communities, with some lots set aside for the Homestead Program, most potential Hawaiian buyers cannot afford the reduced cost. For example, in one project, developers went through 6,000 names on the homestead waiting list before they found 272 who could afford to live in the project.

As of 1997, thousands of people on the list of almost 29,000 applicants have been waiting over 25 years for their land; in fact over 30,000 have died waiting, including former governor John Waihe'e's father. About 75% of Native Hawaiians on the waiting list live below their island's median income (Barrett, 1996). Since a 1994 lands claims settlement that requires the state to pay Hawaiian Home Lands $600 million over the next 20 years, some needed infrastructure is being laid on homestead property. The only Hawaiian governor, John Waihe'e, also gave 16,000 acres of good state land to the program in 1994, before leaving office.

Perceptions that the program is not serving the people have led to a number of protests. In January, 1996, Kahale Smith set fire to himself over frustration with not having his homestead house fixed. This became a rallying point for supporters of the need to fix the program. Toward the end of the year, it was announced that interest-free home loans would be made available to relatively destitute Native Hawaiians to assist them in getting into housing (Office of Hawaiian Affairs, 1996). The program is expected to provide some needed housing for Hawaiians of varying levels of income.

Overall, to many, the Hawaiian Lands Program provides another stark example of how the present efforts to restore to Hawaiians a measure of what was taken have largely failed to meet the level of the Hawaiian community's need. As we suggested, the federal government and several private landowners still control the vast majority of land in Hawai'i. As ceded lands are identified, it has increased debate over the value of such lands and how much should be paid to the Office of Hawaiian Affairs (OHA is owed 20% of the revenues) for land in use and land to be returned to the State of Hawai'i (Kamehameha Schools/Bishop Estate, 1993). Of course, this scenario of broken promises by the federal government was played out countless times with Native Americans through a history of taking land, forced cession of land, land exchanges, relocation to reservations, and, finally, subdivision of reservations and tribal lands into small parcels such that, by the early 1930s, two thirds of tribal lands had passed into White ownership. By the 1940s, the various tribes possessed only 2.3% of the country's land mass (O'Brien, 1985).

THE EDUCATIONAL SYSTEM'S RESISTANCE TO CHANGE OVER TIME

Our previous chapters examining the relationship between political culture and educational policy indicated that, despite considerable local political turmoil, policy change has been more the result of the institutionalization of particular broader cultural values within the public schools. In this section, we consider more closely why the political culture in Hawai'i and its educational system have remained remarkably stable over time, despite periodic calls for educational reform. We focus on several issues relating to the reform of the educational system itself and, more specifically, on problems of educating Native Hawaiian students.

Elsewhere (Benham & Heck, 1994), we classified this culture as traditionalistic or elitist because it emphasized the centralization of authority and privatization of political conflict. As Elazar (1984) argued, in states where political culture is more traditionalistic, the role of government is to maintain accepted social patterns of behavior that are responsive to the needs of the governing elite. Hawai'i's unique history as a people dominated by foreign interests and one-party politics has certainly contributed to a relatively closed political system. Over time, the privatizing of conflict (by limiting or channeling the involvement of others) has led to political and social stability and the acceptance of incrementalism as a policy process.

Because of the State's historical context rooted in colonialism similar to the Southern United States (e.g., plantation living, segregated schooling), fundamental change has been nearly impossible to achieve because of well-established traditions and symbols regarding politics, governance, and school control that are inherent in the state's political culture. The actual effects of increased calls for political and social change during the post-World War II period in Hawai'i were mostly marginal. As we discussed in the previous chapter, this period diluted the power of the Republican oligarchy, provided external economic stimulus through the New Deal mandates, and resulted in the passage of liberal labor laws. The Democrat-controlled governing structure, however, remained highly centralized. For example, both the state legislature and governor's office maintained absolute fiscal control over education.

Despite its geographic separation from the mainland and unique history among the states, however, Hawai'i's educational history mirrored the cultural values of broader policies that had become institutionalized in schools across the United States. These cultural values surrounded important aspects of the educational system such as access to curriculum for particular groups of students, learning of desired social values, and language policy (emphasizing English only) toward diverse groups of voluntary and involuntary immigrants. As Tyack and Cuban (1995) concurred, the basic grammar of schooling including classroom structures, how students are classified, allocated to classrooms, and moved through the system year after year in various vocational or academic tracks has remained remarkably stable over decades. This regularity over time permitted predictable teaching, relatively easy socialization of diverse groups of students, and more efficient control by administrators.

Those who controlled the educational system determined key school policies regarding the language of instruction and the segregated organization of schools that fulfilled different academic missions. In short, the policies reflected a broader organic theory grounded in the values of competitive individualization, labor theory of property and class, and laissez-faire economics. Schools became an effective socialization institution ensuring "stable, peaceful social relations based on the existing social division of labor" (Gonzalaez, 1990, p. 17). The effects of those policies (e.g., English-only instruction, tracking, diminished self-concept, necessity of crossing cultural boundaries to achieve success) were felt over several generations of students educated under them (Huebner, 1985). By the time of Hawai'i's statehood in 1959, the processes of linguistic assimilation (Huebner, 1985) and student socialization to U.S. ways of life were mostly complete. It is not a stretch of the imagination to suggest that the ethnic and linguistic composition of the state were major considerations in the delay toward granting statehood (Huebner, 1985; Tamura, 1994). The issue had arisen periodically, at least since the overthrow of the monarchy in 1893.

Despite policy rhetoric calling for considerable change, the flexibility of Hawai'i's governance structure to bend under stress (by allowing some limited involvement over time, for example, by moving from an appointed to elected board of education) has enabled the various subsystems to isolate tension effectively and remain relatively intact. Efficiency and standardization were goals of a system designed to maintain the islands' colonial social order. Even today, how to modify this entrenched, elite-governed political culture is a major concern for educational policymakers.

This is not to suggest that schools do not undergo change. On the contrary, it appears that policies that emphasize adding to existing structures, ones that are relatively noncontroversial and supported by influential leaders, and ones that are required by laws and easily implemented have the best chance to, or unfortunately do, withstand the test of time (Tyack & Cuban, 1995). As we have come to realize on a national level, however, despite the periodic change, rhetoric surrounding the reform of public education, making fundamental changes to the public schools has remained very difficult.

In our historical and political-cultural analysis of Hawai'i's educational policy system, we found very few political mechanisms in place that encouraged citizen participation in politics and policymaking at the local level across a variety of institutions in the state. While reformers in the United States tinkered with the educational system almost constantly over the 20th century, the resultant changes were mostly incorporated into the existing system incrementally (Tyack & Cuban, 1995). Despite the obvious policy regularities in Hawai'i over time, and although the changes in Hawai'i's public schools have not been far-reaching, our analysis of events unfolding during the last quarter of the 20th century in Hawai'i suggest that there is reason for cautious optimism about the preservation and revitalization of Hawaiian culture and language.

Current Problems and Incremental Changes in Public Education

Consistent with demands for school reform in other states, public dissatisfaction with the schools during the 1980s and 1990s in Hawai'i has produced increasing debate about the structure of the educational system and student outcomes. Currently, the standardized test scores of Hawai'i's students remain near the bottom of the 50 states. Structurally, Hawai'i is unique among the states in terms of the centralization of its public school system, because it is the only state in the United States comprised of one school district.

Considered as a district, however, the system ranks in the Top 10 in size in the United States (Benham & Heck, 1994), with over 180,000 public school students. Moreover, education receives virtually no funding from the local level, but about 10% of its annual funds come from the federal government. In 1978, the state approved an elected Board of Education (moving from an appointed board). Lack of authority at the local level over policy and finance has created public discontent that has been blamed on leaders of the Democratic legislature and the school board (Benham & Heck, 1994).

As we would expect through our earlier analysis of the state's adoption of legitimizing reforms, recent institutional trends across the states to place decision making into local hands have similarly had rippling effects in Hawai'i. For example, site-based management legislation passed in 1989 and charter school legislation in 1994. The site-based management legislation was backed by the Hawai'i Business Roundtable, consisting of Hawai'i's new and old major corporations, with very little representation from educational practitioners and scholars. Although site-based management was mandated as a means to increase community, parent, teacher, and administrative policy participation and to shift accountability to the local school level, the reality was that it was a top-down effort pursued by the State's superintendent through political channels. Orchestrated by Berman and associates (who were very active in achieving similar results in other states) and backed by the Business Roundtable, it represented the adoption of a structure that mimicked a popular educational innovation in the late 1980s.

Proposals for changing the educational system have most often come from groups outside the schools themselves including business interests, politicians, and bureaucrats such as federal policymakers (Tyack & Cuban, 1995). Business still wields considerable policy clout in Hawai'i because of its strong influence on the legislature and governor through, for example, campaign contributions and contracts for state business. Despite rhetoric about lump sum budgeting in site-managed schools, however, fiscal control continues to be centralized. In reality, whereas local schools have applied for a variety of state waivers, only a few isolated schools have actually received waivers that change their local organizational structures and educational practices. For example, one school instituted a 4-day week in an effort to retain teachers; another was becoming a student-centered school, but then became the state's first charter school when that legislation passed.

One preliminary analysis of the implementation of site-based management in Hawai'i's schools indicated that most schools did not target more complex changes at the site level (Tafune, 1994). In retrospect, there has been some lasting marginal impact of the reform, in that the majority (156) of the roughly 240 public schools have implemented site-based management processes with some degree of success. With turnover of superintendents during the 1990s, however, the new state leadership team has pursued an entirely different agenda for school reform. The results of these legislative efforts to free up schools from centralized control, therefore, have been marginal at best. As of November 1996, only two schools had become charter schools (giving them control over their budgets), and some type of site-based management had been implemented in somewhat over half of the state's 240 or so schools.

Other lesser reform efforts have resulted in a relaxing of school attendance policies, with about 7% of Hawai'i's public school students taking advantage of a district exemption program that allows them to attend a school of their choice outside of their neighborhood. Another variation on this theme is that, in two neighborhood schools in Maui, parents supported choice between attending a year-round school or a regular schedule school. This has resulted in a first open enrollment policy between neighborhood schools. It should also be noted that over the past decade or so, about 16% of Hawai'i's schoolchildren attended private schools (DOE, 1994).

It appears, therefore, that there is considerable support in the community for alternative schooling options. Thus, while the structure of governance has been little altered, with the legislature and governor maintaining fiscal control, those outside the elite centralized governance structure have begun to exercise stronger influence in the policy process. Meaningful change to public schools in Hawai'i, however, cannot occur without three elements: the involvement of parents, school or governing boards, professionals, and other agencies that have a stake in the educational welfare of the state; a comprehensive focus that addresses not only structure but also teaching and learning; and reform to institutionalize human diversity in its policies and practices at all levels of school relations.

Problems With Educating Hawaiian Students

As we suggested throughout our presentation, the social stratification in Hawai'i has been played out in politics, economics, and education. Both overtly and covertly, Hawaiians' academic progress over much of the public schools' past was impeded by the structure of classrooms and access to curriculum. The believed superiority of the dominant culture led to classroom activities that negated or denied different cultural traditions.

Researchers over the past decade have come to understand in greater detail the concept of cultural boundaries and how they impact on learning (e.g., Banks, 1988; Ogbu, 1992). For example, D'Amato (1988) identified ways in which peer culture among Hawaiian students is often in conflict with the structures and processes of learning in classrooms. Hawaiian culture favors cooperation, with learning taking place in a variety of informal and formal settings. Classroom structures, however, often foster individual competition, for example, through the assigning of individual grades and actions to gain the teacher's attention. In contrast, Hawaiian children's concerns are more toward staying even with each other. Competition forces some to lead, others to follow, while still others become marginalized.

Several examples of cultural differences that are often neglected in formal school settings include the use of Standard English, the avoidance of eye contact, the need to *talk story*, and the value of family privacy. The use of Standard English by Native Hawaiian children often labels them snobbish or sissy among their peers. This can be attributed to the resistance many Native youth feel toward the *haole* and the need to be accepted by the non-*haole*. Speaking pidgin (Hawai'i Creole English), not Standard English, is an integral component of a Native Hawaiian child's identity. Along this line of learned behaviors, Native children are taught *nānā i lalo* or to look down. This is both an action of respect and protection; that is, staring might easily be misinterpreted as giving someone "the stink eye." Often, lack of eye contact is seen as disrespect by unknowing teachers.

Lack of understanding of Native norms can also lead to novice teachers emotionally hurting a child. Any hint of harsh criticism or contempt is often detected by Native Hawaiian children who, in general, are socialized to be people-oriented. This *'eha* (hurt) often leads to withdrawal and inattentive behavior, and some students will be more vigilant in expressing their anger. Because Hawaiian children are people-oriented and not subject-oriented, they often talk story, exchanging pleasantries and information. This behavior of talking during class time often leads to tensions between teacher and student. Finally, keeping family issues private is a value often challenged by the schools. Show-and-tell or essays about family activities often require students to reveal information they have been taught not to share. Being *nīele* (inquisitive) is often frowned upon, so children often do not question. For most Native Hawaiian children raised with this value, being questioned is often looked upon skeptically. Most often, sharing in either writing or speech is only done after trust has been substantially established.

If the classroom is sufficiently at odds with the children's peer group dynamics, they may begin challenging teacher authority with forms "acting" (general challenges to teacher authority), often led by children who are not satisfied with their peer group roles (D'Amato, 1988). D'Amato argued that organizational features of schools, as well as perceptions about education on wider processes, create a range of student responses. Some submit to these more immediate structures and processes and go along with the organization, whereas others become more resistant over time, the longer they are in conflict with classroom structures inconsistent with their cultural backgrounds. Moreover, some students may not perceive the relevance of school success to wider social institutions (e.g., fewer Hawaiian students than Asian and Euro-American students plan to attend college) such as obtaining a good job after graduation. Unfortunately, many teachers may respond by becoming more authoritarian and punitive. Over time, students' responses to such structures have implications for their success in learning, their participation in activities, and their interactions with peers and teachers.

Policy Toward the Hawaiian Language

Perhaps more profound on the life chances on Native Hawaiians than the structure of classrooms is the larger issue of language policy. Prior to the overthrow of the monarchy, the instruction in the common schools of Hawai'i's public school system was in Hawaiian. English-only instruction was established in 1896 (Department of Education, 1994). A direct result of this policy was that, during the first two decades of this century, Hawai'i underwent a massive language shift from its indigenous Polynesian language to pidgin (Hawai'i Creole English)[4] as the primary language of Hawaiians and other ethnic groups mixed on a daily basis (Kamana & Wilson, 1996). The legislation, therefore, had devastating effects on literacy, academic achievement, and the use of Standard English among Native Hawaiians (Kamana & Wilson, 1996). Out of 200,000 Native Hawaiians in Hawai'i, for example, the 1990 census listed only 8,872 speakers of Hawaiian.

English-only policies also had effects on other cultural groups in Hawai'i, yet different from the effects on Native Hawaiians. From the early 1900s to the 1960s, the Japanese community constituted a plurality in Hawai'i (Huebner, 1985). After World War II, however, this group began to use education to rise economically, politically, and socially. In contrast to Native Hawaiians, the Japanese were relatively successful in establishing autonomous, community-supported schools to maintain the teaching of Japanese language and culture (Huebner, 1985). This was despite a variety of mandated policies to limit instruction or close the schools throughout the Americanization period (Tamura, 1994). Over time, perhaps because of the value placed on education in the family, Japanese students have done quite well in the public and private school systems.

Since the 1960s, large numbers of immigrants have arrived from the Pacific region, including the Philippines, which has further changed the ethnic composition of the State. Many students who attend public schools speak languages other than English or Hawaiian Creole English (HCE). Although the state and the Department of Education have traditionally regulated the use of the Hawaiian language, they have done little to regulate the use of Hawaiian Creole English (e.g., not recognizing it as a language in the Department of Education). While Hawai'i has one of the highest percentages of immigrants in the United States, however, it was one of the last to apply for federal funds for bilingual education (Huebner, 1985). A culturally diverse population and monolingual attitudes toward language instruction suggest remaining vestiges of the English Standard School system of segregated language education, as well as the belief in exhibiting loyalty and nationalism through abandoning previously held cultural traditions (Agbayani, 1979).[5]

Recent concerns with providing educational experiences that are more culturally and linguistically compatible with students' backgrounds have led to the creation of more comprehensive programs, including the infusion of Hawaiian culture in the schools. For example, many speakers of Hawaiian Creole English (e.g., Native Hawaiians) suffer a mismatch between the culture of the home and that of the school (D'Amato, 1988; Huebner, 1985). The recognition of these issues, coupled with Hawaiians' own efforts to regain their political and economic power, have produced some positive results educationally.

Much of the present politicization surrounding Hawaiian educational issues is focused on the long-term survival of the Hawaiian language. There are a variety of legal and academic arguments that support the right of any minority group to have language instruction in its own language. As evidenced by other native peoples such as the Maori in New Zealand, instruction in English led to a decline in the number of speakers, a disregard for the minority language as a socially desirable language, a decline in self-esteem, and an undervaluing of the culture over time (Hastings, 1988). As we presented in previous chapters, all of these conditions were similarly present in Hawai'i. This leads to a stratification of knowledge or a mismatch between what the dominant system values educationally and what the minority group members perceive as important educationally (e.g., arts, music, and the study of their own culture). Whereas Asian groups in Hawai'i were allowed to establish separate (after school) language schools, although they were at times heavily regulated, instruction in the Hawaiian language has always been the purview of the State and the Department of Education.

Since the 1970s, other native groups such as Native Americans and the Maori have also been moved toward self-determination politically and educationally (Deloria, 1985; Hastings, 1988). Most of the claims in the U.S. context stem from Title VI of the 1964 Civil Rights Act, which bans discrimination on race, color, or national origin in programs and activities receiving federal financial assistance. On the heels of that mandate was the Bilingual Education Act of 1968 (PL 90-247; see Elementary and Secondary, 1967), which specifically mentions Native Americans and Native Alaskans in its definition of limited English proficiency. Further definition also came from the sections of Public Law 90-284, referred to as 1968 Indian Civil Rights Act (Chaudhuri, 1985). Native Hawaiians were first included under the definition of Native Americans in the Community Services Act of 1974 (Hammond, 1988). Several other pieces of federal legislation (e.g., PL 98-524, see Carl D. Perkins, 1984; PL 100-297, see Augustus F. Hawkins, 1988) further defined the relationship of Native Hawaiians to the federal government during the 1980s and 1990s, providing them with access to economic, health, education, and social service benefits. The intent of these has been to help bring a measure of parity and self-sufficiency to Native Hawaiians. Recognition of Native Hawaiians as Native Americans makes them a part of the unfolding debate during the past few decades over such issues as Native American rights, religious practices, access to curriculum and other educational programs, and addressing health problems. Recognition thus ensures a wider political forum for concerns—some of which have reached the Supreme Court. Moreover, the Mother Tongue Bill of 1990 (Native American Languages Act, PL 101-477) focused attention on native groups' rights to maintain their cultural practices and develop their languages through education. As we argued, for Native Hawaiians there is also the critical issue of what type of political sovereignty they may hold.

A key policy dilemma is whether the benefits of maintaining thought and communication in the desired language outweigh the further isolation that may be experienced politically, socially, and economically by not maintaining the dominant language exclusively. Thus, the argument goes against assimilation theory, because the minority retains the right to think and communicate in its own language. Forcing the child to be educated in the majority language leads to poor educational outcomes and placement in lower than justified social position (Hastings, 1988). Hastings further argued, however, that the lack of proficiency in the majority language might lead to a denial of access to justice, promotion in employment, and a sense of psychological inferiority. The issue of language survival must be linked to an absence of discrimination against those who use it.

Related academic arguments are divided on the effects of minority language instruction and its benefits to the child. It is difficult often to disentangle the effects of the actual instruction from nonlinguistic factors such as the surrounding community, curricular, and administrative variables that may also be important (Hastings, 1988). As Hastings concluded, most research suggests that minority language instruction can improve academic performance, as opposed to stating that it actually does.

There are several proposed remedies to preserve the existence of a dominated minority's cultural traditions, language, thought, and self-esteem. These include providing language instruction in the schools, increasing cultural studies of the group as part of the standard public school curriculum, and providing greater organizational control for the group over the educational structure (Hastings, 1988). The key issue becomes: How far must the state go in ensuring this right? In reviewing past Supreme Court cases (e.g., Lau v. Nichols, 1973–1974), the answer seems to depend on the particular minority group, its desire to assimilate or not, and the various historical circumstances surrounding the relationship of the group to the dominant culture. In the Lau case, the Supreme Court reasoned that having the same texts, curriculum, and teachers was not enough if the students did not understand the language of instruction and that instruction to learn that language was not available (Hastings, 1988). On the other hand, minorities have not been successful in arguing that equal opportunity in the Fourteenth Amendment guarantees the right to separate language instruction if remedial instruction in English is offered (Hastings, 1988).

EFFORTS TO INFUSE HAWAIIAN CULTURE INTO THE SCHOOLS

In tracing the reintroduction of Hawaiian language into the public schools it is important to understand which domestic laws apply. With Native Americans, some mandates actually provided for federally funded education (Hastings, 1988), as they have an elevated right to a bilingual education derived from a trust relationship (Annis, 1982). An increased awareness of civil rights, therefore, began to focus attention on the needs of people with limited English, handicaps, and disabilities. Similarly, over the past several decades, the federal government once again moved in the direction of recognizing Native Americans' rights of self-determination (O'Brien, 1985).

In response to pressure from the United States Office of Civil Rights, since 1975 Hawai'i's Department of Education has provided bilingual services to immigrant students. The Office of Bilingual Education and Minority Languages Affairs recognized that Hawaiian Creole English qualified for bilingual education funding under the Elementary and Secondary Education Act (Huebner, 1985). This recognition opened the possibility of providing a more culturally appropriate education for these students, many of whom have a mismatch between the culture of the home and that of the school (Au & Jordan, 1977). One early program to address this need was the Kamehameha Early Education Program (KEEP).

At the same time, significant interest in various aspects of Hawaiian culture began in the late 1960s and early 1970s as part of a movement to support Hawaiian music, hula, and language activities (State of Hawai'i, 1986). Hawaiians and others in the community began to seek the development of programs to save the Native language and culture (e.g., Kupuna Language Program, Hawaiian immersion schools). By 1980, the Hawaiian language had been re-introduced into the public school curriculum on a wider basis (Huebner, 1985). From Article X, section 4 of the State Constitution of 1978:

> The State shall promote the study of Hawaiian culture, history and language.
>
> The State shall provide for a Hawaiian education program consisting of language, culture and history in the public schools. The use of community expertise shall be encouraged as a suitable and essential means in furtherance of the Hawaiian education program. (p. 16)

Hawaiian Studies Program

The Constitution of 1978 established Hawaiian, along with English, as official languages of the State (Department of Education, 1994). At the same time, the Constitution created the Office of Hawaiian Affairs, to oversee a variety of issues related to Native Hawaiians. The initial efforts at placing Hawaiian culture in the public schools centered on curriculum and implementation through a *kupuna* (or elder, native speaker) program. This program was called the Hawaiian Studies Program and was largely a response to the new State Constitution (Afaga & Lai, 1994). Although some aspects of Hawaiian culture had been taught in the curriculum prior to 1980, this program represented an effort to incorporate systematically and sequentially elements of Hawaiian culture including language and the historical development of Hawai'i throughout the public school curricular areas and grade levels. It was designed as a program to be integrated with the regular DOE curriculum for all students in kindergarten through grade 12 (Afaga & Lai, 1994).

In its broadest terms, it is the study of Hawai'i including geography, natural environment, cultural heritage, and language. Various strands of study are built around aspects of Hawaiian culture, history, and language. It involves significant instruction by community resources such as *kūpuna* (who are native speakers). There are six objectives including awareness of origin and culture of Native Hawaiians, appreciation of students' own cultures as well as other cultures, knowledge of cultural and historical developments in Hawai'i, opportunities to study further Hawaiian culture and language, understanding of *aloha 'āina* (i.e., love of and harmony with land), and demonstration of *aloha* spirit of cooperation and sharing in interactions with others (State of Hawai'i, 1986).

The most recent evaluation of the program (Afaga & Lai, 1994) indicated that students perceived the program as important and valued what they learned from the *kūpuna*. The evaluation indicated the need for more in-service training of *kūpuna*, as well as for principals and teachers in using curricular materials. A summary of student performance in identifying aspects of culture and geography, however, indicated relatively low performance by students in Grades 4 and 6 (with a mean response of 45% correct at each level). With respect to learning Hawaiian values, students did considerably better in both grades (mean of 67% correct).

Moving Beyond Cultural Studies to Language Immersion

Beginning in the early 1980s, there was developing discussion about a variety of transitional language programs for Native Hawaiians. In the beginning, the discussion focused on students from Ni'ihau, a privately owned island where Hawaiian customs and language have been maintained, who were being sent to Kaua'i for public schooling. Consequently, in 1983 the Board of Education approved the use of Hawaiian as the language of instruction for Ni'ihau School, with English taught as a second language (State of Hawai'i, 1994).

At about the same time, a small group of Hawaiian-speaking educators and parents began to push for various programs to enhance the preservation of Hawaiian culture and language. They formed the 'Aha Pūnana Leo preschool to re-establish school instruction in Hawaiian The effort was to assist the few families trying to revive Hawaiian in the home and in a tiny community that still used Hawaiian at all age levels. In this transitional program, children would learn in their native language as they adjusted to public school (Huebner, 1985). Concurrently, the Kamehameha Early Education Program (KEEP), which was affiliated with the large private school in the state that serves Hawaiians, began to address issues related to the mismatch between the culture of the Hawaiian student and the culture of the school. Eventually, these various programs led to further discussion about immersion programs (e.g., on Kaua'i and Hawai'i) that would teach reading and writing to Hawaiian children in Hawaiian. These widely dispersed programs (e.g., KEEP, transitional, immersion) were perhaps the earliest efforts representing a changing attitude toward the education of Native Hawaiians in the state.

In a significant departure from past practices, therefore, educational policy began to address the needs of Native Hawaiians by giving them greater input into the governance, curriculum, and services provided to students as part of their educational experience in the public schools. This represents a beginning step toward bridging the social and educational inequities of the past. It is important to note that these gains were made by those in the Hawaiian community who insisted that policies and laws reflect the desire of Hawaiians that the Hawaiian language be a living language (Kamana & Wilson, 1996). Moreover, community members took it upon themselves to begin to create these programs at the preschool level.

The language immersion approach to instruction is consistent with the official recognition of the Hawaiian language in 1978 as one of the two languages in the state because of its effectiveness in preserving the language and minority culture. At least in part due to the lobbying of parents of the Hawaiian preschools (Kamana & Wilson, 1996), the ban on English-only instruction in the public schools was rescinded in 1986. The legislation allowed special projects using the Hawaiian language to be subject to the Board of Education's approval.

In the United States context, the language immersion approach is a relatively new concept. It has, however, been used in other native language programs in New Zealand, Canada, Wales, and Spain (Hastings, 1988; Papahana Kaiapuni Hawai'i, 1995). These programs have been particularly successful with minority languages, where the use of the language in the society at large is limited. Immersion education is a form of bilingual education, where students receive part of their instruction through the medium of a second language. In cases where language of instruction is a key issue in retaining native culture and where the implementation of native language instruction would result in separate education's for children of minority and majority status, separate schooling may be recognized as reasonable. The argument is made that if a minority child's right to an education is impeded by English instruction, instruction in the minority language for those children is nondiscriminatory and is necessary to make the right to an education effective, in the sense that minority children derive as much benefit from the right to an education as majority children (Hastings, 1988).

The preschool program serving Hawaiians has now been in existence since 1985, consisting currently of approximately 45 full- and part-time teachers in the 9 preschools with about 175 students (Kamana & Wilson, 1996). Students from the preschool can now continue their Hawaiian language instruction in the public schools. The Department of Education's Hawaiian language immersion program, called Papahana Kaiapuni, has been in existence since 1987. While the program is to accommodate Hawaiian speaking students, it is not limited to those whose ethnicity is Hawaiian (Department of Education, 1994). Papahana Kaiapuni is a complete educational experience provided to students in the Hawaiian language. It has three general purposes: to assist in the revitalization of Hawaiian language and culture, to assist those who wish to integrate into the Hawaiian-speaking community (i.e., school and home language), and to assist those who wish to learn Hawaiian as a second or third language in order to interact with the Hawaiian community (Department of Education, 1994).

The curriculum of Hawaiian Immersion is built around several key principles. These emphasize indigenous teaching practices as well as modern methods and include: use of experience-based education; application of learning to the real world; recognition and tailoring of curriculum to multiple types of intelligence; use of inquiry or problem-based learning; and incorporating learning experiences that emphasize social aspects, including parents (*'ōhana*) and other community resources, living the past, present, and future (e.g., practicing traditional[6] Hawaiian customs). In broad terms, the curriculum emphasizes Hawaiian and Pacific history as well as literature of the Pacific. At the elementary level, the students learn the traditional subjects of reading, writing, and math in Hawaiian. Moreover, they take *'ukelele* lessons, dance *hula*, tend gardens with indigenous Hawaiian plants, listen to Native speakers, and learn on computers programmed in Hawaiian (Harby). Beginning in Grade 5, students study English as part of their daily routine for at least an hour per day. At the intermediate and high school level, curriculum is interdisciplinary, organized around academies (*hālau*). Each *hālau* centers on a common theme emphasizing future studies and traditional cultural activities such as land and sea studies, performing arts, and occupational training.

There are some differences, however, with respect to other native peoples who have sought separate language instruction. For the majority of students entering this program, English is their first language. Some who enter the program have some proficiency in Hawaiian, either through the home or through their preschool education. The intent of the program, however, is to develop dual proficiency in Hawaiian and English. In this manner, the program draws parents into the educational process, as they, too, gain experience with the language. The fact that English is not introduced until the fifth grade has caused some debate within the state's educational circles. Moreover, intermediate and high school children are required to learn a third language (Kamana & Wilson, 1996).

In 1990, the Board approved the formation of an advisory council consisting of representation from the University of Hawai'i, Pūnana Leo preschools, Kamehameha Schools/Bishop Estate, and the Office of Hawaiian Affairs with the State Department of Education to determine long range objectives of the Hawaiian Immersion Program (Department of Education, 1994). A variety of stakeholder groups, therefore, have been involved in governance, in terms of getting the program planned and implemented, as well as charting a course for the future.

In 1992, the Board approved extending the Hawaiian Language Immersion Program to Grade 12. The program has grown gradually, serving 621 students by the fall of 1993 (State of Hawai'i, 1994). In 1995, there were 11 Hawaiian Immersion schools (and two unofficial ones) spread across five islands, serving over 1,000 students (Kamana & Wilson, 1996). Most of these sites share a campus with an English instruction school, but two are totally Hawaiian instruction schools (Kamana & Wilson, 1996).

In 1995, the Office of Hawaiian Affairs awarded a $2.1 million grant to buy a campus for a Hawaiian language high school on the Big Island, and opened an upper-level Hawaiian immersion school on O'ahu (University of Hawai'i, 1996).

The Hawaiian Immersion Program, therefore, complements the educational efforts of Pūnana Leo preschools and also university-level courses and programs focusing on Hawaiian language and culture. The study of Hawaiian culture is further enhanced by the public university system in the state. In contrast to the development of English Standard schools in the 1920s, the Hawaiian language has been taught since 1921 at the University of Hawai'i (Kamana & Wilson, 1996). Consistent with the language revitalization movement in preschools and K–12 schools during the 1980s, language study has greatly expanded in the university system (e.g., University of Hawai'i at Hilo) in recent years. For example, this movement led to the creation of a Hawaiian Studies program and a recently completed Center for Hawaiian Studies at the University of Hawai'i at Mānoa.

Hawaiian is offered at all 2- and 4-year campuses within the University of Hawai'i system, as well as at most private universities (Kamana & Wilson, 1996). Total university enrollments for Fall 1994 were approximately 2,300 (Kamana & Wilson, 1996). Moreover, in late 1996, the Office of Hawaiian Affairs (OHA) and the University of Hawai'i announced another step in the growth of Hawaiian language studies—the creation of a master's degree program in Hawaiian language and literature. As one OHA official said, "it would be the first such program for a native people in America" (University of Hawai'i, 1996). The program follows an already existing bachelor's degree program. Similarly, attempts are underway to establish a teacher education program for those planning to teach in Hawaiian immersion schools (Kamana & Wilson, 1996).

Impact of Educational Policy on Native Hawaiians

In chapter 1 we outlined several important ways in which Native Hawaiians continued to be marginalized in Hawai'i. Some of the current state-level statistics on Native Hawaiian women during pregnancy include lower levels of prenatal care, greater use of drugs during pregnancy, higher infant mortality rate, higher teen birth rate, and more low-birth-weight babies (Kamehameha Schools/Bishop Estate, 1993). These statistics also include children who are less ready to start school and fall behind their peers in terms of academic achievement (Kamehameha Schools/Bishop Estate, 1993). In this section, we provide some additional statistics highlighting the problems and progress of Native Hawaiian educational achievement from the early 1980s through 1996.

As we suggested, academic achievement for Native Hawaiians has remained behind other ethnic groups in the state. Overall, standardized reading scores for public school students and Hawaiian students, more specifically, have dropped from the early 1980s to the early 1990s (Kamehameha Schools/Bishop Estate, 1993). To get a sense of this, while these scores do show some yearly variation, reading scores for Hawaiian and Filipino students across the elementary through high school levels generally range from the 20th to the 35th percentiles over this period, while reading scores for Euro-American and Japanese American students generally range from the 54th percentile to the 65th percentiles (Kamehameha Schools/Bishop Estate, 1993). In math, the scores have remained more stable over the decade (averaging about the 50th percentile), but Hawaiian students do lag behind their Japanese and Euro-American counterparts. For example, Hawaiian students averaged about the 40th percentile in math, whereas Japanese American students averaged slightly over the 70th percentile and Euro-American students averaged at or above the 60th percentile (Kamehameha Schools/Bishop Estate, 1993). Moreover, Department of Education data suggest that Hawaiians, while accounting for 23% of the student population, account for 33% of the identified special education students (Department of Education, 1994).

As these data indicate, there are considerable differences in the academic achievement of Hawai'i's students. Equal access to schooling (or segregation) is a difficult issue in Hawai'i, where no ethnic group represents a clear majority in the state. Students are concentrated in particular communities with widely different socioeconomic status and on particular islands. Hawaiian students tend to be overrepresented in more rural areas, for example, on the island of Hawai'i (33%), the Leeward and Windward O'ahu district (29%), and underrepresented in the Honolulu district (15%) and Central O'ahu district (11%). Because of Department of Education policies regarding transfer, teachers and principals often move away from less desirable schools in outlying rural areas (which tend to produce lower outcome) to more desirable urban or suburban schools when they gain tenure and seniority. In some of these areas, staff turnover can approach 50% per year (Heck & Mayer, 1993). As Heck and Mayer argued, this can lead to a variety of inequities in the allocation of resources and community expectations.

As we suggested earlier, it is difficult to estimate exactly how many Native Hawaiians are in the state. Because of different definitions of ethnicity used by various agencies and the relatively large number of people of mixed ethnicities, we find that Hawaiians were reported in the 1990 census (as cited in Kamehameha Schools/Bishop Estate, 1993) to comprise 13% of the state's population. It is suspected that this figure is too low, however (Kamehameha Schools/Bishop Estate, 1993). For example, Hawaiians accounted for 33% of births (when considering either parent as Hawaiian) in the state in that same year (1990) and were the largest ethnic group (23%) enrolled in the public schools (Kamehameha Schools/Bishop Estate, 1993). Interestingly, Hawaiians also accounted for about the same number in private school enrollments (21%) and home school enrollments (24%) in the 1992–1993 academic year (Kamehameha Schools/Bishop Estate, 1993).

Graduation rates from high school suggest few differences across Hawai'i's different ethnic groups and have remained quite high (averaging 95% of seniors who were enrolled at the beginning of their senior year) throughout the past decade (Kamehameha Schools/Bishop Estate, 1993). Considering data from a variety of sources, it appears that slightly under 10% of Hawaiian students drop out during high school, against a state average of only 8% (Kamehameha Schools/Bishop Estate, 1993). Looking at the percentage of adults over 25 who have completed high school, we find that the graduation rates have steadily climbed in the United States (and Hawai'i) since 1940. For example, in 1940, 23% in the United States had graduated from high school, against 20% in Hawai'i, and 19% of Hawaiians. By 1980, these figures were about 70% in the United States, 75% in Hawai'i, and 68% of Native Hawaiians. For 1990, the figures were nearly 80% in the United States, 81% in Hawai'i, and 80% of Native Hawaiians (Kamehameha Schools/Bishop Estate, 1993).

Similarly, enrollment in colleges has generally increased for Native Hawaiians over the past 20 years. However, graduating from a university provides a somewhat different picture. In Hawai'i, nearly 23% have completed university degrees, while only 9% of Native Hawaiians have done so (cited in Kamehameha Schools/Bishop Estate, 1993). More specifically, data in the 1990s from the University of Hawai'i suggest that recent graduating classes are composed of about 25% Japanese Americans, 24% Euro-Americans, 11% Filipino Americans, 10% Chinese Americans, 8% Hawaiians, and 22% "Other" (University of Hawai'i, 1990–1994). In comparison with 1940, for example, the college graduation rates were about 4% nationally, 5% in Hawai'i, and 2% among Native Hawaiians (Kamehameha Schools/Bishop Estate, 1993). These data reflect that, over this 50-year period, Native Hawaiians' educational attainment at the college level has also lagged considerably behind other ethnic groups in Hawai'i.

Literacy is another area that has garnered much attention in our study. On one hand, Hawaiians had a very strong tradition of basic literacy rate beginning with the arrival of the missionaries (Kamehameha Schools/Bishop Estate, 1993). This tradition is, at least in part, responsible for the high rate of high school completion among Native Hawaiians to this day. The skill level implied by the completion of a basic high school education, however, may be less than might be expected. As we noted, overall standardized achievement data from the Department of Education that we summarized suggest that Native Hawaiians lag behind other groups in a variety of literacy skills, including reading comprehension and writing. Statewide literacy assessment data suggest that almost one third of Native Hawaiians are classified as functionally illiterate, compared with 19% of all others (Kamehameha Schools/Bishop Estate, 1991). The college completion data presented may suggest less support within the Hawaiian community for completing 4 years of college (Kamehameha Schools/Bishop Estate, 1993).

Finally, we looked at Hawaiian representation in the Department of Education, which is responsible for educating well over 180,000 public school students in the state, of which Hawaiians comprise the largest group (23%). Hawaiian representation was 13% of the total Department of Education personnel in 1991 (Department of Education, 1991). Looking more specifically across roles, however, we found that Hawaiians account for only about 11% of school administrators, 8% of classroom teachers, and 6% of district and state administrators. In contrast, Japanese Americans are represented as 51% of school administrators, 51% of teachers, and 61% of district and state administrators (Hawai'i Department of Education, 1991). Of course, Hawaiians are relatively overrepresented in the Department of Education food service (27%), general labor (37%), and trades employees (31%) in that same year (Hawai'i Department of Education, 1991). These numbers have remained fairly stable over the past decade, despite more successful efforts to achieve affirmative action for some underrepresented groups. In contrast, for example, as another underrepresented group, Whites increased from 9% to 15% as district and state administrators, from 10% to 19% as school administrators, and from 16% to 23% as teachers (Hawai'i Department of Education, 1991).

Institutional Theory and Native Voice

As our discussion in this chapter suggested, the re-emergence of a Hawaiian voice in education and politics corresponds with larger movements of Native American rights to self-determination. Since the 1970s, Native Americans have moved toward self-determination and sovereignty (Grell, 1983; Whiteman, 1986). The growing interest by Native American groups in utilizing policy mechanisms to strengthen their control over their education has forced many states to incorporate laws and policies for dealing with them (Este, 1986; Grayson, 1986; Hastings, 1988). Correspondingly, federal law has more recently been developed which recognizes the rights of Native Americans to use, practice, and develop their languages; affords special status to Native Americans in the United States, which includes cultural and political rights; and recognizes that languages are critical to the survival of cultural and political integrity of any people.

An institutional perspective is again useful in helping us understand the responses of native groups to years of domination by policy elites that pursued an agenda of acculturation. The institutional argument suggests that schools across the country came to look similar in structure and activity during the 20th century (e.g., governed by professional elites, pursuing a narrowly defined curriculum, tracking students) because of rationalized myths that conferred legitimacy (Plank et al., 1996). Conforming to these rationalized myths (e.g., the superiority of the dominant culture, the need to Americanize immigrants) maintained the support of policymakers and gained the schools needed resources. We suggested that Hawai'i's schools looked much like schools in the mainland United States during the eras of professional domination of the policy process and Americanization as the policy goal. Schools in Hawai'i looked similar because they were less influenced by local political and social trends and more by the institutionalization of broader cultural values that formed the basis of social and educational policies.

The efforts of native and minority groups marginalized by the institutionalization of a singular set of dominant cultural values over the country's history have been enhanced since World War II by federal policy that grew out of a concern for meeting workforce needs and the civil rights movement (Spring, 1989). As Spring noted, this increasing concern surrounding education at the federal level led to statutes aimed at expanding opportunities for minorities, the discovery of talented youth, and special programs for the disadvantaged. Many of these policies (e.g., economic opportunity, housing, unemployed youth, disadvantaged youths) were pushed forward by Democratic presidents and a more liberal Congress during the 1960s.

Urban riots and student rebellions in the late 1960s also called into question the prevailing definition of a singular education. Added to this was Native American activism such as the confrontation between Native Americans and government at Wounded Knee. Social activism from a variety of special interests, therefore, led to some redefinition of the curriculum during the 1970s and 1980s around multicultural education, bilingual and bicultural education, and improved educational services for special education students. Over time, as Iannaccone (1977) argued, these challenges to the prevailing social and governance structures called into question the underlying educational norms of the municipal reform (i.e., a unitary community, separation of politics and education, neutral competency of professional administrators to govern the schools). The effects of these larger efforts aimed at social activism were also felt in Hawai'i, in terms of greater concern with Native Hawaiian cultural issues and protests surrounding the return of Hawaiian lands.

Similar to other groups such as Native Americans, Hispanics, and Puerto Ricans, the movement toward preservation of language and culture through education has also become an important issue among Native Hawaiians. The gains have been slow to materialize, however, as shown by the underrepresentation of Native Hawaiians in the professions and business ownership (United States Bureau of the Census, 1991). As Spring (1993) argued, the history of education in the United States has not been one of singular pursuit of democratic ideals. In contrast, some groups have had to fight consistently against their marginal status. For Native Americans, who were involuntarily conquered, this has been particularly difficult.

Despite their prolonged marginal status politically and economically in Hawai'i, in recent years, Hawaiians, acting mainly through a variety of special interest groups (e.g., parents for Hawaiian Immersion), have been somewhat successful at first changing the public schools' curriculum to include the study of Hawaiian culture and language and then securing a number of sites throughout the state to start Hawaiian Immersion Programs. Of course, challenges remain. Native Hawaiians have not enjoyed the benefits of social mobility through education that others have (e.g., Japanese Americans) in the state. Among the needs are programs that would provide academic support for Native Hawaiians to seek careers in professional fields, increased resource allocations, and increased community support in public schools that serve primarily the Hawaiian community (Benham, 1993).

The similarities in histories between Native Americans and Native Hawaiians have made possible the closer analysis of the relationship between educational policy and native U.S. groups. A preliminary analysis of previous studies on Native American educational policy (Benham, 1993) identified three primary trends: developing the need to study Native American policy, studying the phenomenon from a historical perspective, and measuring the impact of policy on Native Americans. We chose in this study to focus on the impact of policy on Native Hawaiians. A longitudinal approach is desired because it allows for the tracking of cultural values over time. As Este (1986) suggested, the policy process is twisted into a spiral that generates successive policies. As we discussed in this chapter and preceding chapters, larger cultural values in the U.S. context of government and society have combined to produce profound impacts on the lives of Native Hawaiians. It is clear that these interactions, both historically and legally, are very complex. This makes charting the future very uncertain.

CONCLUSION

As we argued, the policymaking system has definitely opened somewhat during the last quarter of the 20th century due to special interest involvement in a variety of issues surrounding the preservation of Native Hawaiian culture, a political agenda aimed at sovereignty and reacquiring lands, and educational programs to meet the Hawaiian community's needs. Despite good intentions and a variety of agencies that have been involved in promoting Hawaiian culture in the schools, the implementation of these types of educational policies has been uneven across the state's public schools (Afaga & Lai, 1994). Although we are encouraged by some efforts, the reality is that these are just modest beginnings against a devastating past. Although resources have been allocated to redress inequities in some areas, because financial power is still rigidly maintained by the state legislature and governor, proposed allocations for educational and social programs to serve Native Hawaiians compete line by line with all other programs in the governor's budget.

The implementation of the Hawaiian Immersion Program has also raised important debate about how far the state should, or is required, to extend its resources in providing services to Native Hawaiians. A recent example of how this general debate is played out at the local level involves the Hawaiian Immersion parents' request for bus transportation provided to their chosen school site. The Department of Education argued that it did not need to provide this service. Additionally, the Hawaiian Immersion group has also lobbied within the Department of Education to select its own principals and teachers, which is against present policy.

The re-emergence of Hawaiian voice in politics (e.g., land rights, sovereignty) and education (e.g., immersion) represents a fascinating set of issues, because these efforts are at the center of redefining what it means to live in a democracy. With respect to sovereignty, Native Hawaiians have never been considered in quite the same category as Native Americans, who have a much longer history of relationships with the United States government through treaties and court cases (both as groups and individuals) extending back into the 1700s. Thus, the political status of Native Hawaiians as Native Americans, or as a separate colonized indigenous group continues to be debated and contested.

As we suggested in chapter 1, the relationship of Native Americans to the government and its policies for dealing with them was the subject of diverse thought as far back as during the framing of the United States Constitution. In fact, Congress was set up in the Constitution as the proper body empowered to deal with the Native American tribes over a variety of issues including treaties, trade agreements, and land (Chaudhuri, 1985). Ironically, however, while this law is extensive in its scope, span, and law sources (i.e., criminal, property, Constitutional, treaty, agreements, water rights, resources, international law), it is a complex, contradictory, and confusing branch of United States legal thinking (Chaudhuri, 1985).

This is most apparent when dealing with issues surrounding the sovereignty and related rights of self-determination of Native American groups. In U.S. political and legal history, the questions of authority are intertwined with conflicting perceptions of sovereignty (Chaudhuri, 1985); that is, does Congress hold ultimate authority with respect to native groups, or do the groups hold it? Another position is that the native group holds authority over specific, but limited, aspects of its relationship with the government. An example illustrating conflicting views on the status of Native Americans with respect to sovereignty is provided by opinions from one Supreme Court justice (Chaundhuri, 1985). In 1832, Justice Marshall wrote about giving Native American tribes sovereign treaty-making power analogous to that of a Western country such as England:

> The constitution, by declaring treaties already made, as well as those to be made, to be the supreme law of the land, has adopted and sanctioned the previous treaties with the Indian nations, and consequently admits their rank among those powers who are capable of making treaties. The words "treaty" and nation are words of our own language. . . . We have applied the to Indians, as we have applied them to the other nations of the earth. They are all applied in the same sense. [see Samuel A. Worcester v. Georgia, 31 U.S. 515, p. 519 (1832)]

In contrast, on the issue of Native Americans' property rights (e.g., native title to lands), Marshall concluded in 1823 that "Indian inhabitants are to be considered merely as occupants, to be protected, indeed, while in peace, in the possession of their lands, but to be deemed incapable of transferring the absolute title to others" [Johnson v. McIntosh, 21 U.S. 591, p. 591 (1823)].

The two decisions illustrate vastly different conceptualizations of the authority and sovereignty of Native Americans. The Worcester case provides the most liberal view of sovereignty, suggesting that tribes stand in unique status to the United States. In fact, as Chaudhuri (1985) noted, a 1959 Court of Appeals decision, relying on the earlier Worcester case, found that the First Amendment did not apply to tribes in the same manner as to states, since "Indian tribes are not states. They have a status higher than that of states" (Native American Church v. Navajo Tribal Council [272 F. 2d 131 (1959)]). At the other extreme, viewing Native Americans as mere occupants of the land justified political efforts for the United States to gain access to the lands at a time when there was considerable pressure by settlers to acquire these lands. Moreover, religious doctrine in countries that had previously attempted to colonize parts of the United States (e.g., England, France, Spain) held that native groups were childish creatures in need of Christianity and Western commerce (Deloria, 1985).

Of course, the institutionalization of basic cultural values during the history of Native American policymaking is also informative in understanding how the federal government and its various branches dealt with the Hawaiian situation during the last century (e.g., the overthrow of the monarchy, failed treaty to annex in 1893, President Cleveland and McKinley's opposing reactions, eventual annexation in 1898, cession of lands, granting of statehood, return of lands), as well as with Native Hawaiians more specifically. While the recent voting on whether to proceed with Native Hawaiian political sovereignty represents a small first step toward self-determination, there is still a long road to travel because Hawaiian groups themselves are not in agreement. Further, there are a variety of issues to be settled with respect to the authority of the State of Hawai'i and Native Hawaiians themselves over their rights to self-determination (e.g., Hawaiians' rights to live on the beach). For example, Native Hawaiians do not presently have their own governing structures as Native American tribes have. Moreover, the various relationships between the state and Native Hawaiians have not been tested with respect to the federal government, because Native Hawaiians do not have a strong tradition of interacting with the federal government over these types of issues (e.g., property rights, economic activities, water rights, religious practices).

In my first personal Ha'awina No'ono'o, I shared the tragic story of Princess Nahi'ena'ena. Ensnared between the borders of wā kahiko and the advancing Western world of U.S. colonialists, she lost the power and voice to define what her role could be in an evolving cultural milieu. She became a whisper against a wall of silence. It has been nearly 200 years since this event; indeed, the Native Hawaiians have shed the guilt of being Hawaiian, "Onipa'a!"

Me nā mea'oi loa mai nā wā mamua
E holomua kākou I kēia au.
Ua hiki mai ka wana'ao no ka ho'ōla
A me ka ho'āla hou.[7] (Apoliona, 1991)

Let us move forward into the future
Carrying with us the best from the past.
The dawn (the time) has arrived for the
Revitalizing and the reawakening of our community.

ENDNOTES

1. The list of Hawaiian scholars and activists reflects a growing number of talented and passionate warrior voices. People such as Haunani Trask, Mililani Trask, Lilikalā Kame'eleihiwa, Kauanoe Kamana, David Sing, Kaipo Hale, and Mahealani Kamau'u (to name a very few) have benefited from the work of Winona Rubin, Gladys Brandt, Richard

Lyman, Sarah Ke'ahi, Mary Kawena Pukui, Donald Kilolani Mitchell, and George Kanahele.

2. Deloria provides a comprehensive view of Native American policy.
3. For more detailed information see Jocelyn Linnekin, "Defining Tradition: Variation on the Hawaiian Identity," *American Ethnologist 10*(2), 241–252 (1983).
4. Hawaiian Creole English (HCE) is a language distinct from English (Huebner, 1985). Its origins are traced to the plantations as a means of communication between the foreman and his workers. At first, it was a mixture of Hakka and Cantonese from China, Ilocano and Tagalog from the Philippines, Hawaiian, and English. As the immigrant population grew to include Japanese, Puerto Rican, Korean, Spanish, and Portuguese, the pidgin language took on a different flavor determined by locale.
5. This was suggested by A. Agbayani in a paper presented at the National Association of Asian American and Pacific Education Conference as cited in T. Huebner, *International Journal of Social Language, 56*, 22–49 (1985).
6. In this case, traditional means prior to contact with Europeans.
7. From S. Haunani Apoliona's song, "E Mau Ana Ka Ha'aheo" On *Olomana: E mau ana ka ha'aheo* [CD], Honolulu, HI: Better Days (1991).

EPILOGUE: SEEKING A SITUATED UNDERSTANDING OF POLICY

6 'EONO

E MĀLAMA 'IA NĀ PONO O KA 'ĀINA E NĀ 'OPIO (The Traditions of the Land Are Perpetuated by Its Youth)

The intention in developing our presentation in previous chapters was to examine the process of schooling in Hawai'i, with special attention to how institutional values and local changes in the political and social structure of the islands affected the education of Native Hawaiians. We identified broad cultural values that became institutionalized across the United States over time, specified key state policy mechanisms and policymakers, tracked political values such as efficiency, quality, equity, and choice through educational statutes, and, therefore, determined policy and governance patterns. Our concern was with how the institutionalization of broad cultural scripts produced corresponding organizational arrangements such as social, political, and educational structures. Such arrangements outlast the individuals who occupy various roles within the policymaking structure and are products of deep-seated, longitudinal historical and cultural patterns.[1] A variety of social and political relations give these contexts their unique shape at any given moment in time. What we found repeated over time in Hawai'i were institutionalized structures embedded in the policymaking system that served to marginalize Native Hawaiians not only educationally, but also within the wider society.

Borrowing from Gronn and Robbins'[2] (1996) discussion of the relationship between cultural contexts and organizational processes, a relational conceptualization of cultural context and educational policy would attempt to account for the particular institutional forms and patterns that existed over time, would explain why those forms persisted or changed over time, and would account for comparative similarities and differences of form displayed throughout different cultures. Our discussion of the educational system in Hawai'i over time indicated that, despite considerable local turbulence in politics, the form and structure of education has remained relatively stable. As opposed to extensive reform in education, we found smaller, incremental changes incorporated into the existing structure reflecting widely endorsed cultural norms such as missionary values, domination of professionals in decision making, English Standard Schools. Moreover, the changes that were incorporated into the schools (e.g., its centralized governance structure, segregated school system, curricular tracks, emphasis on citizenship) were similar to other reforms that were institutionalized simultaneously in other parts of the United States. With respect to Native Hawaiians, more specifically, we drew parallels between the evolution of federal policy toward other Native American groups and policy toward Hawai'i, as the boundaries of the United States were being shaped during periods of westward expansion and colonialism.

Drawing from our previous discussion, in this epilogue, we continue expanding our discussion of the relationship between context and policy by looking at how the relationships among the state government, federal government, and Native Hawaiians are evolving over time. More specifically, we show how broader cultural values (e.g., missionaries' values, federal policy about Native Americans, Americanization policies) were institutionalized in schools in Hawai'i since the middle 1800s, how state mechanisms were created to provide a structure that mirrored these values, how local political turmoil was only marginally related to these larger trends, and how the relationship of native groups to federal and state governments has shifted over the past two decades. Finally, we review how this book contributes to a wider discussion about Native American educational policy and also speculate about what the major issues are that need to be resolved politically, educationally, and socially with respect to Native Hawaiians.

DEFINING GOVERNMENT'S RELATIONSHIP TO NATIVE HAWAIIANS

In the last chapter, we began to explore the relationship among the federal government, the state, and Native Hawaiians' efforts to regain some of what has historically been taken from them. Underlying the study of the effects of educational policies on Native Hawaiians is an assumption that there has been some continuity to them. We noted that, in the wider context, federal policy toward native groups has been difficult to assess over time because of its conflicting trends, owing from the fact that specific policies have been defined by the executive, legislative, and the judicial branches. While broad institutional values regarding Christianity, the savage–civilization paradigm, and the acquisition of lands obviously formed the foundation to these policies, we observed that political changes in government often conflicted with the actual implementation of specific policies (e.g., Cleveland and McKinley's responses to the overthrow of Hawai'i's monarchy, Justice Marshall's writings that imply conflicting Supreme Court stances on Native American rights and status). Many of these ideas were embedded in the founding fathers' concerns in framing the United States Constitution.

We suggested in chapter 1 that the Native American tribes provided a continuing source of headaches for United States policymakers. First, there were a host of problems related to treaties that were made with the United States or that existed from previous times when the French and English dominated much of North America. Although Congress was identified as the group to deal with Native American nations, and provisions were included in the Constitution for dealing with Native American sovereignty and commerce issues, the reality was that politics dictated the advantages in acquiring these lands. Moreover, there was the widespread belief that these groups were children or savages whose cultures would die out because of contact with superior Western civilization. Thomas Jefferson was committed to the belief that agriculture was the foundation of a republican, participatory type of government. As long as the frontier was expanding, it seemed to encourage the belief that the United States' future was in agriculture. This necessitated settling down on the land, as opposed to occupying (as in roaming) the land to hunt. On the other hand, others were also committed to the idea that native cultures should be assimilated in order to save them from dying out.

As the country expanded westward, however, political pressures increased to give land to the Whites who occupied Native American lands. These pressures were demonstrated in legislation such as tribal removal treaties in 1830, trade policies in 1834, and treaties in 1867 and 1868 that involved giving education benefits in exchange for land.[3] Perhaps beginning with Marshall's decision on Native American's rights to land ownership, federal policy toward Native Americans from the middle 1800s to 1930s shifted gradually to view Native Americans as attachments to the land, as opposed to owners. This was the politics of assimilation. Thus, what had been conceived of as foreign policy at the time of the Constitution's framing gradually became domestic policy for Congress—supervising how Native Americans would use their property. These issues were often referred to as the *Indian problem* because of racial and cultural differences in the 1800s.

The often conflicting policy stances demonstrate the essence of the federalist system in the United States, in that its strength is in its ability to respond by isolating (within a branch or a particular level of government) most sets of policymaking demands. For example, the Constitution considered treaties with Native Americans to be the supreme law of the land—equal in rank with those made by other sovereign nations. In contrast, regarding land rights, Justice Marshall referred to them as "merely occupants" incapable of transferring absolute title to others (Johnson and Graham v. McIntosh, 1823, p. 591). We found some parallels between how federal policy was applied to Native American groups and how it was applied in the Hawaiian context.

Pressures to acquire land for the beginning sugar and pineapple industries in Hawai'i were similar to acquiring land as the United States expanded westward. The Great *Māhele* of 1848 was written to break up the Hawaiian system of land owning to provide large tracts of land for the plantations. This provided impetus for the expansion of these industries throughout the islands and led to the eventual control of politics by the Republican Oligarchy. Land ownership continues to be a major problem in Hawai'i, with the federal government and a few major private land owners holding much of the prime land. This has driven the cost of land ownership to exceedingly high levels for most people.

The historical relationship of Native Hawaiians to the federal government was defined more formally in a series of resolutions and public laws beginning in the middle 19th century. The United States recognized treaties with the Hawaiian monarchy covering friendship, commerce, and navigation in 1849 and reciprocity of harbor entry rights in 1876. At the time of annexation in 1898, all lands were forcefully ceded to the United States. In the joint resolution entitled "A Joint Resolution to provide for annexing the Hawaiian Islands to the United States," approved in 1898, all lands were ceded to the United States, but mandated that revenue generated from these lands be used for the benefit of the inhabitants of the islands for educational and other public purposes. The Hawaiian Homes Commission Act (PL 67-34), enacted in 1921, has been shrouded in controversy, as we developed in the last chapter. Pushed through Congress by Kuhio, who was influenced by the Republican Party, it was to provide land for needy Hawaiians. As we suggested, the program has generally missed this mark.

There is, however, significance in the Act itself beyond the specific substantive intent. This Act was the first to define the special relationship and responsibility of the United States government toward Native Hawaiians. At the time, Secretary of the Interior Franklin K. Lane was quoted in Public Law 103-382 (October 20, 1994; see Improving America's Schools, 1994) as indicating that "natives of the islands who are our wards . . . and for whom in a sense we are trustees, are falling off rapidly in numbers and many of them are in poverty" (3795).[4] Similarly, in 1938, Congress granted special land lease rights for Native Hawaiians in a section of a national park in Hawai'i and extended exclusive fishing privileges to Native Hawaiians in that area (52 Stat. 781 etg seq.). Thus, there is a measure of similarity in how Native Americans and Hawaiians have been defined variously as independent sovereigns and then, after political domination, as wards to a guardian.[5]

The relationship between Native Hawaiians, the State of Hawai'i, and the federal government was partially defined when lands were returned to the State upon entry into the Union in 1959. Congress mandated that returned lands be held by the State in public trust and stated that it would retain legal responsibility to enforce the public trust of the state for the betterment of the conditions of Native Hawaiians as defined in the Hawaiian Homes Commission Act. Congress, therefore, reaffirmed the trust relationship by retaining the exclusive power to enforce the trust, including the power to approve land exchanges and legislative amendments affecting the rights of beneficiaries under the Hawaiian Homes Commission Act.

As conflicting as federal policy has been at times, it appears that there has been a trend since the 1970s to extend equal opportunity rights to Native Americans as a result of their privileged status with the federal government. More specifically, Native Hawaiians were made eligible for participation in the programs of the Administration of Native Americans (Community Services Act of 1974).[6] At that time, the federal government adopted the definition of Native Hawaiian as any person who is "a descendent of the aboriginal people, who prior to 1778, occupied and exercised sovereignty in the area that now comprises the State of Hawai'i" (p. 813). This is the definition that has been used with minor changes since then.

During the 1980s and early 1990s, federal policy appeared to gradually shift toward allowing native groups greater access to education, medical, economic or job-related benefits, and other social programs. Access to these programs was included in a number of separate pieces of legislation. Moreover, other acts recognized the rights of native peoples to preserve their culture, language, and religious practices, as well as safeguard their archeological sites. These separate pieces of legislation are summarized in the Native Hawaiian Education Act as part of Improving America's Schools Act (PL 103-382) in 1994.

The Native Hawaiian Education Act specifically extends equal privileges and rights afforded other Native Americans under other acts (e.g., Native American Programs Act of 1974, American Indian Religious Freedom Act, Native American Graves and Repatriation Act, National Historic Preservation Act, Native American Languages Act). What is of further interest about this Act is that it chronicles the role of the United States government and U.S. citizens in undermining Hawaiian sovereignty (which was recognized by the United States between 1826 and 1893) at the time of the 1893 overthrow of the government. Moreover, it acknowledges the special responsibility of Congress toward Native Hawaiians because of those illegal actions. It is because of this Act that Native Hawaiian groups argue that they have a right to full self-determination under international law—similar to other groups that were colonized in the 1800s and subsequently given full rights of self-determination.

Over time, therefore, we observe that the status of Native Hawaiians with respect to the federal government has obviously changed. Perhaps we are skeptics, but we draw the reader's attention to the use of the terms "occupied" and "sovereignty" in the Community Services Act of 1974 definition of Native Hawaiian, which bring to mind, once again, Justice Marshall's decisions that Native Americans had the status to make treaties as sovereigns, but were occupants of the land when it came to property rights.[7] Thus, the ward and trustee status of Native Hawaiians vis-à-vis the federal government implies a responsibility to provide social and educational programs to take care of them. We suggest that where the Constitution of the United States once dealt with Native American tribes and the Hawaiian monarchy as sovereign nations, the federal government in the 1990s sees native groups as impoverished minorities in need of social programs. Programs, therefore, identify Native Americans as a racial minority, as opposed to sovereign nations.

Because Native American groups have little real self-government, their special status has been described as a mixed blessing.[8] On one hand, they receive a wide variety of social services that other minorities do not receive. On the other hand, these assistance programs serve to stigmatize and further oppress, thereby taking a tremendous toll on Native self-esteem and independence. These issues play into the definition of self-determination and sovereignty that Native Americans have fought for since the 1950s. For Native Hawaiians, sovereignty becomes even more difficult because they do not presently have the same governing structures as various Indian tribes—limited as these governance rights may be. Further, there is not the same length of history of tested relationships with the federal government, especially with respect to the courts.

POLICY IMPLICATIONS

We found support for four hypotheses about culture and policy from our analysis of educational policymaking in Hawai'i. First, viewed culturally and historically, schools in the United States have always been deeply intertwined with political and economic institutions, which together serve to define what David Easton (1965a) argued is the central political question in a democracy: who benefits and who does not? Joel Spring (1989) referred to this phenomenon as ideological management: ". . . the history of education can be considered as part of the study of the political and economic forces shaping both the process and the content of ideas disseminated to the public" (p. 417). Second, over time shifting amalgamations of elite groups defined, or one might argue refined, traditional Euro-American values (e.g., individual wealth and ownership of land, Protestant work ethic, competition, assimilation to a melting pot) that influenced or prescribed ethnic and cultural boundaries and corresponding social and educational priorities.

Third, institutional structures were created within the schools that allowed the implementation of widely endorsed cultural values. For example, policies to track Native Hawaiian children and youth into remedial programs in separate schools from soon after contact with the American missionaries until the last vestiges were removed with the 1960 graduation of the final English Standard high school class promoted a utilitarian, racist, and social caste tradition serving to discipline and acculturate the Native Hawaiian. In this sense, schools acted as sociocultural sorting machines (Spring, 1989), allocating tickets for success and failure.[9] Efforts to improve the educational system largely emphasized progress toward an idealized state of equity and democracy, yet were seldom driven by those outside the centralized (and relatively closed) decision-making elite. The rhetoric of "good for all" carried with it the crucible of "denigrate what is Hawaiian." The institutionalization of this social and educational policy resulted in the near loss of the Hawaiian culture and language. This has resulted in prolonged social marginalization through reduced access to education. Equity has not been adequately promoted, at least as far as statistics tell the story.

Fourth, in the historical cases studied, much of the debate over Native Hawaiian issues can be placed within a larger set of conflicts and relationships among the federal government and its policies toward Native Americans, the states, and the individual Native American groups over such issues as illegally acquired lands (*'āina*), beliefs about governance, sovereignty and self-determination, economic and human resources, and cultural status. What makes the study of these evolving relationships so fascinating to us is that they are at the core of democratic ideals long held as uniquely American. They help define how people will participate in and benefit from our society.

Although the effects of colonialism on indigenous groups is well known, what must not be ignored is how this rhetoric is established. If the message is couched in language that labels difference as inferior and dismisses diversity as unloyalty, thus legitimizing social domination through policy rhetoric, then the activity of schooling will serve to silence—the ultimate assault of marginalization. We identified several wider cultural values that formed the backdrop for the institutionalized organizational structure of Hawai'i's schools. Initially, these included the replacement of Hawaiian values with the missionaries' views of Christianity (e.g., work ethic, morality, beliefs about property) and the belief of Whites in America that native cultures were childlike or savage with a lesser type of social and economic organization. Because of this, indigenous people were mere occupants of their lands, which could be exchanged or taken to protect or save them. Gradually, Americanization also became dominant social and educational policy as a means of ensuring social, political, and economic stability in preparation for eventual Hawaiian statehood.

Within a relatively stable state policy environment, periodic environmental events such as economic instability, a growing immigrant population, or changing social conditions (e.g., after World War II) allowed special-interest coalitions to mobilize (legally or illegally) to assume power. Although sometimes proclaiming their intent to disassemble the previous governing structure, this did not occur. Instead, the closed, elite structure of governance was maintained by reaffirming the traditional values of economic and social efficiency. If there exists any change in value positions, perhaps it is illustrated only in today's reform activities, as increased participation in the educational system by disenfranchised groups is beginning to hasten a move toward decentralization at the state and local school levels to increase choice options.

We are cautiously optimistic in believing that a measure of equity is achieved in opening up educational opportunities for Native Hawaiians after decades of pursuing policies that silenced. For example, attendance of Native Hawaiians at the University of Hawai'i is slowly rising, as is enrollment in Hawaiian Language courses. Additionally, a masters degree in Hawaiian Studies is now offered. More culturally compatible educational possibilities are developing due to greater demands and involvement of parents and other special interests at a grassroots level. Concomitantly, much of this impetus has been encouraged by a changing federal policy orientation toward Native Americans.

The study of educational policy, therefore, is best accomplished in hindsight. For over 150 years, policymakers in Hawai'i have translated their cultural values into concrete public school policies that expressed their educational expectations for the islands' children. In fact, as Tyack and Cuban (1995) argued, the schools have always been a favorite target for those seeking to improve not only educational practices, but society as a whole. Human societies seem always to stumble upward toward a more humane ordering of their domestic relations (Deloria, 1985). Policy toward Native Hawaiians seems to show this same line of progression as other areas of policy consideration. In the late 1800s, our country's leaders sat back and watched as insiders and U.S. citizens crafted an overthrow of Hawai'i's sovereign monarchy. Policy from the early 1900s to the 1970s seemed to dictate that Native Hawaiians would remain tied to vocational education and limited-skills occupations. In contrast, policy over the last two decades, both at the federal and state levels, has begun to provide Hawaiians with some social and educational benefits.

Cultural Institutions Defined Local Policy

From our presentation and analysis we draw several conclusions about Hawai'i and assess our implications with respect to broader issues in educational policy. First, broader cultural trends in the United States (e.g., missionaries' beliefs, federal policy toward Native Americans and other colonized people) were central to the institutionalization of values in Hawai'i's schools since the 1830s. The governance of schools was first written into law by Reverend Richards in Hawai'i's Constitution of 1840. As we suggested, these laws served to establish religious ethics and behavior within the school curriculum, leading eventually to select schools for the missionaries' children and common schools for less-privileged children.

The values embedded in these dominant cultural themes, when translated to legal activity, served to denigrate native traditions and beliefs. In fact, as Deloria (1985) argued, the missionaries played primary roles in implementing federal policy west of the Mississippi aimed at dispossessing tribes from their lands. They also translated the Bible into native languages. Because these values often conflicted with native traditions, they created negative myths and destructive stereotypes. The missionaries' zeal to raise the lowly heathen to a more godly state was the driving force behind the early school curriculum. Schools sought to replace Hawaiian traditions, beliefs, and behaviors with the one Christian god, Calvinistic ethics, and Puritan behavior. Although the school curriculum soon became secularized under governmental control, morals were still a part of the course schedule. "The three R's," plus history, geography, citizenship, and grammar were accompanied by informal lessons concerning how one should behave and what aspirations a person should have.

As we developed throughout this book, other federal policy trends, such as acculturation through Americanization and segregated schools, also became institutionalized in Hawai'i's schools. The effects of these policies were to remove almost all ties between Hawaiians and their cultural traditions. In contrast, when federal policy toward Native Americans began to pursue an equity agenda in the 1970s and 1980s, Hawaiians also received social, educational, and economic benefits from their status as Native Americans.

State Mechanisms Mirrored Larger Intents and Structures

State mechanisms were created to mirror these larger intents, which facilitated the implementation of values into Hawai'i's schools. These mechanisms created institutionalized structures in the public schools. Iannaccone and Lutz (1970) suggested that education is politicized because the process through which schools are governed is defined by political maxims. Policies result from ". . . the process of influence which results in an authoritative decision, having the force of law, by a governmental body such as a school board. . . . (who) act in virtue of their legal competence within a constitutional framework." (Iannaccone & Lutz, 1970, p. 13) For example, operating within an elite-defined policymaking structure, the missionaries managed to move education out of the hands of Native monarchical rule into the domain of a White-dominated, economic authority. Our data suggest that one means of transmitting U.S. values and culture was through school laws—typically reflecting the policy value of efficiency. The pursuit of efficiency as a policy goal ensured that schools where tightly regulated with respect to finance and held accountable to a prescribed school curriculum. Similarly, Americanization ensured social stability in preparation for eventual acceptance into the U.S. family of states. The institutionalization of such values and corresponding structures resulting from previous efforts tends to generate enduring expectations held by generations of educators and the public about their expectations of schooling (Tyack & Cuban, 1995).

Throughout Hawai'i's history, therefore, these expectations of the educational policy process as relatively closed and controlled by the elite enabled a small group to govern schools and define how the predominantly favored values of efficiency and quality were operationalized in the schools. Widely endorsed values were translated into school structures by this group of policymakers. There are three prime examples of elite-dominated, interlocking policy toward curriculum. First was the lack of Hawaiian language, Hawaiian history, and cultural studies as an integral part of the school curriculum for almost 100 years. The curriculum tended to distribute knowledge inequitably across ethnic groups.

A second repercussion of politically closed educational policy was the segregationist policy of English Standard Schools. Translated into actual school activity, this policy meant that the majority of White students received the best preparatory education, whereas the Native Hawaiian and other ethnic minorities received rudimentary and often ill-funded programs. Tracking students into predetermined life roles provided the third example of the elite definition of the educational curriculum. Much of this activity found Native Hawaiians and other ethnic groups funneled into vocational education programs that offered very little in the way of future career opportunity. Although some groups managed to use education to gain social mobility, for Native Hawaiians that has proven more difficult. As a result, Hawai'i had a solid labor force that did not threaten the stability of the colonial social-political system.

Essentially, the domination of elite values in the educational curriculum in Hawai'i dictated that Native Hawaiian students receive fewer life opportunities afforded through education than the foreign White student. In the early 1900s, Hawai'i was growing in economic importance, and education became a desired means to higher occupational prestige—hence, ostensibly, to better incomes. However, the case histories illustrate that, through value-laden educational policy which sought efficient means of acculturating the Native populace, the Native Hawaiian was not afforded formal education that provided increased prospects of high status or better paying employment. These structural constraints that operated to block the advancement of Native Hawaiians have resulted in multiple educational and social problems which are addressed in the following discussion.

The larger themes of Americanization, for example, resulted in institutional structures that tracked Native Hawaiians into lower achieving classes or simply labeled them as either learning disabled or just plain troublesome and ripe for reformatory school. The creation of the dual-school system further separated the already segregated public school system. The English Standard Schools were found in the urban centers, while the ill-funded and understaffed pidgin schools were found in the rural areas of Hawai'i.

Quickly decreasing numbers of full-blooded Hawaiians, due to intermarriages and death, contributed to the success of Americanization programs in Hawai'i's schools. Because many languages were spoken (e.g., Japanese, Chinese, Filipino, and Pidgin), the notion of English as the only central language in schools, religious groups, and business dealings was imperative. The melting pot ideology, which called for Hawai'i's diverse population to become one people, was used to demean what was culture specific and replaced it with a U.S. self-identity. As it was for other indigenous cultures, but more effectively with the Native Hawaiian, once one's history and memories are dismissed, allegiance to another culture is not too far a leap.

In the end, the operationalization of the predominant values of efficiency and quality into school-related mechanisms created a highly centralized school governing system infused within a bureaucratic structure that postulated a stratified school system and Americanism. The schools effectively devalued the Native Hawaiian culture, coerced Native Hawaiians to accept their low social status, and successfully socialized Hawaiians into believing that their Hawaiianness was to blame for their lack of economic acumen, low social status, and failing academic ability. Schooling proved to be an effective means of subjugating Native Hawaiians to a politicized set of moral standards that made it acceptable to dispossess the Natives of their land, to eliminate their mother tongue, to dash a rich Hawaiian oral history and culture from memory, and to overthrow a sovereign government.

Although special interest pressures during the post-World War II period began the dismantling of the formalized dual-school system, the ideal of separatism had become entrenched. The brighter White and Asian American students went to better public schools that were located in the economically affluent centers, whereas the rest of the populace, including the majority of Native Hawaiians, continued to attend the rural schools, many of which were still tied to the plantation system. These settlement patterns served to maintain a type of segregation in Hawai'i beyond the formal dual system that was eventually dismantled. The urban schools approached the student with the vigor or learning and the attitude of success. In contrast, the rural schools maintained the attitude that the intellectual capacity of their clientele was limited to a laborer or service occupation. Vocational education was viewed as an innovative curriculum move, and, although it had merit, its initial intention to mold a compliant labor class tracked many Native Hawaiians into lower paying employment.

Local Political Change Was Only Marginally Related to School Changes

Similar to Plank et al. (1996), who argued that local politics were very different across 100 cities that institutionalized the professionalization of education during the municipal reform period (1890–1920), we suggest that local political turmoil in Hawai'i was only marginally related to the more comprehensive school reforms since the middle 1800s. As we suggested, Hawai'i was very quick to adopt changes that were unfolding simultaneously in other parts of the United States. The adoption of these reforms did create structural changes in education. Some examples include the common school in the 1840s, the professional reform of education in the 1890s with curriculum and values defined by Whites, the segregated schools similar to the United States' South, and the Americanization movement or melting-pot curriculum. In addition, because of the domination of elites over time, it has been very difficult to encourage grassroots-type change to the system. For example, although Hawaiian culture has been infused to some extent into the schools during the 1980s and 1990s, the more comprehensive Hawaiian Immersion Program only serves 1,000 students. The reality is that most of the 45,000 Native Hawaiian public school children are underserved.

Fundamental change in Hawai'i appears to be nearly impossible to achieve, therefore, because of well-established traditions and symbols regarding politics, governance, and school control that are inherent in the State's political culture. We suggest that the effects of increased calls for educational change during the third (post-WW II) and fourth (1970s–present) periods appear mostly marginal. Examples of entrenched ideals are found in the continued high support for private school education (some private schools have existed for well over 100 years), which is a remnant of the previous dual school system. This support stems from the Protestant influence in the early 1800s, where obedience and hard work in school would prepare both Native and Christian students for future success or, more appropriately, to assume their proper places in the social order. In fact, in the fall of 1993, the Hawai'i Supreme Court decided not to hear a case concerning whether a private school serving Hawaiian students could continue to hire Protestant teachers exclusively (thus upholding the circuit court's decision). Another ideal surrounds the current push for Hawaiian language immersion schools as part of a move for Hawaiian sovereignty, yet the program serves only a minute percentage of public students of Hawaiian ancestry.

Wirt and Kirst (1989) reminded us that state policy elites not only impact what value positions are expressed in laws, but also determine what is changed. We believe that the flexibility of the governing system to bend under stress (e.g., by allowing some participation of outsiders in the policy process over time) has enabled it to isolate tension effectively and remain intact. The tradition of one-party domination in politics has also contributed to a relatively closed political system. Thus, despite the periodic policy rhetoric calling for massive change at both the federal and state levels, reform efforts in Hawai'i continue to be somewhat incremental and influenced by trends across the United States as a whole (e.g., site-based management, charter schools), as opposed to revolutionary, because the structure of the system effectively limits the scope of conflict and produces policy responses that are least disturbing to the governing structure. For example, concern with reforming Hawai'i's public schools might be greater if people felt they did not have educational options outside of their neighborhood schools, yet the system has recently provided several options, including limited open enrollment and private school attendance. Tyack and Cuban (1995) referred to this tendency toward incrementalism, despite reformers' larger intentions, in educational policy as "tinkering toward utopia."

In each case, local political turbulence aided change in some aspect of the schools' governing structure, yet these changes were consistent with commonly accepted beliefs about schools held at the time. The first period resulted in the formalization of schools and their governance under constitutional law. After, the second period of political turbulence, governance of schools by an elite group of professionals with political and economic ties to the legislature and Hawai'i's political and social elite became institutionalized. The only real structural change during the third period of political turbulence was the replacing of the appointed school board by an elected body, which was an attempt to bring greater representation of the public, more specifically, American-born Japanese-American (AJA) participation. Yet, this board does not have financial control of the schools. Similarly, during the current period, a number of changes have been made to give the appearance of greater local control (e.g., site-based management, charter schools, Hawaiian Immersion education), but, to date, our assessment is that these reforms have been more in the direction of maintaining social legitimacy than in really freeing up local communities to gain control over the educational process.

Thus, our data concerning these perceived structural changes suggest that, although the change rhetoric was strong in each instance of political change, the school system has remained largely the same. As Tyack and Cuban (1995) noted, most of the assumptions of educational reformers about their abilities to change the educational system failed to give due weight to the resilience of school as institutions to resist change. Essentially, over time school governance was kept within the boundaries of a predominantly centralized political system that kept schools predictable, manageable, and fiscally solvent. This idea of the educational system's ability to stretch and fit political demands without really changing is characteristic of the flexibility of a federalist system.

Changing an Inconsistent Federal Policy Toward Those Colonized or Conquered

With respect to the relationship between Native Hawaiians and senior governments such as the federal government, our fourth conclusion suggests that this relationship has evolved gradually over a period of years, driven by changes in federal policy toward Native groups, establishing a trustee and ward relationship from an initial one of independent sovereigns. It is clear that when we see federal policy toward Native Americans in its historical context, the primary aim was the dispossession of them by those colonizing the Western United States and the Pacific. After dispossessing Native Americans of their lands, efforts were made to integrate them into the dominant culture through education.

Making the picture more complex is that, at another level of generality, the relationship between Native Americans and senior governments has been seen as one of special status and responsibility. From this standpoint, a variety of social, economic, and educational programs have been made available to Native Hawaiians through federal legislation. While these programs have been made available, we suggested that at the implementation level they have often met with little success. We gave the example of the Hawaiian Homes Act that has been a frustration for Native Hawaiians for over 70 years. As Deloria (1985) observed, the implementation of such federal policy for Native Americans has rarely resembled what policymakers actually intended.

With respect to the State government, Hawaiians have also had difficulty in gaining greater self-determination. We gave several examples of ongoing battles between Native Hawaiians and State government over issues such as the right to occupy state lands and the right to conduct a vote among Native Hawaiians for proceeding toward some type of sovereignty. Thus, the relationship of Native Hawaiians to the federal and state governments is one that has been, and will probably remain, in flux.

It is certainly not a new conclusion that the colonial movement in Hawai'i seriously depreciated Native Hawaiians' cultural esteem. To some, the argument that if it were not the Americans, it would have been someone else is still valid. The fact remains that the political values of educational policymakers (i.e., Protestant ideology and capital gain) served to intensify the assimilating effects of schooling. Deeply embedded in the poetic verses of *Kaulana Nā Pua* is a bitter anger that lashes out at the U.S. rhetoric of progress and civilization and calls attention to barbaric acts of land-stealing and back-room politics. Written in 1893 by Ellen Wright Prendergast, this *hīmeni* (hymn) of protest was also entitled *Mele'ai Pōhaku*, the Stone-Eating Song, and *Mele Aloha 'Āina*, the Patriots Song (cited in Elbert & Mahoe, 1970, pp. 62–64). Over 100 years later, this Hawaiian chant still reaches to the heart of what it means to be Hawaiian and presents a stark mirror reflecting the deeper effect of schooling on Native Hawaiians.

As we observed in passing, the pattern we identified in the Hawaiian also appeared to a greater or lesser degree in the educational histories of Puerto Rico, and for the marginalized groups of African Americans, Native Americans, Mexican Americans, and Asian Americans within the boundaries of the United States. Today, all articulate a vision and action of resistance. Economic exploitation of Mexican Americans and Asian Americans has led to their disenfranchisement from the political and economic activity of U.S. society, whereas deculturation coupled with disenfranchisement have disempowered Puerto Ricans, Native Americans, and Native Hawaiians. In effect, schools have been used as a tool for social control "to deny a population the knowledge necessary to protect its political and economic rights and to economically advance in society" (Wirt & Kirst, 1982, p. 326). Resistance to the control of values and ideas have led, in part, to the establishment of tribal schools and tribal community colleges on Native American reservations, to public schools in which English is the second language, and to mainstream schools redefining their work to embrace a multicultural perspective. Yet, this activity is still occurring in the margins of the whole school conversation. Moves to shift this work to the center of local, state, and federal levels have been met with both political and economic barriers.

Therefore, a coalition of men and women who represent, or are sympathetic to, the dominant cultural beliefs, the so-called inner circle (Marshall et al., 1989), are able to establish school policy with relatively little opposition. Aida Negron De Montilla (1971), for example, wrote of this similar use of power to control education in Puerto Rico. She noted that, beginning in the early 1900s, the United States President has appointed Puerto Rico's Commissioner of Education, a process that has resulted, she argued, in an effective control of the island's school system. Early on, the thrust toward Americanization led to "the same system of education and the same character of books" (p. 21), introduction of a large U.S. originated teaching force, and English-only instruction. The notion that Puerto Ricans could be acculturated Americans in one-generation was similar to efforts on the continental United States and in the Hawaiian Islands. Americanization, being "White" under one banner, together with more than 100 years of devaluation and the introduction of diverse cultures led to Native Hawaiian's believing that being Hawaiian was not an asset, but a liability. Marginalization, therefore, suggests that state-level educational policy supports centralized governance by an exclusive elite, U.S. values of democracy, Christian moral ethics, and social stratification by racial lines.

This is an important piece of our study, for the nature of policymaking suggests that it is an applied or practical activity. Therefore, it is not only essential to present theoretical discourse that outlines conceptual lenses and methodological processes through which to evaluate politics and educational policymaking processes, but the impact or outcome of the policy cannot be missed. The fears that Native peoples express so strongly and emotionally about social and linguistic coercion and exclusion has not been shared to the same degree by social, political, economic, and educational policymakers. This has placed enormous obstacles in the way of widespread force to shift conventional values that drive the substantive and practical work of institutions.

In Spring's (1994) assessment, educational policy toward Native Americans, Mexican Americans, and Puerto Ricans, in large measure, was grounded in the move to deculturate and Americanize. He identified six key methods employed in this process: segregation and isolation, forced change of language, curricular content reflecting dominant group's culture, texts reflect dominant culture, those who are being oppressed have no voice and so cannot express their culture, and teachers are from the dominant group. Hawai'i's schools mirrored much the same activity in policymakers' efforts to deculturate and Americanize a growing and diverse ethnic population. The effect of this action resulted in overall poor

Native Hawaiian performance in school and in the larger society. In this way, Native Hawaiians resemble other indigenous populations in the sense that their overall educational levels are low, high school completion and college completion are consistently lower than for other racial groups, and their representation in high-income employment is considerably lower than most other minority groups.

IMPROVING EDUCATIONAL EXPERIENCES

How might we go about improving educational experiences for Native Hawaiians, and what should be the goal of such reforms? The historical and personal stories related in this book reveal that educational policy promoted U.S. beliefs and negative stereotypes of Native Hawaiians, thereby leading Hawaiians to believe that what was Hawaiian was not good. This suggests that both current policy and resource allocation should focus on academic and cultural support designed to create parity and develop positive role models. Indeed, this conclusion further leads us to suggest that educational policymakers, school leaders, and practitioners be collectively responsible to developing far-reaching policies and practices that facilitate the inclusion of differences in school governance, that present avenues and incentives to highlight teaching and learning, that balance the conservation of cultural traditions with preparation of children for the 21st century, and that places at the center of school decision making the values of equity, respect, and responsibility.

Ogbu (1992) explained that, "Most problems caused by primary cultural differences are due to differences in cultural content and practice" (p. 12). A solution to bridge misunderstanding between differing cultures is to support programs which increase the educational policymakers', educational leaders', and teachers' knowledge of the cultural needs of Hawai'i's children and youth and to strive for equity in the allocation of resources to fulfill these needs. Provisions must be made to support ongoing training which fosters stereotype breaking, focus on issues and behavior of indigenous people, and develop skills in culturally appropriate curriculum and teaching methods.

We argue for a clear and substantive articulation of a multicultural perspective. Perhaps the greatest danger of educational policy and curriculum change, especially when it entails a change in the expressed belief system, is that the curriculum becomes heavily in favor of one culture while opposing all other cultural traditions. The analysis of each of the preceding case histories identifies this as a typical result of educational policy and curriculum programs in Hawai'i over time. A solution to this dilemma is to support ongoing educational efforts that are multicultural in focus for children, adults, and families—providing opportunity for the transference of ethnic traditions. Thus, in becoming pro-Hawaiian, a person does not become anti-every other ethnic group.

This suggestion requires much flexibility on the part of both Hawai'i's policymakers and curriculum planners as well as the many racial groups who call Hawai'i home. As difficult as this may sound, Showers and Cantor (1985) explained that people are capable of

> . . . (a) adjusting interpretations in response to situational features; (b) taking control of their thoughts and their plans; (c) seeing multiple alternatives for interpreting the same event or outcome; and (d) changing their own knowledge repertoire by adding new experiences and by reworking cherished beliefs, values, and goals. (p. 277)

Support for community programs that enable a variety of ethnic groups to learn and positively incorporate traditional values to current situations is the first step toward this flexible multicultural focus. In addition, support must be given to teachers and administrators to develop courses that address racism and social action as well as emphasize multiculturalism and flexibility. Providing school and community programs that focus on the cooperative spirit and sensitivity of multiculturalism will support Native and ethnic empowerment and can more effectively channel the anger between ethnic groups into a more positive and constructive future.

In essence, it is incumbent on the policy analysts and educational policymakers to look beyond the ethnic biases and the special interests needs, to stop playing one ethnic decision against another, and to accept the idea that multiculturalism can work. Also, care needs to be practiced so that the mistakes of the past are not made in the future. Much debate today pits those seeking cultural conservation against those who see educational goals as preparing children for modern life. These two forces, however, are not as contradictory as might at first be expected. Of course, the old ways of the Native Hawaiian ancestors are anachronistic, and no one wants to live in a world that avoids new knowledge. But traditions are not passé; on the contrary, they provide a stable foundation from which is taught tolerance and respect, competition and the value of education, of *kokua* (help) and *ukupau* (to work together), of *'ōhana* (family) and *ho'oponopono* (to put to right).

REFLECTIONS

In this last section, we speculate about where current conditions are likely to lead and what the major issues to be resolved are politically, educationally, and socially. Our study identified the misdirection of academic work, but this is not our only indictment. We believe that the school institution has also suffered from economic dysfunction. That is, the primary flow of financial support has been invested in schools and students who are in the elite. In effect, legislative control of school financing has also led to legislative fiat of school curriculum. What has been described in all four case histories is the funding of politically charged school-related programs that frequently were in opposition to the needs of Native Hawaiians. Therefore, a practical solution to this centralized and very constricting form of financing is to take resource allocation power out of the political domain and put it into the hands of the practitioners who are close to the needs of their community and school clientele. In addition, increased resource allocation in the forms of financing, materials, and services must be made available to school-level administrators to create and support programs that are both culturally sensitive and maintain high levels of academic excellence. This decision-making power would provide the school-level administrator the freedom to establish schools that build cultural diversity and provide quality cultural choices such as immersion.

Increased leverage in financial decisions by school-level administrators enhances the opportunity for monies to be directed to needed programs. Resources can be used to develop or purchase materials that are current and appropriate to the needs of each school's students. Additionally, resources could be directed to provide academic programs that address a range of individual student needs as well as provide needed educational community programs (e.g., preschool and adult learning). An asset of this school-based financial responsibility is that it could counteract the effect of Hawai'i's unique problem of geographical isolation. Resources could be designed to facilitate efforts to alleviate educational problems associated with schools in rural settings. For example, development of technology could enhance this effort. In sum, the quality of a school's curriculum would be dependent upon how it fulfills its dual responsibility to the cultural and academic needs of its students and how it responds to the future of an ever-changing 21st century.

Finally, we argue that the deep structure of schooling must reflect a shift from educating a meritocratic elite to the empowerment of all. The politics of institutional structures and the preponderance of byzantine processes and conventional academic traditions has presented us with a classic contradiction. As long as political values embrace social stratification and racial and gender preference, which is then translated to the work of social, political, and economic institutions, an elite social status quo will be preserved. Equity will not be realized.

In the end, what has been learned is that, as the State of Hawai'i moves through other incremental changes, the fundamental values of its political culture must broaden to appreciate cultural diversity, thereby valuing equity and choice. This requires educational policymakers to validate cultural plurality and challenges teachers to depart from long-held Western modes of pedagogy and research to apply new combinations of ideas and practices that are effective with their unique group of students.

This historical study revealed the devastating silence of the Native Hawaiian. As many groups before have sought and gained control of Hawai'i, it is time that Native Hawaiians ground their values in Hawaiian tradition and act with the skill and knowledge afforded in today's modern society. Not only must we claim our personal sovereignty that will lead to claiming our voice, our power, and our authority for self governance, but we must take responsibility to dispel the noble savage myth and, instead, identify ourselves as leaders, not children, of Hawai'i Nei.

HA'AWINA NO'ONO'O PAU

(The end of our writing)

ENDNOTES

1. See Peter Gronn & Peter Robbins, "Leaders in Context: Postpositivist Approaches to Understanding Educational Leadership," *Educational Administration Quarterly* 32:3 (1996) 452–473.
2. Gronn & Robbins, op. cit.
3. For more information see: Vine Deloria, "The Evolution of Federal Indian Policy Making," in Vine Deloria, Jr. (ed.), *American Indian Policy in the Twentieth Century* (Norman, OK: University of Oklahoma Press), pp. 239–256.
4. Quoted on p. 3795 in the Improving America's Schools Act of 1994, P.L. No. 103-382, §9202, 108 Stat. 3518 (1994).
5. Deloria, op. cit.
6. This is also referenced in Ormand Hammond, "Needs Assessment and Policy Development: Native Hawaiians as Native Americans," *American Psychology* 43:5 (1988) 383–387.
7. Deloria, op. cit.
8. Joel Spring, *The American School 1642–1993*, 3rd Ed. (New York: McGraw Hill, 1994).
9. See Aaron Cicourel & John Kitsuse, *The Educational Decision Makers* (Indianapolis, IN: Bobbs-Merrill, 1963).

Appendix A

TABLE A.1
Hawai'i's Monarchy

Royal Rulers	*Dates*	*Kuhina Nui (Regent)*
Kamehameha I	1795–1819	
Kamehameha II (Liholiho)	1819–1824	Ka'ahumanu I (1819–1832)
Kamehameha III (Kauikeaouli)	1824–1854	Ka'ahumanu II (Kīna'u) (1832–1839) Kekauluohi (1839–1845) Keoni Ana (John Young) (1845–1855)
Kamehameha IV (Alexander Liholiho)	1854–1863	Victoria Kamāmalu (1855–1863)
Kamehameha V (Lot Kapūaiwa)	1863–1872	Mataio Kekūanao'a (1863–1864)
William Lunalilo	1873–1874	None
David Kalakaua	1874–1891	None
Lili'uokalani (Lili'u Kamaka'eha)	1891–1893	None

Appendix B

TABLE B.1
Territorial Governors of Hawai'i

Governor	*Years of Tenure*	*Appointed By*
Sanford Ballard Dole	1898–1903 (President of the Republic of Hawai'i, 1893–1898)	President McKinley
George Robert Carter	1903–1907	President Theodore Roosevelt
Walter Francis Frear	1907–1913	President Theodore Roosevelt
Lucius Eugene Pinkham	1913–1918	President Woodrow Wilson
Charles J. McCarthy	1918–1921	President Woodrow Wilson
Wallace Rider Farrington	1921–1929	President Warren G. Harding and reappointed by President Calvin Coolidge (1925)
Lawrence McCully Judd	1929–1934	President Herbert Hoover
Joseph Boyd Poindexter	1934–1942	President Franklin Delano Roosevelt
Ingram Macklin Stainback	1942–1951	President Franklin Delano Roosevelt
Oren E. Long	1951–1953	President Harry Truman
Samuel Wilder King (first Native Hawaiian)	1953–1957	President Harry Truman
William F. Quinn	1957–1959 1959 first elected Governor of the State of Hawai'i	President Harry Truman

Appendix C

TABLE C.1
Distribution of Values Among School Policy Mechanisms (SPM), 1905–1969

SPM	*Year*	*Quality*	*Efficien.*	*Equity*	*Choice*	*Total*
Finance	1905		1	1		2
	1924		10			10
	1947		1			1
	1966		8			8
Personnel	1905	1			1	2
	1924	4	3	1	2	10
	1947		1			1
	1961				1	1
	1966		1			1
Testing						0
Program	1905	12	1			13
	1924		1			1
	1947	3				3
	1961	1				1
	1966	3				3
Governa.	1905		25			25
	1924		18			18
	1947		1			1
	1961		2		1	3
	1966		15		1	16
	1969		5			5
Curricul.	1905		2			2
	1924		2			2
Bldg./Fac.	1905		3			3
	1924		6			6
Total		24	106	2	6	138

Glossary of Hawaiian Language

ahupua'a—a land division from the mountain to the ocean

'āina—land

akua—god

'alamihi—black crab

ali'i—chief

aloha—love, greetings, farewell

auwana—(cannot be translated)

'eha—hurt

Ha'awina No'ono'o—Sharing thoughts

hana—work

hānai—adoption

haole—foreigner, often white foreigner

heiau—Hawaiian temple

heluhelu—reading

honu—sea turtle

ho'oponopono—a process to put right

hui—club

hula hālau—house of hula instruction

'ihi—respect

i'iwi—Hawaiian honeycreeper bird

imua—to move forward

Kalākaua—is the name of the last Hawaiian King

kahiko—(see wā kahiko)

Kahuna—an expert in a particular profession

Kahuna Lapa'au—medical expert

kai—ocean

kaikamahine—girl

kākau lima—writing

kamali'i—children

kānaka maoli—indigenous people of Hawai'i

kane—male

kaona—(cannot be translated into English)

kapu—forbidden

keikikāne—boy

kīhāpai—small piece of land

kōkua—help

kuhina nui—regent

Kūlia—(part of an 'ōlelo no'eau, cannot be translated alone)

kumu—teacher

kupuna/kūpuna (plural)—grandparent, ancestor

luna—boss

maha'oi—bold

māhele—to cut into parts

maka'āinana—the common people

makua—parent

mana—power

Mānoa—this is a place

moku—a land division

nānā—to look

nīele—inquisitive

nīnau—to question

'ōhana—family

'ōlelo no'eau—a Hawaiian saying

oli—chant

Pī-ā-pā—Hawaiian alphabet

pueo—owl

uka—upland

ukupau—labor

wā kahiko—ancient times

wahine—female

References

Adams, D. W. (1988). Fundamental considerations: The deep meaning of Native American schooling, 1880–1900. *Harvard Education Review, 58*(1), 1–27.

Adams, D. W. (1995). *Education for extinction: American Indians and the boarding school experience, 1875–1928.* Lawrence, KS: University Press of Kansas.

Afaga, L., & Lai, M. (1994). *Evaluation of the State of Hawai'i Department of Education's Hawaiian Studies Program.* Honolulu, HI: College of Education, Curriculum Research and Development Group.

Agbayani, A. (1979). *Bilingual education and public policy in Hawai'i: Historical and current issues.* Cited in T. Huebner (1985), Language education policy in Hawai'i: Two case studies and some current issues, *International Journal of Social Language, 56,* 29–49.

Alexander, W. D., & Atkinson, A. T. (1888). *A historical sketch of education in the Hawaiian Islands.* Honolulu: Daily Bulletin Steam Print.

Allen, H. G. (1982). *The betrayal of Lili'uokalani last queen of Hawai'i 1838–1917.* Honolulu: Mutual Publishing.

Alu Like, Inc., and the Office of Hawaiian Affairs. (1989, June). *A compilation recommendations from needs assessments and research reports pertaining to Native Hawaiians.* Honolulu: Authors.

American Board of Commissioners. (1838). *Report of the American Board of Commissioners for Foreign Missions, 1838.* Boston: ABCFM.

Anderson, J. D. (1988). *The education of Blacks in the South, 1860–1935.* Chapel Hill, NC: University of North Carolina Press.

Andrews, L. (1835). *Mission to the Sandwich Islands: Report of the American Board of Commissioners for Foreign Missions, 20.* Unpublished report. Honolulu: State Archives of Hawai'i.

Annis, B. (1982). Indian education: Bilingual education—a legal right for native Americans. *American Indian Law Journal, 10,* 333–356.

Apoliona, H. (1991). E mau ana ka ha'aheo (Enduring pride). On *Olomana: E mau ana ka ha'aheo* [CD]. Honolulu, HI: Better Days.

Apology, PL No. 103-150, 107 Stat. 1510. (1993).

Appleton, N. (1983). *Cultural pluralism in education: Theoretical foundations.* New York: Longman.

Armstrong, R. (1848, November). *Journal of a tour around the Windward islands, Hawai'i, Maui, and Moloka'i, in the months of September, October, November, 1948.* Honolulu State Archives of Hawai'i.

Aronowitz, S., & Giroux, H. (1985). *Education under siege: The conservative, liberal, and radical debate over schooling.* South Hadley, MA: Bergin & Garvey.

Atkinson, A. (1864). *Biennial report of the President of the Board of Education to the Legislative Assembly, 1864.* Kingdom of Hawai'i: Dept. of Public Instruction.

Atkinson, A. (1890). *Biennial report of the President of the Board of Education to the Legislative Assembly, 1890.* Kingdom of Hawai'i: Dept. of Public Instruction.

Atkinson, A. (1892). *Biennial report of the President of the Board of Education to the Legislative Assembly, 1892.* Kingdom of Hawai'i: Dept. of Public Instruction.

Atkinson, A. (1894). *Biennial report of the President of the Board of Education to the Legislative Assembly, 1894.* Kingdom of Hawai'i: Dept. of Public Instruction.

Au, K. H., & Jordan, C. (1977). Teaching reading to Hawaiian children: Finding a culturally appropriate solution. In G. Treuba & K. Au (Eds.), *Culture and the bilingual classroom: Studies in classroom ethnography* (pp. 139–152). Rowley, MA: Newbury House.

Augustus F. Hawkins–Robert T. Stafford Elementary and Secondary School Improvement Amendments of 1988, PL No. 100-297, 102 Stat. 1. (1988).

Banks, J. (1988). *Multiethnic education: Theory and practice.* Boston: Allyn & Bacon.

Banks, J. (1993). The canon debate, knowledge construction, and multicultural education. *Educational Researcher, 22*(5), 4–14.

Barrett, G. (1996, October 20). Hawaiian Homelands: Long, bitter wait. *Honolulu Advertiser,* pp. A1, A8–A9.

Bell, D. A. (1992). *Faces at the bottom of the well: The permanence of racism.* New York: Basic Books.

Bell, R. J. (1972). Admission delayed: The influence of sectional and political opposition in congress on statehood for Hawai'i. *Hawaiian Journal of History, 6,* 45–68.

Bell, R. J. (1984). *Last among equals: Hawaiian statehood and American politics.* Honolulu: University of Hawai'i Press.

Benham, M. (1993). *Political and cultural determinants of educational policymaking: Their effects on Native Hawaiians.* Unpublished doctoral dissertation, University of Hawai'i-Mānoa, Honolulu, HI.

Benham, M., & Heck, R. (1994). Political culture and policy in a state-controlled educational system: The case of educational politics in Hawai'i. *Educational Administration Quarterly, 30*(4), 419–450.

Berman, P., Izu, J., McCelland, R., & Stone, P. (1988). *The Hawai'i plan: Educational excellence for the Pacific area. Recommendations to the Hawai'i Business Roundtable.* Honolulu, HI: Hawai'i Business Roundtable.

Bishop, C. R. (1881). *The Biennial report of the President of the Board of Education to the Legislative Assembly, 1881.* Kingdom of Hawai'i: Dept. of Public Instruction.

Bishop, C. R. (1882). *The Biennial report of the President of the Board of Education to the Legislative Assembly, 1882.* Kingdom of Hawai'i: Dept. of Public Instruction.

Blaisdell, K. (1997, May 18). Kānaka Maoli are not "Native Americans." *Honolulu Advertiser,* p. B3.

Blount, J. H. (1894). *Blounts Report. House Ex. Doc., no. 47, 53 Congress, 2 session.* Washington, DC: Foreign Relations of the United States.

Borman, K., Castenell, L., & Gallager, K. (1993). Business involvement in school reform: The rise of the Business Roundtable. In C. Marshall, (Ed.), *The new politics of race and gender* (pp. 69–83). Washington, DC: Falmer Press.

Brieske, P. R. (1961). *A study of the development of public elementary and secondary educators in the Territory of Hawai'i.* Unpublished doctoral dissertation, University of Washington, Seattle.

Brown, K. (1993). Do African American males need race and gender segregated education?: An educator's perspective and a legal perspective. In C. Marshall, (Ed.), *The new politics of race and gender* (pp. 107–127). Washington, DC: Falmer Press.

Carl D. Perkins Vocational Education Act, PL No. 98-524, 98 Stat. 2435. (1984).

Carneiro, R. L. (1970). A theory of the origin of the state. *Science, 169*, 733–738.

Carneiro, R. L. (1978). Political expansion as an expression of the principle of the competitive exclusion. In R. Cohen & E. R. Service (Eds.), *Origins of the state* (pp. 205–223). Philadelphia: Institute for the Study of Human Issues.

Carneiro, R. L. (1980). The chiefdom: Precurser of the state. In G. D. Jones & R. R. Kautz (Eds.), *The transition to statehood in the new world* (pp. 37–79). Cambridge: Cambridge University Press.

Castle, A. L. (1981). Advice for Hawai'i: The Dole-Burgess Letters. *The Hawaiian Journal of History, 15*, 24–30.

Castle, W. R. (1915). Sketch of constitutional history in Hawai'i. In the *23rd Annual Report of the Hawaiian Historical Society* (pp. 13–27). Honolulu: Paradise of the Pacific Press.

Chamberlain, L. (1824). *Journals of Levi Chamberlain*. Honolulu, HI: Hawaiian Mission Children's Society Library.

Chaudhuri, J. (1985). American Indian policy: An overview. In V. Deloria, Jr. (Ed.), *American Indian policy in the twentieth century* (pp. 15–33). Norman, OK: University of Oklahoma Press.

Cicourel, A. V., & Kitsuse, J. I. (1963). *The educational decision makers*. Indianapolis, IN: Bobbs-Merrill.

Civil Rights Act, PL No. 88-352, 78 Stat. 241. (1964).

Cody, C., Woodward, A., & Elliot, D. (1993). Race, ideology, and the battle over curriculum. In C. Marshall, (Ed.), *The new politics of race and gender* (pp. 48–57). Washington, DC: Falmer Press.

Coffman, T. (1973). *Catch a wave: A case study of Hawai'i's new politics*. Honolulu: University of Hawai'i Press.

Coleman, M. C. (1993). *American Indian children at school, 1850–1930*. Jackson, MS: University Press of Mississippi.

Cooper, G., & Daws, G. (1985). *Land and power in Hawai'i*. Honolulu: University of Hawai'i Press.

Cornbleth, C., & Waugh, D. (1996). *The great speckled bird: Multicultural politics and education policymaking*. Mahwah, NJ: Lawrence Erlbaum Associates.

Crawford, D. L. (1931–1932). *Biennial report of the Department of Public Instruction, 1931–1932*. Territory of Hawai'i: Dept. of Public Instruction.

Crawford, J. (1989). *Bilingual education: History, politics, theory, and practice*. Trenton, NJ: Crane.

Crowningburg-Amalu, S. (1974). *Jack Burns: A portrait in transition*. Honolulu: Mamalahoa Foundation.

Cuban, L. (1990). Reforming again, again, and again. *Educational Researcher, 19*(1), 3–13.

D'Amato, J. (1988). "Acting": Hawaiian children's resistance to teachers. *The Elementary School Journal, 88*(5), 529–544.

Daws, G. (1969). *Shoal of time: A history of the Hawaiian Islands*. Honolulu: University of Hawai'i Press.

Delay angers backers of Hawaiian vote. (1996, September 10). *Honolulu Advertiser*, pp. A1–A2.

Deloria, V., Jr. (1985). The evolution of federal Indian policy making. In V. Deloria, Jr. (Ed.), *American Indian policy in the twentieth century*. Norman, OK: University of Oklahoma Press.

Department of Education. (1991). *Affirmative action program, annual report fiscal year 1990–1991*. Honolulu, HI: Hawai'i Department of Education.

Department of Education. (1994). *Information system services*. Honolulu, HI: Hawai'i Department of Education.

Department of Public Instruction. (1931). *Policy Handbook, Education Policy, 1931*. Territory of Hawai'i: Author.

Department of Public Instruction. (1947). *School policy*. Territory of Hawai'i: Author.

Dillard, C. B. (1995). Leading with her life: An African American feminist (re)interpretation of leadership for an urban high school principal. *Educational Administration Quarterly, 31*(4), 539–563.

DiMaggio, P., & Powell, W. (1983). The iron cage revisited: Institutional isomorphism and collective rationality in organizational fields. *American Sociological Review, 48*, 147–160.

Easton, D. (1953). *The political system*. New York: Knopf.

Easton, D. (1965a). *A system analysis of political life*. New York: Wiley.

Easton, D. (1965b). *Framework for political analysis*. Englewood Cliffs, NJ: Prentice-Hall.

Elbert, S. H., & Mahoe, N. (Eds.), *Nā Mele o Hawai'i Nei: 101 Hawaiian songs*. Honolulu, HI: University of Hawai'i Press.

Elazar, D. (1984). *American federalism: A view from the states*. New York: Crowell.

Elementary and Secondary Education Act of 1967, PL No. 90-247, § , 81 Stat. 783. (1967).

Este, R. A. (1986, October). *A policy process model as a tool of educational governance*. Paper presented at the Mokakit Conference, Winnipeg, Manitoba, Canada.

Eulau, H. (1972). Political science and education: The long view and the short. In M. Kirst (Ed.), *State, school, and politics: Research directions*. Lexington, MA: Heath.

Everhart, R. (1988). Fieldwork methodology in educational administration. In N. J. Boyan (Ed.), *Handbook of research on educational administration* (pp. 703–726). New York: Longman.

Everly, H. (1965). Education in Hawai'i—Yesterday and today. In the *Kamehameha Schools 75th Anniversary Lectures* (pp. 45–52). Honolulu: Kamehameha Schools.

Feher, J. (1969). *Hawai'i: A pictorial history*. Honolulu: Bishop Museum Press.

Finkelstein, B. (1978). Pedagogy as intrusion: Teaching values in popular primary schools in nineteenth century America. In D. R. Warren (Ed.), *History, education, and public policy* (pp. 239–270). Berkeley, CA: McCutchen.

Freire, P. (1985). *The politics of education: Culture, power, and liberation*. New York: Bergin & Garvey.

Fried, M. (1967). *The evolution of political society*. New York: Random House.

Friedberger, M. (1996). Country schooling in the heartland. *American Journal of Education, 104*(2), 148–153.

Fuchs, L. H. (1961). *Hawai'i pono: A social history*. New York: Harcourt Brace.

Garms, W., Guthrie, J. W., & Pierce, L. C. (1978). *School finance: The economics and politics of education*. Englewood Cliffs, NJ: Prentice-Hall.

Gay, F. T. (1945). *A study of the development of the senior high school*. Unpublished master's thesis, University of Hawai'i, Honolulu, HI.

Gibson, A. (1985). Philosophical, legal, and social rationales for appropriating the tribal estate, 1607 to 1980. *American Indian Law Review, 12*, 3–37.

Gibson, W. M. (1884). *Biennial report of the President of the Board of Education to the Legislative Assembly, 1884*. Kingdom of Hawai'i: Dept. of Public Instruction.

Givens, W. E. (1924). *Report of the Superintendent for the biennium ending December 31st, 1924*. Territory of Hawai'i: Dept. of Public Instruction.

Gonzalaez, G. G. (1990). *Chicano education in the era of segregation*. Cranbury, NJ: Associated University Press.

Governor's Office. (1955). *A report of the Governor's Conference on education*. Honolulu: Territorial Department of Public Instruction.

Graber, R. B., & Roscoe, P. B. (1988). Circumscription and the evolution of society. *American Behavioral Scientist, 31*(4), 405–415.

Grayson, W. L. (1986). *New Mexico's policy in Indian education. A report on the development of New Mexico's policy on Indian education*. Santa Fe, NM: New Mexico State Department of Education, Santa Fe Division of Indian Education.

Grell, L. S. (1983, November). *Indian self-determination and education of the Kickapoo Nation school*. Paper presented at the 82nd Annual Meeting of the American Anthropological Association, Chicago, IL.

Gronn, P., & Robbins, P. (1996). Leaders in context: Postpositivist approaches to understanding educational leadership. *Educational Administration Quarterly, 32*(3), 452–473.

Hammond, O. (1988). Needs assessment and policy development: Native Hawaiians as Native Americans. *American Psychology, 43*(5), 383–387.

Harby, W. (1993). Living the language. *Island Scene*, Fall, 1–3.

Hastings, W. (1988). *The right to an education in Maori: The case from international law*. Wellington, New Zealand: Victoria University Press.

Hawai'i Education Association. (1946). *Proceedings of the Hawai'i Education Association*. Honolulu: Author.

Hawai'i Education Association. (1947). *Proceedings of the Hawai'i Education Association*. Honolulu: Author.

Hawai'i Education Association. (1948). *Proceedings of the Hawai'i Education Association*. Honolulu: Author.

Hawaiian Homes Commission Act of 1920, PL No 67-34, §1881, 42 Stat. 108. (1921).

Headstart, Economic Opportunity, and Community Partnership Act of 1974, PL No. 93,644, § , 88 Stat. 1368. (1975).

Heck, R. H. (1991–1992). Systems dynamics and Chicago school reform: A model for redefining who governs. *Administrator's Notebook, 35*(4), 1–6.

Heck, R. H., & Mayer, R. (1993). School characteristics, school academic indicators and student outcomes: Implications for policies to improve schools. *Journal of Education Policy, 8*(2), 143–154.

Holman, L. R. (1986). *Journal of Lucia Ruggles Holman*. Brookfield Center, CT: Congregational Church of Brookfield.

Huebner, T. (1985). Language education policy in Hawai'i: Two case studies and some current issues. *International Journal of Social Language, 56*, 29–49.

Hyde, C. M. (1885, January 21). The Hawaiian public school system. *Hawaiian Gazette*, pp. 2–4.

Iannaccone, L. (1977). *Three views of change in education politics*. Chicago, IL: National Society for the Study of Education.

Iannaccone, L., & Lutz, F. W. (1970). *Politics, power and policy: The governing of local school districts*. Columbus, OH: Merrill.

Iannaccone, L., & Lutz, F. W. (Eds.). (1978). *Public participation in school decision-making*. Lexington, MA: Lexington.

Improving America's Schools Act of 1994, PL No. 103-382, §9202, 108 Stat. 3518. (1994).

Indian Affairs Federal Recognition Administrative Procedures, H.R. 671, 104th Cong., 1st sess. (1995a).

Indian Affairs Federal Recognition Administrative Procedures, S.479, 104th Cong., 1st sess. (1995b).

Johnson and Graham's Lessee v. William McIntosh, 21 U.S. 543. (1823).

Kaestle, C. (1983). *Pillars of the republic: Common schools and American society*. New York: Hill & Wang.

Kahananui, D. M. (Ed. & Trans.). (1984). *Ka mo'o'ōlelo Hawai'i*. Honolulu, HI: University of Hawai'i Press.

Kamakau, S. M. (1992). *Ruling chiefs of Hawai'i* (rev. ed.). Honolulu, HI: Kamehameha Schools/Bishop Estate.

Kamana, K., & Wilson, W. (1996, March 15). Hawaiian language programs revisited. American Indian Bilingual Education. *NABE News*, pp. 13, 42.

Kame'eleihiwa, L. K. (1992). *Native land and foreign desire. Ku Hawai'i 'ana a me na koi pu'umake a ka po'e haole: A history of land tenure in Hawai'i from traditional times until the 1848 māhele, including an analysis of Hawaiian ali'i and American Calvinists.* Honolulu, HI: Bishop Museum Press.

Kamehameha Schools/Bishop Estate. (1965). *Kamehameha Schools 75th Anniversary Lectures.* Honolulu, HI: Author.

Kamehameha Schools/Bishop Estate. (1983). *Native Hawaiian educational assessment project: Final report.* Honolulu: Author.

Kamehameha Schools/Bishop Estate. (1991). *Office of Program Planning and Evaluation* (unpublished report, 12–91). Honolulu, HI: Author.

Kamehameha Schools/Bishop Estate. (1993). *Native Hawaiian Educational Assessment Project: 1993 survey report.* Honolulu, HI: Author.

Kanahele, G. S. (1986). *Kū kanaka, stand tall: A search for Hawaiian values.* Honolulu, HI: University of Hawai'i Press, Waiaha Foundation.

Kelly, M. (1981–1982). Some thoughts of education in traditional Hawaiian society. In *To teach the children: Historical aspects of education in Hawai'i* (pp. 4–13). Honolulu: Bernice Pauahi Bishop Museum.

Kemmis, D. (1990). *Community and the politics of place.* Norman, OK: University of Oklahoma Press.

Kent, H. W. (1965). *Charles Reed Bishop man of Hawai'i.* Palo Alto, CA: Pacific Books.

Kingdom of Hawai'i. (1839a, June). *Declaration of Rights.* Kingdom of Hawai'i.

Kingdom of Hawai'i. (1839b, June). *Edict of Toleration.* Kingdom of Hawai'i.

Kingdom of Hawai'i. (1840, October). *Constitution and Laws of His Majesty Kamehameha III.* Kingdom of Hawai'i.

Kingdom of Hawai'i. (1842). *Constitutional Laws of Hawai'i 1842.* Kingdom of Hawai'i.

Kingdom of Hawai'i. (1845–1846). *Organic Acts.* Kingdom of Hawai'i.

Kingdom of Hawai'i. (1850). *School Tax Law.* Kingdom of Hawai'i.

Kingdom of Hawai'i. (1855). *Reorganization Act of 1855.* Kingdom of Hawai'i.

Kingdom of Hawai'i. (1859). *Hawai'i's Codified Laws of 1859.* Kingdom of Hawai'i.

Kingdom of Hawai'i. (1870). *Statue Law.* Kingdom of Hawai'i.

Kingdom of Hawai'i. (1887). *Constitution of 1887, Act 57.* Kingdom of Hawai'i.

Kirst, M. W. (1984). *Who controls our schools? American values in conflict.* New York: Freeman.

Kitaguchi, L. S. (1962). *Organized labor and public education in Hawai'i 1945–1960.* Unpublished doctorate dissertation, New York University, New York, NY.

Kittleson, D. (1981). Native Hawaiians as western teachers. *Educational Perspectives, 20*(3), 10–16.

Kuykendall, R. S. (1938). *The Hawaiian Kingdom 1778–1854, Vol. I.* Honolulu: University of Hawai'i Press.

Kuykendall, R. S. (1940). *Constitutions of the Hawaiian Kingdom: A brief history and analysis* (Pamphlet). Honolulu, HI: Author.

Kuykendall, R. S. (1953). *The Hawaiian Kingdom 1854–1874, Vol II.* Honolulu: University of Hawai'i Press.

Kuykendall, R. S. (1967). *The Hawaiian Kingdom 1874–1893, Vol. III.* Honolulu: University of Hawai'i Press.

Lau et al. v. Nichols et al., 414 U.S. 563. (1973–1974).

La Croix, S. J., & Roumassett, J. (1984). An economic theory of political change in premissionary Hawai'i. *Explorations in Economic History, 21,* 151–168.

Lili'uokalani. (1964). *Hawai'i's story by Hawai'i's Queen.* Rutland, VT: Charles E. Tuttle.

Lind, A. W. (1967). *Hawai'i's people.* Honolulu: University of Hawai'i Press.

Lind, A. W. (1980). *Hawai'i's people.* (4th ed.) Honolulu: University of Hawai'i Press.

Linnekin, J. (1983). Defining tradition: Variations on the Hawaiian identity. *American Ethnologist, 10*(2), 241–252.

Linnekin, J. (1985). *Children of the land: Exchange and status in a Hawaiian community.* New Brunswick, NJ: Rutgers University Press.

Linnekin, J. (1990). *Sacred queens and women of consequence: Rank, gender, and colonialism in the Hawaiian islands.* Ann Arbor, MI: University of Michigan Press.

Literary Digest. (Feb. 10, 1897). *Volume 14,* 499.

Littler, R. (1927). *The government of the Territory of Hawai'i.* Honolulu: Honolulu Star Bulletin Pamphlets.

Logan, D. (1897). Education in the Hawaiian Islands. *The North American Review, 164,* 20–25.

Lowrie, S. G. (1951). Hawai'i drafts a Constitution. *University of Cincinnati Law Review, 20*(2), 217.

Lutz, F. W., & Iannaccone, L. (1969). *Understanding educational organizations: A field study approach.* Columbus, OH: Merrill.

Lyman, S. (1860). *Journal of Sarah Lyman, 1830–1860.* Honolulu, HI: Hawaiian Mission Children's Society Library.

MacCaughey, V. (1909). Public elementary schools in Hawai'i. *Paradise of the Pacific,* 33–35.

MacKenzie, M. K. (Ed.). (1991). *Native Hawaiian rights handbook.* Honolulu: University of Hawai'i Press.

Makanani, R. K. (July 15, 1991, April 6, 1992, May 12, 1992). Native Hawaiian historian and educator (Interviews).

Malo, D. (1898). *Hawaiian antiquities.* Honolulu, HI: Bishop Museum, No. 2.

Mann, H. (1876). *American pedagogy: Education, the school, and the teacher in American literature* (2nd ed.). Hartford, CT: Brown & Gross.

Mann, H. (1957). *The Republic and the school: The education of free men.* New York: Columbia University Press.

Mann, H. (1965). *Horace Mann on the crises in education.* Yellow Springs, OH: Antioch Press.

Marcoulides, G., & Heck, R. H. (1990). Educational policy issues for the 1990s: Balancing equity and excellence in implementing the reform agenda. *Urban Education, 25*(1), 55–67.

Marshall, C. (1984). Elites, bureaucrats, ostriches, and pussycats: Managing research in policy settings. *Anthropology and Education Quarterly, 15*(3), 235–251.

Marshall, C. (1985). Field studies and educational administration and policy: The fit, the challenge, the benefits, and costs. *Urban Education, 20*(1), 61–81.

Marshall, C. (1993). Politics of denial: Gender and race issues in administration. In C. Marshall (Ed.), *The new politics of race and gender.* Washington, DC: Falmer Press.

Marshall, C., Mitchell, D., & Wirt, F. (1989). *Culture and education policy in the American states.* New York: Falmer Press.

Martin, M., Lyman, N. H., Bond, K. L., & Damon, E. M. (Eds.). (1970). *The Lymans of Hilo.* Hilo, HI: Lyman House Memorial Museum.

McLaughlin, W. G. (1984). *Cherokees and missionaries, 1789–1839.* New Haven, CT: Yale University Press.

Meehan, K. A., & Meha, A. T. (1989, March). *Recruiting, retention and achievement of minority students: The case of Native Hawaiians.* Community Colleges Paper presented at the 1989 Annual Meeting of the American Association of Community and Junior Colleges, Honolulu, HI.

Meller, N. (1971). *With an understanding heart: Constitution making in Hawai'i.* National Municipal League, State Constitution Convention studies No. 5. New York: National Municipal League.

Merton, R. (1972). Insiders and outsiders: A chapter in the sociology of knowledge. *American Journal of Sociology, 78,* 9–47.

Meyer, J. W., Boli, J., & Thomas, G. (1987). Ontology and rationalization in Western cultural account. In G. Thomas, J. Meyer, F. O. Ramirez, & J. Boli (Eds.), *Institutional structure: Constituting state, society, and the individual.* Newbury Park, CA: Sage.

Meyer, M. A. (1996). *Native Hawaiian epistemology: Nānā I ke kumu—Look to the source.* Unpublished qualifying paper, Harvard Graduate School, Cambridge, MA.

Missionary influence in Hawai'i. (1897, February 20). *Literary Digest, 16,* p. 499.

Mitchell, D., Marshall, C., & Wirt, F. (1986, Winter). The context of state-level policy formation. *Educational Evaluation and Policy Analysis, 8*(4), 347–378.

Moore, J. A. (1889, April). *A paper on methods of teaching the studies of the primary course in the public English schools in the Hawaiian Kingdom.* Pamphlet presented at the Teachers Convention, Honolulu, HI.

Native American Church of North America v. Navajo Tribal Council, 272, F. 2d 131. (1959).

Native American Languages Act, PL No. 101-477, 104 Stat 1153. (1990).

Native American Languages Act, PL No. 101-477, 104 Stat. 1153. (1990).

Negron De Montilla, A. (1971). *Americanization in Puerto Rico and the public school system, 1900–1930.* Rio Piedras, PR: Editorial Edil.

O'Brien, S. (1985). Federal Indian policies and the international protection of human rights. In V. Deloria, Jr. (Ed.), *American Indian policy in the twentieth century.* Norman: University of Oklahoma Press.

Office of Hawaiian Affairs funds home loans for destitute Hawaiians. (1996, November 5). *Honolulu Advertiser,* p. B1.

Office of the Governor of Hawai'i. (1983). *Hawai'i basic data and information book on Hawaiians.* Honolulu, HI: Office of Youth and Children.

Ogawa, R. T. (1992). Institutional theory and examining leadership in schools. *International Journal of Educational Manangement, 6*(3), 14–21.

Ogbu, J. U. (1992). Understanding cultural diversity and learning. *Educational Researcher, 21*(8), 5–14.

Ogbu, J. U. & Gibson, M. A. (1991). *Minority status and schooling: A comparative study of immigrant and involuntary minorities.* New York: Garland.

One-party dominance jolted but still intact. (1996, November 10). *Honolulu Advertiser,* pp. A1–A2.

Papahana Kaiapuni Hawai'i. (1995). *Program design for the Hawaiian Language Immersion Program.* Honolulu, HI: Department of Education.

Patton, M. Q. (1990). *Qualitative evaluation and research methods.* Newbury Park, CA: Sage.

Paul, J. F. (1975). The power of seniority: Senator Hugh Butler and statehood for Hawai'i. *Hawaiian Journal of History, 9,* 140–147.

Pierce, R. H. (1965). *Savagism and civilization: A study of the Indian and American mind.* Baltimore: Johns Hopkins University Press.

Pierce, R. H. (1965). *The savages of America: A study of the Indian and the idea of civilization.* Baltimore: Johns Hopkins Press.

Plank, D., Scotch, R. K., & Gamble, J. L. (1996). Rethinking progressive school reform: Organizational dynamics and educational change. *American Journal of Education, 104*(2), 79–102.

Popkewitz, T. (1981). Qualitative research: Some thoughts about the relation of methodology and social history. In T. Popkewitz & B. Tabachnick (Eds.), *The study of schooling: Field-based methodologies in educational research and evaluation* (pp. 155–178). New York: Praeger.

Pukui, M. K., Elbert, S. H., & Mo'okini, E. T. (1975). *The pocket Hawaiian dictionary.* Honolulu: University of Hawai'i Press.

Pukui, M. K., Haertig, E. W., & Lee, C. A. (1972). *Nānā i ke kumu (Look to the source)* (Vols. 1–2). Honolulu: Hui Hanai.

Quinn, W. F. (1984). The politics of statehood. *Hawaiian Journal of History, 18,* 1–12.

Reich, R. B. (1991). *The work of nations: Preparing ourselves for 21st century capitalism.* New York: Knopf.

Richards, W. (1938). Unpublished personal journal. Honolulu: Hawaiian Mission Children's Society.

Republic of Hawai'i. (1894). *The First Constitution of the Republic: Constitution of the Republic of Hawai'i Draft Submitted to the Constitutional Convention by the Executive Council* (Sen. Ex. Doc. 117 [53 Congress, 2 sess.]) Archives of Hawai'i.

Republic of Hawai'i. (1896). *Act 57.* Republic of Hawai'i.

Russ, W. A., Jr. (1959). *The Hawaiian Revolution, 1893–1894.* Selinsgrove, PA: Susquehanna University Press.

Russ, W. A., Jr. (1961). *The Hawaiian Republic 1894–1898 and its struggle to win annexation.* Selinsgrove, PA: Susquehanna University Press.

Sachen, D. M., & Medina, M. Jr. (1990). Investigating the context of state-level policy formation: A case study of Arizona's bilingual education legislation. *Education Evaluation and Policy Analysis, 12*(4), 378–399.

Sahlins, M., & Barrere, D. (Eds.). (1973). William Richards on Hawaiian culture and political conditions of the islands in 1841. *Hawaiian Journal of History, 7,* 18–40.

Sahlins, M., & Kirch, P. V. (1992). *Anahulu the anthropology of history in the Kingdom of Hawai'i Vol. I.* Chicago: Chicago University Press.

Samuel A. Worchester v. The State of Georgia, 31 U.S. 515. (1832).

Schattschneider, E. E. (1960). *The semisoveriegn people.* New York: Holt, Rinehart & Winston.

Schattschneider, E. E. (1969). *Two hundred million Americans in search of a government.* New York: Holt, Rinehart & Winston.

Schatzman, L., & Strauss, A. (1973). *Field research: Strategies for a natural sociology.* Englewood Cliffs, NJ: Prentice-Hall.

Schmitt, R. C. (1968). *Demographic statistics of Hawai'i, 1778–1965.* Honolulu: University of Hawai'i Press.

Schmitt, R. C. (1973). *The missionary census of Hawai'i.* Honolulu: Anthropological Records, No. 20, Department of Anthropology, Bernice P. Bishop Museum.

Schmitt, R. C. (1977). *Historical statistics of Hawai'i.* Honolulu: University of Hawai'i Press.

Scott, E. B. (1968). *The saga of the Sandwich Islands.* Crystal Bay, Lake Tahoe, NV: Sierra-Tahoe Publishing Co.

Scott, J. (1895). *Biennial report of the President of the Board of Education to the Legislative Assembly 1895.* Republic of Hawai'i: Dept. of Public Instruction.

Selznick, P. (1957). *Leadership in administration.* New York: Harper & Row.

Serlin, R. C. (1987). Hypothesis testing, theory building, and the philosophy of science. *Journal of Counseling Psychology, 34*(4), 365–371.

Service, E. R. (1975). *Origins of the state and civilization.* New York: Norton.

Showers, C. & Cantor, N. (1985). Social cognition: A look at motivated strategies. *Annual Review of Psychology, 36,* 275–305.

Sinclair, M. (1995). *Nahi 'ena'ena sacred daughter of Hawai'i: A life ensnared.* Honolulu: Mutual Publishing.

Spindler, G. (1968). Psychocultural adaption. In E. Norbeck, D. Price-Williams, & W. M. McCord (Eds.), *The study of personality: An interdisciplinary appraisal* (pp. 337–343). New York: Holt, Rinehart & Winston.

Spring, J. (1989). *The sorting machine revisited: National educational policy since 1945.* New York: Longman.

Spring, J. (1993). *Conflict of interests: The politics of American education* (2nd ed.). New York: Longman.

Spring, J. (1994). *The American school 1642–1993* (3rd ed.). New York: McGraw-Hill.

Staff. (1994, February 11). Educational governance is hot issue: Who runs Hawai'i's public schools? Should this be changed? *Honolulu Advertiser,* pp. A1, A3.

State of Hawai'i. (1961). *Hawai'i Session Laws of 1961, Act 182*. State of Hawai'i.

State of Hawai'i. (1966). *Hawai'i School Laws*. State of Hawai'i.

State of Hawai'i. (1969). *Constitution of the State of Hawai'i as Amended by the Constitutional Convention of 1968*. State of Hawai'i: Archives Div., Dept. of Accounting and General Services.

State of Hawai'i. (1986). *Department of Education. Hawaiian Studies Program Guide*. Honolulu, HI: Office of Instructional Services.

State of Hawai'i. (1993). *The State of Hawai'i data book: A statistical abstract 1992*. Honolulu, HI: Department of Business, Economic Development, and Tourism.

State of Hawai'i. (1994). *Long-range plan for the Hawaiian Language Immersion Program*. Honolulu, HI: Office of Instructional Services.

Steuber, R. K. (1964). *Hawai'i: A case study in development education 1778–1960*. Unpublished doctoral dissertation, University of Wisconsin, Madison, WI.

Steuber, R. K. (1981–1982a). An informal history of schooling in Hawai'i. *To teach the children: Historical aspects of education in Hawai'i* (pp. 16–34). Honolulu: Bernice Pauahi Bishop Museum.

Steuber, R. K. (1981–1982b). Twentieth-century educational reform in Hawai'i. *Educational Perspectives, 20*(4), 4–19.

Stevens, S. K. (1945). *American expansion in Hawai'i 1842–1898*. Harrisburg, PA: Archives Publishing.

Sullivan, W. M. (1982). *Reconstructing public philosophy*. Berkeley, CA: University of California Press.

Tafune, S. (1994). *Hawai'i's school reform: A content analysis of the School community based management system*. Unpublished master's thesis, University of Hawai'i at Mānoa.

Tamura, E. (1994). *Americanization, acculturation, and ethnic identity. The Nisei generation in Hawai'i*. Urbana: University of Illinois Press.

Territory of Hawai'i. (1900). *Organic Law of 1900*. Territory of Hawai'i.

Territory of Hawai'i. (1905). *Revised School Laws of the Department of Public Instruction of the Territory of Hawai'i, 1905*. Territory of Hawai'i: Hawaiian Star Print.

Territory of Hawai'i. (1924). *School Laws and Laws Relating to Child Welfare, 1924*. Territory of Hawai'i: Dept of Public Instruction.

Territory of Hawai'i. (1927). *Information pamphlet*. Honolulu: Honolulu Star Bulletin.

Territory of Hawai'i. (1931a). *Governor's committee on education: Survey of schools and industry [Prosser Report]*. Honolulu: The Printshop Co.

Territory of Hawai'i. (1931b). *Session Laws of Hawai'i, Act 284 (Sec. 1)*. Territory of Hawai'i.

Territory of Hawai'i. (1948, January). *Program of studies for the secondary schools of Hawai'i*. Territory of Hawai'i: Dept. of Public Instruction.

Territory of Hawai'i. (1949). *Session Laws, Act 227 (Sec 1–2)*. Territory of Hawai'i.

Territory of Hawai'i. (1950). *Constitution of 1950*. Territory of Hawai'i.

Territory of Hawai'i. (1951). *School survey 1957* (Vols. 1–3). Territory of Hawai'i: Dept. of Public Instruction.

Territory of Hawai'i. (1958). *Program of studies for the secondary schools of Hawai'i*. Territory of Hawai'i: Dept. of Public Instruction.

Thrum, T. B. (1900). *The Hawaiian almanac and annual 1896–1900: A handbook of information*. Honolulu, HI: State Archives of Hawai'i.

Thurston, L. A. (Ed.). (1904). *The fundamental law of Hawai'i, 1840–1842*. Honolulu: The Hawaiian Gazette.

Thurston, L. A. (1936). *Memoirs of the Hawaiian Revolution*. Honolulu: Advertiser Publishing Company.

Title II Rights of Indians, PL No. 90-284, B2 Stat. 73. (1968).

Tom, H. Y. K., Furushima, L. Y., & Yano, P. T. (Eds.). (1965). *A hundred years: McKinley High School 1865–1965*. Honolulu: McKinley High School Publishing Dept.

Townsend, H. S. (1896). *Biennal report of the President of the Board of Education to the Legislative Assembly of 1896.* Republic of Hawai'i: Dept. of Public Instruction.

Townsend, H. S. (1897). *Biennial report of the President of the Board of Education to the Legislative Assembly of 1897.* Republic of Hawai'i: Dept. of Public Instruction.

Townsend, H. S. (1899). *Biennial report of the President of the Board of Education to the Legislative Assembly of 1899.* Republic of Hawai'i: Dept. of Public Instruction.

Turner, F. J. (1894). *The frontier in American history.* Washington, DC: Government Printing Office.

Twain, M. (1966). *Letters from Hawai'i.* Honolulu: University of Hawai'i Press.

Tyack, D. (1974). *The one best system.* Cambridge, MA: Harvard University Press.

Tyack, D., & Cuban, L. (1995). *Tinkering toward utopia: A century of public school reform.* Boston: Harvard University Press.

U.S. Bureau of Census. (1940). *16th Census of the United States: 1940. Population, Second Series Characteristics of Population, Hawai'i.* Washington, DC: U.S. Government Printing Office.

U.S. Bureau of the Census. (1991). *Survey of minority-owned business enterprises.* Washington, DC: U.S. Dept. of Commerce Bureau of the Census.

University of Hawai'i to offer master's degree program in Hawaiian language and literature. (1996, October 25). *Honolulu Advertiser*, pp. A1–A2.

Wagner, J. (1993). Ignorance in educational research: Or, how can you not know that? *Educational Researcher, 22*(5), 15–23.

Ward, J. G. (1993). Demographic politics and American schools: Struggles for power and justice. In C. Marshall (Ed.), *The new politics of race and gender.* Washington, DC: Falmer Press.

Whiteman, H. (1986, Spring). Historical review of Indian education: Cultural policies United States position. *Wicaza Saturday Review, 2*(1), 27–31.

Wirt, F., & Kirst, M. W. (1982). *Schools in conflict: The politics of education* (2nd ed.). Berkeley, CA: McCutchen.

Wist, B. O. (1940). *A century of public education in Hawai'i.* Honolulu: Hawai'i Educational Review.

Zinn, H. (1980). *A people's history of the United States.* New York: Harper & Row.

Author Index

N–O

P

Q

R

S

T

W

Z

Subject Index

D

E

W

Y